The Economic and Social Research Institute

The Economic and Social Research Institute (ESRI) is a non-profit organisation which was founded in 1960 in the Economic Research Institute. The Institute is a private company, limited by guarantee, and enjoys full academic independence. It is governed by a Council consisting of 32 members who are representative of business, trade unions, government departments, state agencies, universities and other research institutes.

The ESRI's *General Research Series* is the primary research series of the Institute and is intended for the publication of the findings of a substantial research project. It is concerned mainly with research undertaken by the author on topics which lend themselves to the use of more scientific and technical methods of analysis. The conclusions drawn in the paper tend to be confined to those that stem directly from the author's own research findings. Papers published in the series are subject to a rigorous refereeing procedure. The first draft of the paper is read by two staff members, who evaluate the paper as a whole. The revised version is then sent for comment to organisations with a more direct interest in the subject matter, such as government departments, trade unions, employers' organisations, state agencies, etc. The paper may be revised in the light of their comments. The revised draft is then sent to an external referee known only to the Director of the Institute, at an academic institution in Ireland or abroad. The recommendation of this referee in regard to publication is normally decisive, though the final responsibility for deciding whether and in what form all work undertaken at the ESRI is published rests solely with the Director.

COEDUCATION AND GENDER EQUALITY

Exam Performance, Stress and Personal Development

Damian F. Hannan
Emer Smyth
John McCullagh
Richard O'Leary
Dorren McMahon

Oak Tree Press

Dublin

Oak Tree Press
Merrion Building
Lower Merrion Street
Dublin 2, Ireland

ISBN 1-86076-022-8

Printed in Ireland by Colour Books Ltd.

Contents

The Authors

DAMIAN F. HANNAN Ph.D., MRIA, is a Research Professor at the Economic and Social Research Institute. He was formerly Professor of Social Theory and Institutions at University College Cork.

EMER SMYTH, Ph.D., is a Research Consultant at the Economic and Social Research Institute. She holds a doctorate in Sociology from University College Dublin.

JOHN McCULLAGH holds an M.Sc. in Public Sector Analysis from Trinity College, Dublin. He is currently an Assistant Principal (Analyst) in the Department of Education, and was seconded to the Economic and Social Research Institute for the duration of the study.

RICHARD O'LEARY, MA, is a former Research Assistant at the Economic and Social Research Institute. He is currently a doctoral student at Nuffield College, Oxford, where his D.Phil. thesis is on religious intermarriage.

DORREN McMAHON, Ph.D., is a former Research Officer at the Economic and Social Research Institute. She is currently a College Lecturer in the Department of Sociology, University College Dublin.

List of Figures

List of Tables

Acknowledgements

This study was initiated in November 1993 by Noel Lindsay, then Secretary in the Department of Education who, in co-operation with Denis Healy, Assistant Secretary, arranged the contract and main funding for the project. We sincerely acknowledge their help and support for the project.

The study is based on analyses of extensive interviews with school principals, guidance counsellors and, particularly, students in 116 second-level schools. We are especially grateful for their willing help and co-operation in situations of considerable work overload for them. We hope that the quality of the book to some extent recompenses them for their help.

We owe a special debt of gratitude to the members of the project's Advisory Committee, all of whom have been unfailingly helpful and vigilant in guiding the study to its successful completion: Carmel Foley (EEA), chairperson of the committee; Eileen Aiken (ACS); Maureen Bohan (Department of Education); Richard Breen (QUB); Frances Comerford and Pauline O'Shaughnessy (Department of Equality and Law Reform); Siobhán Corry (JMB); Mary Dowling Maher (ASTI); Máirín Ganley and Helen Mahony (TUI); Nuala Henry (National Parents' Council); Tony McKenna (IVEA); Des Ormond (Department of Education). Much of the value of the study depends on their invaluable critiques and guidance.

Without the full backing of the Department of Education staff, we could not have carried out the project successfully. In particular we would like to thank: Seán MacGleannáin, Cearbhaill Ó Dálaigh and Gearóid Ó Conluain of the Inspectorate; Torlach O'Connor, Austin Vaughan and their colleagues at the Psychological Service; Tom Kavanagh of the Planning Unit; and Catherine Kelly of the IT unit, Athlone. We are also grateful to staff of the ERC, Drumcondra, for scoring the ability-test results.

The book owes much to the critical comments and suggestions of the two internal ESRI referees, Tony Fahey and Dorothy

Watson, as well as those of the anonymous external referee. In addition, we would like to acknowledge the generous and continuing help and advice of Richard Breen of Queen's University; as well as thanking Peter Daly of QUB, whose comments on an earlier draft were particularly helpful. The comments of the NCCA review group were also very helpful.

Within the ESRI, we would like to thank Kathleen O'Higgins, Selina McCoy and Justine Horgan. The staff of the ESRI Survey Unit worked energetically to code and check over 10,000 extended student interviews in a very short time. We are especially grateful to Brendan Whelan (Head of the Survey Unit) and to Miriam Murphy, Maura Cagney, Pauline Needham and all the coders and support staff of the Survey Unit. We also wish to thank Pat Hopkins, Maura Rohan, and the general office staff, especially Annette O'Connell.

Much of the value of this work is a result of the assistance and support of our colleagues and helpers. Any remaining errors or omissions are the sole responsibility of the authors.

1

The Gender Fairness of Coeducation

Coeducation is of relatively recent origin in Western Europe, with the greatest expansion taking place since the late 1950s. This expansion was related to the rapid growth of comprehensive educational provision which took place in many European countries from the mid-1950s onwards. The new comprehensive schools were intended to cater for all groups within society — boys and girls, and pupils of different abilities and from different social backgrounds. It was argued that comprehensive education would contribute to an improvement in economic and social conditions, firstly, by ensuring human capital growth, and secondly, by reducing or eliminating social inequalities in educational achievement. Coeducation was also seen as having potentially positive effects on gender equality: enhancing the performance of girls in traditionally "male" subjects, and providing a more natural social setting for adolescent development.

By the late 1970s, however, increasing concern was expressed about the gender fairness of coeducational provision. Several research studies suggested that coeducation had negative effects for girls in terms of both their educational achievement and their personal development. Three main factors were seen as contributing to the negative effects of coeducation. Firstly, girls-only schools appeared to provide a more supportive environment for girls' academic and personal development through, for example, the presence of female role models in senior staff positions in the school, and less gender-biased organisational and curricular arrangements. Secondly, there appeared to be significant differences between coeducational and single-sex schools in the nature of classroom interaction, with girls receiving less teacher attention than boys in coed schools. Finally, it was argued that coeducational schools tended to reproduce gender inequalities within the wider society. If positive action in favour of girls was not taken, then, it was argued, the academic performance and personal development of girls in coeducational schools would be inferior to that of their counterparts in girls-only schools.

Whether these conclusions hold true across all types of co-educational schools and in all societies remains open to question, however. A number of studies (reviewed in detail in Chapter 2) have been carried out on coeducational/ single-sex differences, but the findings have often been inconsistent and far from definitive. In order to determine the impact, if any, of coeducation on academic performance and personal development, it is essential to take account of, or to control for, the effects of other factors which may influence these outcomes. Many of the most quoted studies of coeducation have failed to do so, in particular neglecting to control for the selectivities by social class and academic ability that are characteristic of single-sex schools. This is particularly problematic in relation to countries like Britain or the United States, where single-sex schools form a minority, disproportionately drawing on pupils of higher ability and social background. This selectivity results in wide variations between different types of schools in the social class and ability composition of their pupils, which, in turn, leads to wide disparities in academic achievement. There must, therefore, be considerable doubt over the findings of studies which have failed to take these compositional differences into account. Even more recent, statistically sophisticated studies have failed to reach agreement on the impact of coeducation, with findings varying according to the kind of background and schooling factors taken into account. In spite of the lack of consensus on the impact of coeducation, however, these international studies raise a number of questions about the potential negative effects of coeducational schooling on girls' academic achievement and personal/social development, and highlight the need for a comprehensive Irish study in this area.

1.1 COEDUCATION IN IRELAND

In comparison with other Western countries, the Irish educational system has been characterised by a strong emphasis on single-sex provision. (See Appendix 1.1 for a more detailed description of the

Irish educational system). The predominance of gender-segregated education must be seen in the context of the role of Catholic religious organisations in educational provision, and the associated impact of Catholic social teaching on the development of the school system. The stance of the Catholic Church is perhaps best illustrated in Pope Pius XI's Encyclical, *Christian Education of Youth* (1929):

> False and harmful to Christian education is the so-called method of "coeducation". This ... is founded upon naturalism and the denial of original sin, ... a deplorable confusion of ideas that mistakes a levelling promiscuity and equality for the legitimate association of the sexes.

The Encyclical went on to say that these principles of forbidding coeducation must be applied in all schools, but particularly "in the most delicate and decisive period of formation, that namely of adolescence". These proscriptions were, for the most part, adhered to by the Catholic hierarchy in Ireland, evidenced particularly in the high proportion of single-sex schools among Church-run secondary schools, and in their then opposition to coeducational schooling within the vocational and community school sectors (see O'Connor, 1968).

The emphasis on gender-segregated education was linked with an equal concern regarding "gender-appropriate" education: with, for example, a requirement that Home Economics should be provided in all schools catering for girls; the existence up to the mid-1960s of a separate lower level Mathematics syllabus primarily for girls; and different subject groupings for boys and girls taking the junior cycle "Group Certificate" in the vocational sector. This gendered system led to very significant differences in the nature of the education received by girls and boys at second level up to the late 1960s.

The trend towards coeducational provision only began to gain pace during the 1970s. This trend initially reflected a growth in "comprehensive" educational provision (with an increasing number of community/comprehensive schools established), but more recently has resulted from the amalgamations of single-sex schools owing to declining pupil enrolments in many areas of the country. By 1994, a majority (almost 60 per cent) of pupils were being educated in coeducational schools. Given the projected demographic trends over the next decade, coeducational provision is likely to increase in importance as smaller single-sex schools become amalgamated into larger coeducational schools.

The trend towards coeducational provision has occurred at a time when gender equality issues within the educational system have come increasingly to the fore. Firstly, educational achievement has become much more important to young people's employment and career chances. Consequently, gender inequalities in achievement are likely to translate into labour-market inequalities between women and men. Secondly, rapid change in the occupational and industrial structures of the economy (see Canny, Hughes, Sexton, 1995) has highlighted the central role of education and training in helping women and men to adjust successfully to these changes. Thirdly, an increasing proportion of young women are remaining in the labour force after marriage and childbirth. In the context of these changes in women's roles, it is extremely important to assess whether coeducation enhances or reduces the educational achievement of young women.

As in many other OECD countries, young women in Ireland outperform their male counterparts in second-level schooling (OECD, 1995). More girls than boys go on to sit the Leaving Certificate, and girls achieve higher grades at both Junior and Leaving Certificate levels (Kellaghan and Dwan, 1995a; 1995b). Why then should we be concerned about girls' potential underperformance in coeducational schools? Firstly, girls' higher performance may, in fact, result from their disproportionate presence in single-sex schools; as a result, increasing coeducational provision may result in a reduction in girls' educational achievements. We need, therefore, to assess the impact of coeducation on girls' overall performance. Secondly, while girls outperform boys on average, they remain significantly under-represented in mathematical, scientific and technical subject areas both at second and third level. If, as some research has suggested, girls are even less likely to take "male" subjects in coeducational schools, then the impact of a shift towards coeducational provision must be assessed.

Education has, of course, much wider functions than the achievement of high examination grades. Most school authorities and individual school managements — at least in their mission statements and prospectuses — emphasise the moral, social and personal development of the young person. "Nurturing the holistic development of the individual and promoting the social and economic welfare of the society" (White Paper, 1995: 4) is put forward as one of the main principles justifying the State's involvement in education; and the Department of Education sets the preparation of pupils for entry to open society as one of the main objectives of the senior-cycle programme in schools (*Rules and Programmes for Secondary Schools*). Schools have become increasingly important in the socialisation of adolescents, as young people have remained in the educational system for longer and can anticipate rapidly changing economic and social roles as adults. Consequently, it is vital to assess the potential impact of coeducational schooling on the personal and social development of young people.

1.2 THE STUDY

Coeducational provision in Ireland has increased rapidly in recent years and is likely to continue to expand in the future. In this context, it is extremely important to assess the impact of this policy on pupils' educational performance and personal and social development. Concern about the potential impact of coeducation was heightened by the publication of a small-scale regional study (Hanafin, 1992), which indicated that coeducation was detrimental to girls' Leaving Certificate exam performance. As a result of this growing concern, the study on which this book is based was initiated in November 1993 at the request of the Department of Education. The main objective of the study was to determine whether coeducational schools, relative to single-sex schools, have negative effects on girls' educational achievements and personal and social development. In keeping with the policy objectives expressed in the Green Paper, *Education for a Changing World* (1992), the Department was particularly concerned with issues of gender equality in the curricular and organisational arrangements, and pedagogical practices of schools. Four key objectives were specified for the study:

(1) To determine whether, and to what extent, gender inequalities in educational achievement exist between pupils in single-sex and coeducational schools, particularly whether girls in coeducational schools underachieve relative to their male peers or to girls in single-sex schools

(2) To assess the effects of coeducation on certain aspects of girls' and boys' personal and social development, specifically on

their academic self-image, sense or locus of control, body image, and gender role stereotyping, as well as on current stress levels

(3) To determine the factors explaining any such differences between coeducational and single-sex schools

(4) To assess the implications of the findings for policy on co-education, and to make recommendations for corrective action, if required.

The approach taken in this study has a number of advantages over previous research carried out on coeducation in Ireland and internationally. Firstly, it is based on a large-scale, national survey of schools and pupils in Ireland. A survey of over 10,000 pupils in their Junior and Leaving Certificate years in a national sample of schools was carried out in the Spring of 1994. (Details of the research design are presented in Chapter 3.) The large-scale nature of the survey means that we can generalise from our results to the national population of coeducational and single-sex schools.

Secondly, very detailed information was collected on pupils and schools. School Principals and Guidance Counsellors were interviewed to elicit information on school organisation and characteristics, along with the nature of subject provision and choice for pupils. Pupil questionnaires focused on pupils' social background, their perceptions of their schooling, and their educational and occupational aspirations. In addition to the survey, tests of academic ability were conducted on the Junior Certificate sample, in order to assess pupil ability prior to the examination (see Chapter 3). The detailed nature of the information collected means that we can compare "like with like" in assessing the impact of co-education on pupils' academic performance and personal/social development.

Thirdly, we use "state-of-the-art" statistical techniques (including Multi-Level Modelling) to analyse the information collected on schools and pupils. These techniques allow us to provide more accurate estimates of the effects of coeducation, over and above the impact of social background, ability and certain school-level factors. Details of this technique are presented in Chapters 3 and 6.

Fourthly, the educational outcome measures we use are multi-dimensional: focusing on educational achievement as well as on important aspects of personal and social development. Educational achievement is measured in terms of examination grades at the Junior and Leaving Certificate levels. Given the crucial role of examination grades in access to employment and further education, these measures tap a very important outcome of the schooling process. While many studies in Ireland and internationally have focused exclusively on coeducational/single-sex differences in exam performance, this study is equally concerned with the developmental outcomes of the educational process. We measure five dimensions of pupil development: pupils' conceptions of their own academic capability (academic self-image), the extent to which they feel in control of their lives (locus of control), their evaluations of their physical appearance and attractiveness (body image), their gender role stereotyping (both in terms of their expectations for the future and their present involvement in domestic labour within their households), and current stress levels. These measures give us a broader picture of the impact of education on pupils' experiences and outcomes than focusing on academic performance alone. All of these measures are discussed in detail in Chapters 3, 8 and 9.

Finally, while the study draws specifically on information about the Irish context, it highlights issues which are of relevance to educational policy in other countries. In particular, the relatively even balance of coeducational and single-sex schools in Ireland provides a more accurate test case for comparing "like with like" in assessing the impact of coeducation on girls' and boys' achievements.

1.3 OUTLINE OF THE BOOK

The presentation of the results of the study starts with Chapters 4 and 5. Differences are described in the type of pupils attending coeducational and single-sex schools, as well as differences in the way schools "process" their pupils. The results of the analyses of the effects of coeducation on Junior and Leaving Certificate examination performance are presented in Chapters 6 and 7. While the analyses focus on school differences in overall academic achievement, they also provide information on whether coeducation impacts differently on pupils of different abilities, and whether the effects differ across subject areas (using English and Mathematics as examples).

Chapters 8 and 9 present detailed analyses of the impact of

coeducation on aspects of personal and social development and current stress levels. They highlight gender differences in the way boys and girls perceive themselves, and indicate disturbingly high stress levels for pupils (particularly girls) in examination years.

The conclusions, policy implications and recommendations following from the research are presented in Chapter 10. This chapter discusses the implications of coeducational provision for pupil achievement and personal/social development. In addition, it highlights important aspects of the schooling process which may facilitate (or hinder) the full development of girls and boys within the educational system. It is hoped that the issues raised will contribute to the debate on coeducation in particular, and second-level schooling in general, and assist government, school management, principals, teachers, and parents in developing a system which maximises educational, personal and social development for both girls and boys.

2

Literature Review and Hypotheses

In this chapter we provide a brief overview of the extensive research literature on gender differences in educational achievement, and on the effects of coeducation on gender equality in achievement. We first distinguish four main sets of causal variables affecting educational achievement: individual and family background variables, school and pupil–teacher interaction characteristics, gender differences in educationally relevant abilities/ aptitudes, and educationally relevant attitudes and aspirations. Finally, we review research on coeducational effects on educational achievement and on personal and social development. This research review is then used to develop a set of broad hypotheses about the extent and nature of coeducational effects on gender differences in achievement and on personal and social development. These general hypotheses are used to guide the subsequent analyses.

Most of the studies we review have been carried out in the United States, Britain and other English-speaking countries, with a small number carried out by Irish researchers (Madaus et al., 1979, 1980; Hanafin, 1992; Lewis, Kellaghan, 1993; Daly, 1994). Given the significant economic, sociocultural and institutional differences between Ireland and these other countries, why should we expect research findings from these other countries to be generalisable to Ireland?

There are, however, a number of reasons why we might expect consistent findings from such international studies to be generalisable to Ireland. Firstly, there are substantial similarities in the nature of gender relationships — particularly in terms of the gendered division of labour and power — across these countries.

Although there are still significant cross-national differences in the participation rate of married women in the labour force, similar gender inequalities occur in the household division of labour, in the persistence of occupational segregation in the workforce, and in the gender income-gap, in all countries. Secondly, there are some consistencies across countries in the research findings about the gender differentiating effects of co-education on the type and level of education achieved. This holds particularly for studies of the minority Catholic school system in Britain and the United States. This system contains a dispropor-tionate number of single-sex schools, and has recently been the subject of some of the most sophisticated empirical studies on the effects of coeducation. Therefore, while acknowledging the sub-stantial cultural and institutional differences between Ireland and other English-speaking countries, there are sufficient simi-larities to allow us to generate hypotheses concerning the likely effects of coeducational schooling on gender differences in achieve-ment in Ireland.

The main purpose of this chapter, therefore, is to review the main research findings from Ireland and other (mainly English-speaking) countries, in order to generate hypotheses about: (i) the extent to which coeducation influences the type and level of educational achievement by girls and boys, and (ii) the main explanatory factors shaping any gender differences which occur.

2.1 ACCOUNTING FOR GENDER DIFFERENCES IN EDUCATIONAL ACHIEVEMENT

Although our main research interest is in coeducational effects on educational achievement, we need to place these differences within the context of "school effects" on educational achievement in general. To what extent do schools have differential effects on educational achievement, effects that are clearly independent of background differences in the ability level and the socioeconomic and sociocultural background of their pupil bodies? Do state control and resourcing mean that most schools are so similar in their resource levels, in the qualifications of teachers and the nature of the curriculum and pedagogy applied, as well as in other organisational arrangements, that the remaining variance between schools has very little effect on pupil performance? Pupils of the same ability level and similar socioeconomic background may achieve much the same results whichever school they attend. This effectively was the conclusion reached in Coleman et al.'s (1966) study for the US government: that is, that schools have no discernible additional effects on performance once the effects of individual ability and family socioeconomic background had been controlled for. Numerous further studies of Coleman's research data bases effectively came to the same conclusion (see especially Jencks et al., 1972).

Since the late 1970s, however, a growing body of new research in the United States, Britain and elsewhere has come to different conclusions, primarily because these studies have focused on different "causal variables". Coleman and his co-workers had dealt primarily with the amount and quality of resource differences amongst schools, employing a very limited set of "educational process" variables. The new research focused not on the amount and quality of school resources used, but on the manner and effectiveness with which they were used or managed; concentrating on the manner in which schools "process" and bring about educational improvements in their pupil intake from first entry to final exit. Critical school-level dimensions examined in these studies include school organisation and process, school culture and ethos, instructional/pedagogical practices and classroom interaction processes. Hence, the research literature on the differential effects of coeducation on boys' and girls' educational progress needs to be firmly rooted in the wider context of the "school effectiveness" literature (Madaus et al., 1979; Rutter et al., 1979; Madaus et al., 1980; Mortimore et al., 1988; Smith and Tomlinson, 1989; Bryk et al., 1993).

In categorising the set of variables that affect educational achievement, or the effects of being educated in coed rather than in single-sex schools, it is useful to think of them in terms of a "nested decision-making system". Individuals make choices, but institutions and organisations (including schools) pattern, shape or constrain the alternative choices that are available, even influencing the probability of people making one choice rather than another (see Epstein, 1988).

Schools as organisations, however, also make choices, and may change their decisions over time — for example, by appointing a new principal, adding to their curriculum or teaching body, changing the nature of the qualifications or gender mix of the teaching staff; or even changing the way in which they categorise pupils and allocate them to classes (see Hannan, Breen et al., 1983; Hannan, Boyle, 1987). Equally, schools may change over time from being conservative, culturally reinforcing institutions (reinforcing the traditional gender role values of a gender-stratified society, for example) to institutions which challenge gendered definitions of pupils' abilities, potentialities and likely career paths (see Lee et al., 1994). So schools can vary significantly from each other in their schooling process characteristics; can change over time; and can function as either conservative or liberating organisations. These variations are not necessarily related to whether the school is coed or single sex.

As we shall see later in Chapter 4, coed schools in Ireland differ from single-sex schools in many important respects, particularly in the type of school (whether secondary or vocational, for instance) as well as in the social class and academic ability characteristics of their pupil intakes (Hannan, Boyle, 1987). Therefore, "raw" differences in examination outcomes between coed and single-sex schools may be caused by pre-existing differences in pupil intake, rather than by coeducation per se. In the first part of the following review, therefore, we discuss the factors which are most likely to affect educational achievement — paying particular attention to those variables that might affect boys' and girls' achievements differently. In the final section we review the most relevant evidence on the "net effects" of coeducation.

Relevant research literature is considered under the following headings, each of which will be considered in detail in sections 2.2 to 2.7.

(1) Family and socioeconomic background characteristics of pupils

(2) School choice, the social composition of school intakes as well as other school-type characteristics

(3) Differences in aptitudes, abilities and attitudes of girls and boys existing prior to entry to second-level schools

(4) Gendered differences in attitudes towards subjects and occupational/family-role expectations

(5) Interaction between pupils and teachers and amongst pupils in single-sex and coed schools

(6) The effects of coeducation.

2.2 FAMILY BACKGROUND, SOCIAL CLASS AND EDUCATIONAL ACHIEVEMENT

Since the earliest post-war studies of educational achievement and equality of opportunity, the central role played by family socioeconomic and sociocultural factors has been emphasised (Coleman et al., 1966; Jencks et al., 1972; Halsey, 1972, 1975; Karabel and Halsey, 1977; Halsey, Heath and Ridge, 1980). The earliest sophisticated statistical models of individual educational achievement (Sewell, Haller and Portes, 1969; Duncan et al., 1972) included a number of family socioeconomic background variables, in addition to measures of academic ability, as the most important initial predictor variables.

In the Irish context, the socioeconomic characteristics of pupils in schools, and other pupil selectivity characteristics, have been found to explain around half of the variance in the average academic achievement levels of schools (Hannan, Boyle, 1987: 143); while social-class effects on individual pupil achievements are highly significant (Breen, 1986; Breen, Hannan and O'Leary, 1995; Breen, 1995). In addition, family size and birth order have been shown to be important, with those from smaller families and older siblings doing better (Breen, 1986; Blake, 1989).

Parental encouragement for educational achievement also operates independently of social class of origin and, combined with support, supervision and help with homework and study, is a very important influence on educational achievement levels (Davies and Kandel, 1981; Heath and Clifford, 1990). Having a west of Ireland rural background as well as being a farmer's daughter — presumably a cultural residue of the traditionally gendered inheritance system — operate as important influences on parental expectations and encouragement for high educational achievement in Ireland (Hannan, Ó Riain, 1993; Clancy, 1995).

There are a number of underlying reasons why social class has significant effects on children's educational achievements. There is obviously a direct economic effect, with higher social class and income groups better able to afford household and education resources (such as separate bedrooms, study areas, books and reading materials) that facilitate higher educational achievements. In addition, higher-income families can directly or indirectly purchase access to better resourced schools as well as bear the extra (direct and opportunity) costs of senior-cycle and third-level education. Besides economic influences, social and cultural differences become more elaborated in societies like our own where there is a relatively low degree of mobility between classes (see Breen and Whelan, 1992). As a result, significant class differences arise in familial cultures, which have substantial effects on the linguistic development appropriate to educational achievement (Bernstein, 1977). Equally significant differences arise in parental educational expectations and attitudes. These become internalised by children early in their lives and come to have substantial effects on their subsequent educational motivations and achievements. Different social class settings, in addition, generate different family and personal habits and practices — such as ability to concentrate and study for long periods, or extent to which parents supervise and help with homework and study — which also come to have substantial effects on educational achievement (Bourdieu and Passeron, 1977).

2.2.1 Maternal Education, Employment Status and Occupation

Most researchers include mother's educational level in regression-type models predicting children's educational achievement, net of the effects of father's occupational status or familial social class, and his level of education (Sewell and Hauser, 1975; Mare, 1981; Breen, 1986). These studies have found that the additional net effect of mother's education is generally more important than that of father's (see Murnane et al., 1981; Kalmijn, 1994). The greater effect of maternal education is presumed to be the result of the more direct "transmission", through greater time involvement and more emotionally supportive relationships with younger children, of maternal "cultural capital": the socially conditioned attitudes, expectations and habits/skills differentially characteristic of families in the social-class hierarchy (see Bourdieu and Passeron, 1977; Murnane et al., 1981; Drudy and Lynch, 1993).

Besides maternal education, the influence of maternal employment has been extensively studied. While some American studies have concluded that maternal employment appears to have a slight negative effect on intellectual development and educational achievement early in life (see Kalmijn, 1994), others have found that it may have a positive effect resulting from increased household income (Haveman, Wolfe and Spaulding, 1991) and involvement in higher status occupations (Blau and Grossberg, 1992; D'Amico et al., 1983). In general, the effect of maternal employment is highly conditional on parental education, occupational status of the mother, the quality of substitute care, as well as on the timing and extent of work commitments after childbirth (Murnane et al., 1981; Heynes and Catsambis, 1986; Baydar, Brooks-Gunn, 1991).

Mother's employment has also been found to have significant effects on the gender role attitudes of sons and daughters, with daughters of working mothers appearing to be more independent-minded, ambitious and self-confident, and displaying less traditional sex-role attitudes — particularly if mothers are employed in higher status occupations (Walshok, 1978; Cherry et al., 1979; Keith, 1988; Hoffman, 1989). Such effects may also be translated into the adoption of less traditional subject choices and occupational orientations by daughters of working mothers (Steinberg et al., 1984; Keith, 1988). These effects, where present, appear most marked amongst working mothers with higher levels of education and higher occupational status (Carpenter, 1985; Keith, 1988; Kalmijn, 1994). In many of these studies, however, not all of the other relevant variables were adequately controlled.

2.3 SCHOOL-LEVEL FACTORS

There are three aspects of schools attended that appear most relevant: parental/pupil choice of schools, the composition and characteristics of the pupil body, and schooling management/ processing characteristics. We deal with each of these in turn below.

2.3.1 Choice of School

In addition to the direct and indirect effects of parental background on pupils' educational expectations and achievements, there is another effect which needs to be considered: the conscious choice of schools by parents/pupils. Parental choice of school may be influenced by considerations of the school's curriculum, academic reputation and ethos, parental educational ambitions for the child, the social status of the school and the socioeconomic level of the students attending it (Madaus et al., 1980: 4). Rutter et al. (1979) have shown that parental "subscription rates" for entry into chosen schools were related to the proportions of higher-ability children in the intake and the proportion of children with parents holding non-manual jobs. Parental subscription rates were not, however, significantly associated with educational achievement measures once pupil composition effects were controlled for. The study suggested, however, that the motivation of children might vary according to whether they had gained a place in the school of their choice (*Ibid*: 52).

There is some evidence in Ireland of a parental preference for single-sex education for their adolescent daughters (Lynch, 1989a). This is reflected in the fact that girls are more likely to attend single-sex schools at second level than boys. In addition, girls in coed schools may be somewhat more likely to come from homes of lower socioeconomic status (Lee and Bryk, 1986; Hannan, Breen et al., 1983).

Thus, the research discussed indicates the significant role of parents' socioeconomic status, employment status, educational background and attitudes in influencing the educational expectations and achievements of pupils, influences which may be significantly mediated by choice of school. Research also highlights the potential impact of school-choice factors on the cultural and social-psychological characteristics of the pupil body of a school, all of which needs to be controlled for in comparing the outcomes of single-sex and coed schools.

2.3.2 School-Composition Characteristics

Besides the obvious necessity to control for the effects of individual differences in ability and social-class background on performance, the additional compositional and structural effects of the "social profile" of a school's pupil intake (in terms of average social class and ability characteristics, for instance) on school ethos and educational processes, also needs to be examined before one can validly examine whether one school type is more effective than another. There is, for instance, significant evidence of an additional positive contextual effect from having a concentration of pupils from middle-class backgrounds, or a high proportion of pupils of high academic ability, in the school. At the other extreme, there is also evidence of a negative contextual effect from having a high proportion of the school intake from very disadvantaged families, or with very low academic abilities (Hoffer, Greeley and Coleman, 1985; Willms, 1985; Bryk, Lee, Holland, 1993). Rutter et al. (1979), however, found that although such structural effects were evident, their influence appeared to operate more indirectly through their impact on school culture and ethos, and thereby on the attitudes and expectations of pupils.

The most influential intake variable found by Rutter et al. (1979) was the ability characteristics rather than the socio-cultural background of pupils. For children at all levels of ability, outcomes tended to be less positive if the majority of the students consisted of those in the lowest ability band (op. cit.: 200). Outcomes were likely to be most favourable where there was a reasonable balance of academically successful children, more liable to be rewarded for their good attainments at school and, therefore, more prone to identify with the school goals (op. cit.: 159).

In the Irish context, Hannan and Boyle (1987) found that co-educational community/comprehensive schools have a broader and more varied social-class intake than other school types. This is in keeping with their educational objectives, as well as reflecting the fact that they are usually much less subject to competition within their local catchment areas (Hannan, Boyle, 1987: 40). On the other hand, they noted the negative effects of local competition, particularly on vocational schools, where some local secondary schools "cream off" the top-ability pupils, leaving other schools with a concentration of the lower-ability and problem children from the local community (1987: 125). Lynch (1989b) also noted that single-sex secondary schools were more selective in their intake. Hence, Irish coed schools have many other things in common besides having girls and boys in the same classrooms. These factors obviously need to be controlled for in any assessment of their effects.

2.3.3 School Organisation, Gender Differentiation and School Effectiveness

School-effectiveness studies from the late 1970s onwards have not only indicated that schools "make a difference" but have isolated some organisational and cultural features which have been consistently found to be characteristic of more effective schools (Mortimore et al., 1988: 219–62; Sammons et al., 1995). In addition, a large number of studies on gender differences in educational achievement have isolated features of school management and organisation which appear to be consistently related to gender inequalities in achievement and to gender differentiation in the type of education received (review by Kelly, 1987; Marsh, 1989a, 1991).

Extensive research has demonstrated the importance of schools as socialisation agents, in most cases reinforcing the dominant values and beliefs of society (Oakley, 1985; Garrett, 1987). The gender-differentiated socialisation of the home may, therefore, be further nurtured in the school, as school ethos, teacher and peer group influences reinforce home and community values. Conversely, family-background influences may be challenged and even changed as schools (through, for example, curricular and instructional programmes, teacher expectations and peer-group influences) moderate differential gender-role cultures in both overt and subtle ways. It is likely, however, that the quite clear gender-role stereotyping characteristic of Irish schools in the early 1980s (Hannan, Breen et al., 1983) is still present, though more subtly textured than it was previously. Thus, particular attention needs to be paid to the effects of gender biases in curricular provision and allocation, and in streaming or tracking practices — found to be so important previously (Hannan, Breen et al., 1983).

2.3.4 School and Class Size

Research on the impact of school size on attainment levels has indicated either negative or contradictory effects on achievement (Rutter et al., 1979; Mortimore et al., 1988). Mortimore's work showed a curvilinear relationship between school size and effectiveness at primary level, with the very small schools and the very large schools both at a disadvantage. The larger schools tend to be more formally and hierarchically organised, with less subject-teacher involvement in the everyday running of the school, results which conform closely with the literature on medium-sized and large organisations (see Mortimore et al., 1988: 236). The obvious benefits from economy of scale, such as a more extended curriculum and more specialised teachers (see Hannan, Breen et al., 1983), are often lost through greater formalisation.

Earlier research on the impact of class size on attainment was ambiguous or somewhat contradictory in its conclusions. Rutter and Madge (1976) concluded that increasing class size does not seem to be consistently associated with negative school behaviour or attainment levels. On the other hand, recent reviews of the research literature on class-size effects indicate that significant improvements in achievement occur only with substantial reductions in class size (less than 15 pupils), and that class-size effects vary both by the social class and ability levels of the pupil body (Glass, Cahan, et al., 1982; Finn and Achilles, 1990; review by Martin and Morgan, 1994). Ability grouping within classes may also mediate the effects of class size on pupil achievement levels, with the effectiveness of such ability groups themselves being sensitive to size (Hallinan and Sorensen, 1985; Hallinan, 1994).

2.3.5 Pupil Differentiation: Streaming and Banding

The relationship between the grouping of students by their ability levels (whether mixed ability or hierarchically streamed) and achievement levels has been extensively studied. Research has indicated that within streamed schools some advantage accrues to pupils in the top stream, even after differences in ability or pre-vious achievement and social background have been taken into account (Rutter et al., 1979; Sorensen and Hallinan, 1984); but often at the cost of lower achievements for those in the bottom classes. In the Irish context, Hannan and Boyle (1987) found that increasing levels of rigidity and differentiation in the schooling process had no discernible effects on average attainment levels but significantly increased the variance in overall attainment levels. If, as that study found, girls' schools are least likely to stream, and lower-ability girls in coed schools are, therefore, more likely to be in lower-ability streams/bands, the disadvantage of coeducation may be limited to certain ability groups, and operate through factors other than coeducation per se.

Streaming influences children's attitudes and behaviour, with a tendency for lower-streamed children to be labelled as failures and to perceive themselves as such (Hargreaves, 1967; Rutter et al., 1979). Similarly, Hannan and Boyle (1987) found that stream-ing was linked to higher dropout rates from school, while alloca-tion to lower streams had a marked negative effect on educational aspirations. Highly streamed schools encourage the formation of "closed" class-based peer groups who take the maximum number of subjects together. As a result, reference-group judgments appear to be much more consistent and cumulative within streamed classes and associated peer groups. Thus, negative self-images/concepts may be more strongly reinforced in lower-streamed classes. In addition, streaming has substantial effects on curricu-lar allocation (*Ibid*: 147). For example, girls in the lower streams tend not to be allocated Science while similarly located boys are not excluded from Science in this way. Hence, the way in which streaming and "curricular tracking" in the large coed schools affect the allocation and take-up of subjects and levels, as well as gender-differentiated achievement, needs to be studied in detail.

2.3.6 Teacher Characteristics

In general, the research literature on this subject — though not always consistent — indicates little consistent relationship between school "quality", as judged in terms of the qualifications of their teachers, and overall school effectiveness (Rutter et al., 1979; though see also Dale, 1974; Ainsworth and Batten, 1974). A similar pattern is found in the Irish context in spite of substantial between-school variation in teacher qualifications (Hannan, Breen et al., 1983).

Teacher gender may also be significant. Irish single-sex schools have predominantly single-sex teacher bodies. Coed secondary and community/comprehensive schools are roughly evenly balanced, though, among coed secondary schools, those which developed from convent schools have a majority of female teachers, while those which were originally boys' schools have a predominantly male teacher body (Hannan et al., 1983: 233). Gender differences have also been found in teachers' attitudes to equal opportunities. In an English survey of teachers, male respondents were much more likely to indicate opposition to equal opportunities than female respondents. Teachers of Maths, physical sciences and technical crafts (mainly male) were least in favour of equal gender opportunities (Pratt, 1985: 24). Again, however, such gender, qualifications and attitudinal differences amongst teachers may have more effect on students' take up of, and performance in, particular subjects and on third-level and occupational aspirations than on overall performance (see Hannan, Breen et al., 1983: 233–4).

2.3.7 School Curriculum and School Type

There appear to be at least three aspects of school type and curriculum that are relevant to educational achievement. The first is attendance at a more academic (secondary/grammar) school, in countries like our own with a differentiated school system, where it appears to increase level of educational achievement (Allmendinger, 1989; Shavit, 1990). In Ireland, controlling for the substantial social class and previous ability/performance differences between pupils and schools, attendance at a vocational

school has a slight but clear negative effect on Leaving Certificate performance for girls, though not for boys (Breen, 1986: 65–86). Secondly, however, even in almost completely comprehensive school systems, such as the United States, substantial "curricular tracking" occurs within schools, with allocation to these tracks being significantly affected by social class of origin as well as by academic ability and previous performance (Oakes, 1985). Allocation to a non-academic curricular track appears to have a significant depressing effect on overall educational performance as well as on third-level entry chances (Oakes, op. cit.; Shavit, 1984, 1990; Bryk, Lee and Holland, 1993).

However, focusing solely on the level of educational attainment or on overall examination grades yields only a partial assessment of the effectiveness of vocational education or allocation to vocational/technical tracks. For the majority of pupils who do not go on to third-level education, placements in a vocational track, or specialising in vocational-technical subjects, appear to have significant positive effects. In the Irish case, for instance, this group is more likely to be employed on leaving school (Hannan, Ó Riain, 1993: 109); and those in the group are also more likely to be satisfied with the quality of the education they received (Hannan and Shortall, 1991: 128–63). This Irish research is supported by more recent international studies which show that taking such vocational-technical courses increases both the chances of employment and the skilled quality of that employment (Shavit, Muller, Kraus, Katz-Gerro, 1994). It appears, therefore, that schools can vary significantly in the nature of the curriculum they provide and in the extent to which they use it to maximise the educational chances of pupils of moderate to low academic ability.

2.3.8 School Ethos and Academic Press

In many studies, variables related to school ethos, climate and policy have been found to be moderately predictive of average school achievement scores (Brookover et al., 1979; Madaus et al., 1979; Rutter et al., 1979; Mortimore et al., 1988; Smith et al., 1988). These school-climate variables include students' academic achievement expectations, along with school and teachers' "academic press", that is, school and teacher expectations and support for high academic performance. Hannan, Breen et al. (1983), for instance, found significant variation in the "achievement ethos" of Irish schools. Boys' schools tend to have a higher achievement ethos with a clear instrumental bias (towards Maths/Science rather than arts) while girls' schools have, on average, a more modest achievement ethos with less specialised liberal curricula (op. cit.: 197); but, generally, more concern for those of average to below-average academic ability.

Amongst the variables found to be important by Madaus et al. (1980) were teachers' estimates of the extent to which their classes conformed to "academic press", as well as classes' perceptions of the extent to which teachers expected them to conform to it. In overall terms, students tended to perform better in schools with a strong academic emphasis. The Rutter et al. (1979) study also found that schools which scored high on measures of academic emphasis (such as more homework, and higher teacher expectations) tended to secure better outcomes (op. cit.: 109).

To some extent, such variation in the academic climate of schools is a function of school and class organisation. One English study, for instance, found that pupils in comprehensive (coed) schools with large sixth forms did as well in Maths and Science as those in grammar schools (traditionally more academic and disproportionately single sex). The presence of large sixth forms helped to create and maintain a climate for academic study in the lower forms (Bryan and Digby, 1986). However, it is not just the presence and prestige of academic-level classes in the school that is important, but the nature and quality of the "schooling process". The effectiveness and commitment of management and staff, the provision and structuring of an intellectually challenging, highly organised and disciplined classroom work environment, effective interpersonal communication between pupils and teachers, and between teachers and management, as well as a general positive climate for academic achievement, are all important (Mortimore et al., 1988).

Creating and maintaining a high value on academic attainment amongst pupils may be very difficult, however, if the intake to a school consists of a high proportion of less able children, which increases a tendency to form non-academic peer groups, indifferent, or even opposed, to academic success (Rutter et al., 1979: 202).

2.3.9 Homework and Study

Time spent on homework and study has been found to be strongly and positively related to exam performance (Madaus et al., 1980:

105; Cooper, 1989; Postlethwaite and Ross, 1992); as well as to achievement levels in Maths and Science (Martin, Hickey and Murchan, 1992). There appear to be some differences between coed and single-sex schools in the amount of study undertaken (Trickett et al., 1983; Lee and Bryk, 1986; Marsh, 1989a) — with students in single-sex schools spending more time each day doing homework and independent study. However, controls for pupil composition differences amongst schools were not always adequate in these studies.

2.3.10 Discipline

Discipline has a positive effect on school academic achievement (Madaus et al., 1980: 100; Coleman et al., 1982; Coleman and Hoffer, 1987). It has been observed that good discipline, the involvement of pupils in discipline (through the use of the prefect system) and a low use of corporal punishment are most likely to be associated with good attendance and higher levels of student achievement (see Rutter et al., 1979: 17). Mortimore et al.'s (1988) sophisticated study of school effectiveness in the London region showed that the provision of a highly structured and disciplined work environment in the classroom and the school were some of the most important aspects of effective schools. In terms of the association of discipline with coeducation, a number of studies have shown that students who had attended both single-sex and coeducational schools perceived the single-sex schools to be stricter than the mixed schools (Dale, 1969: 232; Schneider and Coutts, 1982); with Lee and Bryk (1986: 385) finding that girls in single-sex schools reported fewer discipline problems.

2.3.11 Summary of School-Level Factors

Besides their more obvious effects at the individual level, pupil compositional characteristics (such as average social class) have been found to impact on average student performance at a school level. The particular impact of coeducation on pupil achievement will be discussed in greater detail in a later section. While research findings on the effect of certain school organisational factors (such as school and class size) have been ambiguous, a number of factors are found to have a strong relationship with pupil achievement and gender differentiation. Firstly, rigid streaming within a school tends to have a significant polarising effect on pupil attainment levels, as well as reinforcing negative self-concepts and poorer achievements in lower streamed classes, resulting in higher dropout rates among these groups. Secondly, certain aspects of the school ethos, particularly a strong academic emphasis and a supportive, structured and disciplined work environment, have positive effects on overall pupil performance. However, such a priority on academic achievement may inadvertently disadvantage pupils of lower academic ability. Attention, therefore, also needs to be given to pupils of average to below-average academic ability, who perhaps have strong capabilities in other areas of the curriculum, such as vocational-technical subjects, Music or Art.

2.4   DIFFERENCES IN ATTITUDES AND ABILITIES EXISTING PRIOR TO SECOND-LEVEL SCHOOLING

2.4.1 Early Family Socialisation and the Development of Gendered Roles and Attitudes

Deeply rooted cultural differences by gender exist in virtually every culture and result in the socialisation of girls and boys into gender role models that are often so deeply entrenched that they are unselfconsciously reproduced in child-rearing practices. From the child's earliest learning experiences gendered attributions are used to define who one is, what one should do and why. By the age of five, most children's views on appropriate behaviour and expectations are gender-typed, and their behaviour is monitored and adapted in the light of these distinctions (Weinreich, 1978; Davies and Kandel, 1981; Maccoby, 1988). Central to this development are parental attitudes and behaviours, reinforcing traditional gendered roles even when the parents themselves consider that they are acting in a totally egalitarian manner (Lewin and Tragos, 1987). Hence, parents play a crucial role in moulding their children's gender identification (Hunt and Hilton, 1981; Block, 1983; Garrett, 1987; Berk, 1989); with almost a direct link between the beliefs, attitudes and values of parents (particularly mothers) and the attitudes and behaviour of children (Youniss and Smollar, 1985). Mothers, on average, tend to treat babies differently according to their gender, with girls expected to be more delicate and needing to be protected. Similarly, fathers tend to discourage evidence of "feminine behaviour" in boys. Boys are also more likely to be encouraged to develop their independence earlier, and thus their sense of autonomy and self-confidence is often much stronger than that of girls, even at an early age (Fitzgerald and Crites, 1980).

2.4.2 Interpersonal Interaction Styles

Maccoby (1990), in a critical review of the research literature on the subject, suggests that, although significant gender differentiation may occur in early family socialisation (which has subsequent effects on young male and female infants' attitudes, expectations and personality traits), it cannot so easily explain the very early development of distinctive sex-typed interpersonal interaction styles. She concludes that, even in early and middle childhood, peer-group interaction amongst young children shows clear sex differences in interpersonal interaction styles. Gender segregation in peer interaction is widespread in most cultural settings at very young ages — being greater in situations which are not structured by adults, and increasing as children age. Besides segregating themselves, young boys' and young girls' styles of interaction differ significantly — young boys being more directive, aggressive and potentially controlling; while girls are more facilitative, indirect and more emotionally supportive of others. The presence of adults significantly moderates the more directive and aggressive behaviour of boys, and reduces the gender inequalities in interaction. Obviously, managements and teachers in coed schools need to take these gender differences in interaction styles into consideration in order to ensure equality of treatment — otherwise boys would clearly dominate in classroom interactions.

2.4.3 Gender Differences in Language, Maths and Spatial Ability

Gender differences in ability, aptitude, expectations and attitudes are strongly associated with preceding differences in socialisation — varying, therefore, to some extent by culture. A review of the international literature shows, for instance, significant cross-cultural differences in what is regarded as "masculine" and "feminine". Thus, our interpretation of male- and female-associated characteristics is often based on assumptions drawn from our own cultural perspective (Kelly 1978; 1981; Eccles et al., 1983; Giorgi and March, 1990).

Despite this cultural variation, however, most studies have

shown female superiority in verbal ability from an early stage of development. Girls, on average, speak significantly earlier and develop linguistic skills at a faster pace than boys (Eccles et al., 1984; Linn and Petersen, 1985). This accelerated verbal development from infancy may give girls a head start which is maintained throughout childhood. Consequently, girls have been found to have fewer learning problems in verbal skills than boys, who display more and larger learning deficits (Wittig and Petersen, 1979).

The male advantage in mathematical ability tends to emerge later, at the post-puberty stage, with boys having a slight average advantage, but a significantly greater tendency to show exceptional ability (Maccoby and Jacklin, 1974; Eccles et al., 1984). Even then, the strongest predictors of mathematical performance appear to be the perceived value of Maths and Maths "self-concept" (that is, the perception of own Maths ability) of participants (Eccles et al., op. cit.). Girls, on average, are more likely to avoid the tougher, higher level Maths options or do less well in tests because they see Maths as less relevant to their future lives and/or because they have lower perceptions of their own ability, even when their own previous performance equalled that of boys (Hannan, Breen et al., 1983: 248–82). Furthermore, girls are more likely to attribute good performances in Maths to external factors, such as luck or good teachers, rather than to their own ability (Stipek, 1984; Kimball, 1989).

The implications of the above research are clear. Differences in Maths ability cannot simply be innate, since variance in Maths ability and performance increases in the post-puberty stage, and differences in ability even then are too small to explain the lower performance by females in Maths. Secondly, findings, which show how self-concept, curricular and pedagogical practice, and the gender-typing of Maths as a masculine area influence Maths choices and performance, suggest that wider and more complex social-psychological and social (including schooling) factors are at work.

Of all the areas in which gender differences in ability have been identified, spatial abilities have been amongst the most widely reported. The implications of lower levels of spatial ability for subject choice are considerable, since such aptitudes are so beneficial for subjects such as Physics, Computing, Engineering and some practical subjects. While the degree of difference varies according to the nature of the task involved (see Halpern, 1986), results in general have shown consistent differences in favour of boys. Spatial tasks are usually of three types: mental rotation, spatial perception and spatial visualisation (Witkin et al., 1954). These tasks require imaginative visual manipulation of three-dimensional objects and interpretation of spatial relationships. While mental-rotation tasks show the most consistent and greatest differences in favour of boys, average abilities are higher for boys in all three areas (Halpern, 1986).

Explanations for these gender differences have been divided between those who maintain that the differences are biologically (usually hormonally) based (Berk, 1989), and those who maintain that spatial ability is learned — for example, through differential childhood play experiences (Baeninger and Newcombe, 1989). In the latter view, boys' toys, such as blocks, puzzles and building sets, can encourage manipulation and innovative play with objects from a very early age, thus improving spatial ability for males. Specific "spatial training", using various tasks and games, can, however, significantly reduce observed gender differences in spatial ability (Tracey, 1987).

These gender differences in cognition or aptitudes, whether biologically or environmentally determined, become evident at a relatively young age. There are other social-psychological factors, emerging much later, which also show significant gender differences and which have substantial effects on educational achievement. We deal with a number of these social-psychological variables here: differences in academic self-concept, in levels of self-confidence and self-esteem, in levels of educational expectations, and in level and type of occupational/career aspirations.

2.4.4 Self-concept

At least two separate aspects of self-concept are important: the more narrow "academic" aspect — self-concepts of own ability, aptitude or performance potential, and the more general one of beliefs about one's self in terms of general competencies, moral worth and overall value and attractiveness to self and others (Rosenberg and Pearlin, 1978; Leahy, 1985; Rosenberg et al., 1985; Rosenberg, 1995).

Self-concept in academic areas is substantially correlated with academic achievement, but non-academic facets (for example, physical appearance, relationships) of self-concept are not (Marsh et al., 1988). There appears to be a marked difference by gender in the direct effect of self-concept on academic achievement. For females, such self-concepts of academic ability appear to mediate significantly the impact of ability and subject/level choices on educational attainment, whereas this mediating affect of self-concept effect is less marked for males (Turritin et al., 1983: 407).

In the Irish context, girls tend to have significantly lower educational self-concepts than boys, even at the same level of academic performance (Hannan et al., 1983). However, such self-concepts vary by subject area — girls having higher self-concepts (or sense of competency) than boys in some areas, such as languages; and lower self-concepts in other areas, like Mathematics. These differences tend to be consistent with gender stereotypes (Dusek and Flaherty, 1981; Hannan, Breen et al., 1983; Marsh et al., 1988; Rowe, 1988). These gender differences in educational self-concepts appear to be well established at primary-school level, with boys more likely to rate themselves more favourably than girls in a range of subject areas — not only in Maths but also in English, as well as in intelligence and memory (Kellaghan and Fontes, 1988). Girls' level of "subject confidence", however, is also significantly influenced by parental and teacher support (Hannan, Breen et al., 1983: 276–82).

2.4.5 Educational and Occupational Aspirations

Besides objective family-background effects, research has consistently shown a clear impact of parental and pupil educational and occupational aspirations and expectations on levels of educational achievement (Sewell, Haller and Portes, 1969; Sewell, Haller and Ohlendorf, 1970). Schools and teachers also play important roles in affecting pupil expectations and subsequent performance. Parental and teacher expectations and support appear to be particularly important in girls' "non-traditional" subject choices and examination performance (Hannan, Breen et al., 1983: 262–82; Carpenter, 1985; Breen, 1986).

2.5　GENDERED ATTITUDES TO SUBJECTS

One consequence of differential socialisation on the development of gendered self-concepts and occupational aspirations is the gradual evolution of different attitudes towards subjects as girls' and boys' school careers evolve over time. Pupils enter second-level schools knowing little about certain subjects. As a result, their growing awareness and experience of these subjects, the increased significance of the views of their peers and teachers, and the general attitudinal climate of the school, as well as the development of differentiated educational/career plans, gradually lead to the development of differential attitudes toward different subject areas. This attitudinal process seems to become more crystallised, or more salient, at senior-cycle level. Gender differences in attitudes toward different subjects are most obvious in Maths, Science (particularly the physical sciences) and in the language/literature area. Each of these is examined in turn below.

2.5.1 Maths

There appear to be a number of reasons why Maths is male dominant: cognitive/aptitude differences between the sexes (Maccoby and Jacklin, 1974); the historical dominance of males in these subjects, the nature of the rational-technical logic involved and the often "male" nature of the examples used (Kelly, 1978; 1981; 1987; Spender, 1982); parents', teachers' and peers' attitudes and expectations; the lack of successful role models in schools and society for girls; and the lack of fit between Mathematics and the educational/career expectations of girls (Hardin and Dede, 1973; Kahle and Lakes, 1983; Oakes, 1990).

Compared to boys, girls have been found to have more negative attitudes to Maths (Hannan et al., 1983), though the extent of these differences appears to vary by school type. Some studies indicate that attitudes may become more polarised over time in coed schools, with older girls tending to draw away from Mathematics because boys are perceived as better, and boys correspondingly drawing away from literary subjects because girls are seen as better (Dale, 1974; Stables, 1990). This finding is consistent with the hypothesis that each gender, when educated with the other, may tend to use subject preferences to assert gender role identity (Ormerod, 1975). In contrast, results from the Irish context do not support these findings on polarisation of attitudes to subjects and choices in coed schools, but suggest that the greatest gender differences occur in single-sex schools (Hannan et al., 1983: 34–6).

In interpreting differences in subject preference between coed and single-sex schools, Ormerod (1975) argued that attitudes of, and towards, teachers play an important mediating role. In support of this view, Hannan et al. (1983) found that pupils' perceptions of teacher expectations for them were more important for girls choosing higher level Maths. Class composition may also be important, even within coed schools. Rowe (1988), for example, found that being placed in single-sex classes in a coed school was associated with greater confidence among girls, which in turn significantly increased the likelihood of their subsequent participation in senior-cycle Mathematics courses (see also Smith, 1980).

2.5.2   Science

In some respects, gender differences in attitudes toward Science reflect those toward Mathematics. However, significant differences arise between the physical and biological sciences, with the former generally perceived as "male" subjects. Differential attitudes, previous experience and differential school/teacher encouragement for the physical sciences all interact to affect physical science take-up by girls. Keys and Ormerod (1976), for instance, record that a significant number of girls with a high preference for Physics dropped Physics, while a significant number of boys with low Physics preference took it for O-levels. Head (1987) linked subject choice to "ego-development", arguing that male adolescents going through a period of questioning and reformulation of identity toward a more secure adult identity, are more likely to perceive Science as a conventional and acceptable subject/career choice for boys — offering firm, clear and methodically derived answers to complex questions. Girls at a similar stage of development are more likely to avoid Science, partly because it is a less conventional choice, and partly because of some aptitude and value differences in approaching scientific reasoning, with girls who choose Science at the senior level being more likely to be emotionally mature and more self-confident. Research on the "Girls into Science and Technology" (GIST) project indicates that girls perceive Science as a man's world, and not particularly useful in getting a job (Whyte, 1986; Kelly, 1987).

2.5.3   French

Most studies show a clear gender difference in attitudes to French. In the Irish case, for instance, girls are more likely than boys to think that French is interesting, useful and less difficult (Hannan, Breen et al., 1983: 34). As to the effects of co-education on such attitudes, Dale (1974) found some evidence of a polarisation effect for French, with girls' liking for French being increased by the presence of boys in the classroom, with these sex differences increasing with age. However, these differences in attitude did not appear to result in a consistent tendency for coed boys to perform worse in French than those in boys-only schools. However, other studies have indicated that attainment in French was enhanced for both sexes by single-sex schooling (Steedman, 1983a; Willis and Kenway, 1986).

2.5.4 Summary

Both parental and teacher expectations appear to shape pupils' educational aspirations, which in turn influence the take-up of, and performance in, particular subjects. Research, both national and international, indicates marked gender differences in attitudes towards, and take-up of, many subjects — particularly Mathematics, Science and languages. A number of British and American studies have suggested that this gender polarisation is more pronounced in coed than in single-sex schools. However, not all studies support these findings: research in the Irish context providing some evidence that the greatest gender differences occur amongst those in single-sex schools (Hannan, Breen, et al., 1983).

2.6   INTERACTION BETWEEN PUPILS AND TEACHERS AND AMONGST PUPILS

2.6.1 Pupil–Teacher Interaction

Gender-differentiated treatment by teachers of girls and boys within the same classroom may significantly affect equality of outcomes. The allocation of classroom work tasks to primary-school pupils by teachers shows significant gender differences. Stereotypical allocation is more obvious at a younger age, with "caring roles", like looking after younger children, being allocated to girls and the more physically demanding tasks, like shifting around classroom furniture, being allocated to boys (Lewis and Kellaghan, 1993). Many observation studies of classroom interaction in coeducational schools have shown a consistent tendency for boys to get more attention from teachers; though, when questioned, girls in Irish schools (including those in coed schools) reported more positive interaction with teachers, and boys reported more frequent sanctioning by teachers (see Hannan, Breen et al., 1983: 36–43). It is estimated in some studies that boys receive almost two-thirds of a teacher's attention in coed class-rooms, principally through a higher incidence of teacher-demand-ing behaviours and teacher–student disciplinary interactions involving boys (Wernersson, 1991; Spender, 1982).

Teachers initiate more behavioural, disciplining, procedural and academic interactions with boys than with girls, while boys are more likely to initiate communication with the teacher — by calling out answers without being first recognised, for instance (Brophy and Good, 1974; Wilson, 1991). In general, male pupils in coed classes appear more likely to take chances and to be more impulsive and intuitive in their answering, whereas female stu-dents take more time, are more careful and reflective and are less likely to be adventurous in answering questions. Hence, girls are less likely to put up their hands straight away and, as a result, are less likely to be called upon by the teacher to answer (Krupnick, 1985; Fiske, 1990). In the Irish context, Lewis and Kellaghan's (1993) study shows clear gender differences in the frequency and type of sanctions used by teachers at primary level, with gender differences being greater in mixed than in single-sex schools (29–32).

Pupil–teacher interaction appears to differ between single-sex and coed schools. Single-sex school classrooms were rated higher in student involvement in the class, particularly for girls (Cocklin, 1982; Trickett et al., 1983). Dale (1974), despite his overall posi-tive conclusions about coed schools, found that younger girls from coed schools expressed rather more reluctance to speak out in class than did their counterparts in girls-only schools. This differ-ence was still apparent at 17 years of age. Coed boys had a mini-mal advantage, but those aged 17 years were also rather more reluctant to speak out than were the boys from single-sex schools. However, very few girls in coed classes attribute their fear of speaking out to the presence of boys (1974: 135). Some later studies did, however, find some negative class "put downs" and even harassment of girls in coed schools (Jones, 1985; Mahony, 1985; Stanworth, 1983).

Gender differences in pupil–teacher interaction appear to be more marked in particular subjects. A study of Science teachers, for instance, concluded that they interact more with boys than with girls in Science lessons, although the difference is most marked in teacher sanctioning and control of boys (Crossman, 1987).

Some research indicates that boys and girls have different

learning and classroom interaction styles and respond differently to various teaching strategies and types of teacher behaviour (Ormerod and Duckworth, 1975; Maccoby, 1988; 1990). If so, this could mean that in coeducational classes teachers may unwittingly adopt practices which encourage boys, while reinforcing girls' less assertive styles of interaction and gendered beliefs about Maths and the physical sciences (Ormerod, 1975). Some research studies of coed classes, for instance, show that the teaching style and expectations of Science teachers vary according to whether boys or girls predominate. Classes having a majority of girls are more likely to be characterised by lower-order intellectual activities (like rote learning), whereas classes having mostly boys are more likely to engage in higher-order intellectual activities such as abstract problem-solving, analyses, inference and hypotheses generation (Willis and Kenway, 1986). In Mathematics teaching, Fennema and Peterson's (1986) findings suggest that what constitutes effective teacher behaviour depends both on the gender of the student and on the cognitive level of the Mathematics task. Neutral feedback, for instance, to correct student responses, particularly to more difficult Maths/Science questions, may be much less effective for girls than for boys.

The impact of teacher sanctions and rewards on student attainment levels has been well documented. The use of positive (verbal) feedback/rewards by teachers tends to be associated with a higher level of student achievement, though the use of formal prizes shows only a weak and inconsistent association with achievement outcomes (Rutter et al., 1979). While some research suggests that teachers praise boys as often as they praise girls (Brophy and Good, 1974), Hannan et al. (1983) found that girls across all school types reported higher levels of perceived reward and positive feedback from teachers than did boys. Punishment, or negative (verbal) sanctions, on the other hand, whether for academic or social/behavioural failures, appears to be more frequent for boys (Brophy and Good 1974; Hannan, Breen et al., 1983; Fennema and Peterson, 1986). The Hannan et al. (1983) results, however, were based on questionnaires completed by pupils rather than on classroom observations and, hence, reflect pupils' expectations as well as actual experiences. Thus, if girls in coed classes have lower expectations of teacher interaction than boys, their reported level of supportive contact will overstate the actual level achieved relative to boys.

In contrast to the above results, Carpenter (1985) found that girls in coed schools were less likely to report teacher encouragement for post-secondary studies than were their counterparts in single-sex schools. However, girls at coed schools who experienced teacher encouragement for further study were more likely to achieve higher grades than girls experiencing similar influences at single-sex schools. Although less frequently occurring, such encouragements were more influential. Thus, the social context of classes — whether mixed or single sex — may significantly mediate the differential impact of teacher support or sanctions on girls and boys. However, the results from different studies in this area are not consistent — some studies showing, for instance, that students of both sexes from coeducational schools had more positive attitudes towards teachers than had students from single-sex schools (Feather, 1974; Schneider et al., 1988), in contrast to Carpenter's (1985) findings.

In interpreting differences in subject preference and performance between pupils in coeducational and single-sex schools, attitudes towards, and responsiveness to and by, teachers play an important mediating role (Ormerod, 1975). Girls appear to be more affected by teacher attitudes and behaviour, whether implicit or explicit, particularly in non-traditional subject areas (Sears and Feldman, 1974; Hannan, Breen et al., 1983; Stables, 1990).

The significant effects of teacher expectations on pupil attainments have also been shown in many studies (Pilling and Pringle, 1978; Rutter et al., 1979; Carpenter, 1985). In an Irish context, Hannan et al. (1983) found that teacher expectations had clear effects on pupils' performance and educational and career expectations, particularly in choice of higher level Maths for girls, while no such effect was evident for boys (op. cit.: 273). Thus, in general, teacher expectations and encouragement appear to be more important for girls than boys, especially for performance in "male" subjects.

2.6.2 Pupil–Pupil Interaction

Hannan, Breen et al. (1983) found that girls are significantly less competitive or assertive in class than boys, in both single-sex and coed schools. If this pattern applies generally, it would have substantial implications for teaching styles in coed classes.

Inter-pupil expectations may be highly influential in the perpetuation of gender role stereotypes, even influencing perceptions of cognitive ability, as well as subject choice (Pearson and Ferguson, 1989). The adolescent period, during which important academic decisions must be made, having major implications for future life courses, is a time when physical differences between the sexes become highly apparent and salient. Motivation to conform to peer group expectations, which provide a reference framework for all actions, is at its greatest at that period (Medrich et al., 1982). For adolescent girls in particular, the cultural definition of what it means to be "feminine" is especially strong and is constantly evaluated and sanctioned by peers and teachers within the school environment. Research has highlighted the possibility that girls, in order to appear more attractive to the opposite sex, strive to appear less clever and may avoid such subjects as higher level Maths and the physical sciences because they are perceived to be male domains and thus incompatible with ideal images of femininity (Whyte, 1986). Girls may also feel more pressurised by male peers in coed schools to conform to the traditional gender role stereotype. Girls who confront these norms and take male-dominated subjects are often regarded as self-determined, strong-willed — judgments which may not be welcomed (Orlofosky, 1977; Wetter, 1977).

Research points to the higher level of self-esteem required, and the advantages of supportive significant others, particularly parents and teachers, for those girls taking non-traditional routes (Erickson, 1968; Hannan, Breen et al., op. cit.). This often provides the social support necessary to withstand peer-group pressure and adopt a more "deviant" orientation (Landsbaum and Willis, 1971). Kandel and Lesser (1972), however, point out that, although peer acceptance is crucial to adolescents, parents and teachers are usually more influential in the development of educational aspirations.

2.6.3 Summary

Research indicates marked gender differences in pupil–teacher interaction, with boys both initiating and receiving more interactions from teachers. In spite of this, however, girls report a higher level of positive feedback from teachers. Teacher encouragement of, and expectations for, pupils appears to have a marked effect on subject take-up and exam performance. This effect appears to be stronger for girls than for boys, especially in gender-typed subjects. Peer-group interaction and pressures also appear to be important in the development and reinforcement of gender differentiation, especially in coed schools.

2.7   THE EFFECTS OF COEDUCATION

The questioning of the value of coeducation for girls is a relatively recent phenomenon; indeed, coeducation itself is of relatively recent (post-war) origin in most Western countries. Up to at least the mid-1950s, with the general exception of the United States, single-sex education had been the norm in most Western countries, particularly at second level. Such gender-differentiated schooling corresponded closely to the prevailing traditional division of labour and patriarchal authority system in society at that time. From a much earlier period in the United States, but generally corresponding to the rapid growth and comprehensivisation of post-primary education in Britain and most of the white Commonwealth countries, coeducation grew rapidly from the mid to late 1950s onwards. The main political driving forces behind this rapid growth of comprehensive coeducational expansion were twofold. Firstly, it was widely believed to be necessary to expand educational participation for economic growth reasons. Secondly, comprehensivisation was viewed as a mechanism to tackle the glaring class inequalities in educational achievement characteristic of the older wide divisions between the (upper and middle class) grammar schools and the (working class) vocational/technical and general secondary schools. Tackling the gender inequalities in provision and outcomes that, in retrospect, were glaringly obvious in the schooling of the time had a low priority during that expansionary phase from the late 1950s to the early 1970s. These inequalities were so deeply institutionalised and so taken for granted that they, by and large, remained unquestioned.

The first major study of coeducation in Britain — Dale's three-volume study *Mixed or Single Sex Schools?*, published in 1969, 1971 and 1974 — was framed in a context of general acceptance of the prevailing gender-differentiated power and division of labour relationships of that time. His general conclusions were that co-education provided the optimal preparation for adult life for both sexes and (somewhat more cautiously) that girls' educational progress was not held back by coeducation, although his results indicated some minor educational achievement disadvantages for girls, especially for Maths and Science.

Soon after the publication of Dale's 1974 study, however, a series of British studies raised serious doubts about girls' educational achievements in coed schools and classes. Findings suggested that girls had higher average achievements and took more "male" subjects — like Maths and Science — in single-sex classes (within coed schools), if not in girls' schools (Ormerod, 1975; Shaw, 1976; Spender et al., 1980; Arnot, 1983; Deem, 1984). However, most of these studies had inadequate designs or statistical controls for social class and academic-ability differences between single-sex and coed schools (which were unrelated to their co-educational status), or were based on unrepresentative case studies of single-sex and coed schools. However, two later studies, which were more statistically sophisticated and larger scale, came to either neutral or negative conclusions about the effects of coeducation on girls' achievement. Bone's (1983) comprehensive review and meta-analysis of the more statistically sophisticated studies of the effects of coeducation, carried out for the UK's Equal Opportunities Commission, came to the conclusion that, taking into consideration the substantial social class and ability differences between single-sex and coed schools and other unrelated school-type characteristics:

> the subject mixes taken by girls, their academic results and the responses of the schools to their more personal needs have been conditioned far more by the type of school they attend (comprehensive, grammar, modern or independent) and by the style of school (traditional or not) than by whether their school was single sex or mixed (op. cit: 1–2).

At the same time, she concluded that, although there was some consistent evidence of greater sex role stereotyping in pupil attitudes in coed schools ("where girls look more favourably on male areas of study when they are educated with other girls"), there was no evidence that girls' schools actually used this educational advantage to any great effect. However, girls did appear to enjoy mixed schools more, with some evidence that both sexes acquired less stereotyped attitudes towards the other sex in coed settings, even though girls had to compete more with boys for the teachers' attention (op. cit.: 4).

Steedman's (1983a; 1983b) studies, based on the large-scale longitudinal Child Development Study data, with good statistical controls for prior pupil ability and family social background, found that "very little in their examination results is explained by whether schools are mixed or single sex once allowance is made for differences in intake" (op. cit., 1983a: 98).

The development of new computer statistical packages in the late 1980s ("multi-level modelling"), which could more adequately model the specific effects of schools as instructional/learning organisations, allied to the availability of longitudinal educational performance data for pupils attending schools in the Inner London Education Authority area, allowed more accurate estimation of the independent effects of school type on educational performance. The resultant research either came to conclusions (in the early reports) that girls in single-sex schools had higher achievements, or came to ambiguous conclusions, controlling for prior ability differences. However, later studies of schools in the same area, using multi-level statistical models, which provided more accurate estimates of school effects (ILEA, RS 1277/90; Goldstein et al., 1993), concluded that there was no significant advantage in the educational achievement (public examination results) of girls in single-sex schools, once prior intake differences amongst schools and students' prior performance were taken into consideration. However, they did find in this, and an earlier study, that schools appeared to differ in their effectiveness with different kinds of students and for different subjects (Goldstein et al., 1993), as had Steedman (1983a; 1983b) in her earlier study. Similarly, other studies by Nuttall et al. (1992), and by Thomas et al. (1994) of samples of schools from a number of local education authority areas, using multi-level models and sophisticated controls for prior ability and family circumstances, found the single-sex/coed schools difference to be insignificant. Not all of the more recent and more statistically sophisticated British studies, however, came to the same conclusion (see Thomas et al., 1993).

We might draw three preliminary conclusions from these British studies. First, it is essential to control for all relevant "extraneous" variables when comparing coeducational and single-sex schools, including social class and ability/prior performance differences between pupils attending coeducational and single-sex schools. Secondly, if there are any such coed effects, these inter-school differences appear to be small on average, but may be quite important for particular subgroups: for example, pupils of lower academic abilities or those from very deprived backgrounds. Thirdly, it appears more likely that, if such coed effects exist, they are likely to be more prevalent in subjects like Maths and the physical sciences, where boys have traditionally been more successful.

A substantial amount of research on the effects of coeducation has been carried out in Australia, where, in some of its provinces, a high proportion of schools are still single sex. Most satisfactorily designed studies of the effects of coeducation on girls' academic achievements carried out there come to much the same conclusions as their British equivalents, indicating no effects or slight negative ones, particularly on Maths/Science achievements. Carpenter's (1985) study showed that, controlling for the complex of confounding variables involved, coed schools had little overall effect. However, there was significant interaction between mothers' employment, occupational status, school type and girls' educational achievement. Young and Fraser's (1990) study of achievements in Science suggested significant advantages of single-sex education for girls. However, Young's (1994) later study of Physics showed no such effect. An earlier study by Yates and Firkin (1986), however, found that high performers in Mathematics were more likely to come from single-sex schools, controlling for most confounding variables. This result was supported by Ditchburn and Martin's (1986) study about participation in Maths and Science courses, as well as in attitudes towards Maths and physical science courses (Bryan and Digby, 1986; Stables, 1990; Gill, 1992; Daly, 1995).

In a number of longitudinal case studies of the effects of amalgamations of single-sex schools in Sydney, the research showed that, at least in terms of overall academic achievement, girls did not suffer any decline in achievement levels or in self-esteem (Marsh et al., 1988; Sampson, 1989). In contrast, another Australian study of coeducational amalgamations (Jones, Kyle and Black, 1987) found that, although students' views of coeducation were positive — particularly in terms of personal and social development (as it was for ex-pupils in Ireland (Hannan, Ó Riain, 1993)) — perceived levels of inter-pupil competition and inequalities in allocation of teachers' time had increased with amalgamation.

Thus, it would appear from these British and Australian studies that, although there may be no, or only very slight, advantages to girls' overall academic achievements in single-sex schools, some consistent findings indicate that, particularly in subjects like Maths and the physical sciences, there are some advantages to girls' education in single-sex settings, if not necessarily in single-sex schools. In addition, at least in the initial period after amalgamations, coeducation may have some overall academic disadvantages for girls — a warning note that had originally been struck by Dale (1971: 162, 284–8), even though his overall evaluation of coeducational provision was positive.

The American research literature on coeducational comprehensive (high-school) education has a much longer pedigree, at least as far back as Coleman's (1961) study of school adolescent peer groups and adolescent subcultures. This study showed some clear negative effects for adolescent girls, warning at one point that "coeducation in some high schools may be inimical to both academic achievement and social adjustment" (op. cit.: 50). However, most of the critical studies of coeducation were not carried out until the mid- to late 1980s — primarily because of the increasing saliency of gender inequalities, with the growing power of the feminist movement, as well as, paradoxically, a growing interest in Catholic schools where most single-sex provision still occurs. Moore et al.'s (1993) extensive review of the research literature, in a special report commissioned for and published by the United States Department of Education, severely criticised existing research for its inadequate statistical design. Essentially, many studies compared non-equivalent schools, in terms of the social class and ability of their pupil intakes and differences in school characteristics unrelated to coeducation per se.

Some of the more statistically sophisticated studies — mostly of Catholic schools — have found small but statistically significant negative effects for girls in coed schools (Lee and Bryk, 1986; 1989). However, even these results were strongly contested on the basis of research design because of their limited controls for other pre-existing differences in pupils and other statistical flaws. Marsh (1989b; 1989c) claimed, from his re-analyses of their results and other results based on the longitudinal or follow-up studies of the "High School and Beyond" national survey, that coed/single-sex school differences were not significant, once adequate controls for pupil intake differences and prior achievements had been taken into consideration. However, a later and more substantial study by Bryk, Lee and Holland (1993), with an array of social-background controls for pupil characteristics, showed clear positive effects for girls' academic achievement as well as for social and personal development outcomes (self-image/concept, locus of control, educational aspirations and less stereotyped gender role attitudes) in girls' schools. Their main finding was a "broad base of positive effects for single-sex schools across a broad array of educational outcomes" (op. cit.: 239). This more recent and more statistically sophisticated study supports earlier less statistically conclusive results which indicated that girls in coed schools had less favourable attitudes to "male" subjects like Maths and physical sciences (Finn, 1980; Blin-Stoyle, 1983; Vockell and Lobonc, 1987; Lee and Lockheed, 1990).

The main Irish study on coeducation (Hanafin, 1992; Hanafin and Ní Chárthaigh, 1993) was based on 17 second-level schools in the Limerick area. It included controls for social-class differences in pupil intake and school differential dropout rates to the Leaving Certificate, but not for prior ability differences. The study found that single-sex schools significantly advantaged girls in terms of academic achievement at Leaving Cert level. However, an earlier unpublished study reported in Drudy and Lynch (1993), based on the original *Schooling and Sex Roles* (1983) data base, had found no significant difference, although again no controls for prior ability/achievement differences were used. Neither study, however, used the newer statistical software packages for multi-level modelling, which provide more accurate and reliable estimates of school-level effects.

On the other hand, Daly's (1994) study of the effects of attendance at coed schools in Northern Ireland on overall examination results at second level did use sophisticated multi-level statistical models of analysis. He found no coed effect as such, once social background and previous ability/performance had been controlled for (Daly, 1992; 1994). The coed coefficient was negative for girls, but not statistically significant, though the number of pupils per school was low. Nevertheless, his results agree broadly with Bone's (1983) and Steedman's (1983a) studies of English and Welsh schools.

In concluding this review of research on the effects of coeducation on girls' academic achievements, a number of factors appear clear. Firstly, it is very difficult to asses the "pure" or independent effect of coeducation per se. There are such substantial ability and social-class differences between coed and single-sex schools in their pupil intake, as well as in the nature and structure of these school types, that to ensure that one compares "like with like" requires not only substantial background knowledge on pupils and schools, but also the use of sophisticated statistical methods to analyse such data.

Secondly, apart from average differences between single-sex and coed schools, it appears likely that coed schools themselves vary significantly from each other in the extent of gender fairness in their schooling practices and processes. Coeducational schools which reflect the values, expectations and social practices of their surrounding communities in their policies, practices and teacher expectations, cannot expect to have different socialisation effects than would otherwise occur in pupils' families and social networks. In so far as a majority of coed schools reflect the external social environment, they are, therefore, likely to reproduce those gender inequalities in achievements and roles characteristic of the communities which they serve. It is the balance between the predominance of culturally reinforcing or liberating tendencies in the population of coed and single-sex schools that will, therefore, determine whether the average effects of coed schools are positive or negative.

Schools, however, are expected not only to reflect current social realities, but are expected by the State to intervene actively to socialise their pupils for their expected future roles, as well as to counter those strongly ingrained inequalities in class, race and gender that may be characteristic of their surrounding environment and which bring about serious inequalities in educational achievement. These educational inequalities have serious consequences for adult life chances. One of the main stated aims of second-level schools, for instance, is to prepare pupils for their adult roles or "for immediate entry into open society" (*Rules and Programmes for Secondary Schools, 1987/88 to 1993/94*). Adult society is, however, changing rapidly, not least in women's roles in the economy and the family. Hence, in their anticipatory socialisation practices — in the formal and informal/hidden curriculum — schools are at least implicitly expected to have a "positive engenderment" policy, or to make a "conscious effort to provide an equitable education for both sexes, including attempts to counter sexism and its residual effects" (Lee, Marks and Byrd, 1994: 98). As is the case with social class inequalities, schools may either reinforce gender inequalities or they may challenge them, serving as either conservative or liberating forces in their society (Wrigley, 1992). From the Irish State's point of view, one of the primary aims of education is to help in the "breaking down of stereotypes, the opening up of opportunities, and the growth and self-esteem of all, irrespective of sex" (*Green Paper*, 1992: 68), and thus to promote equality of treatment, treating "all students, female and male, on the basis of equality" (*White Paper*, 1995: 7). However, it is unlikely that without conscious and sustained effort, schools — whether coed or single sex — can have much independent impact on gendered socialisation. Coed schools may not, therefore, be the only schools within which traditionally gendered education occurs. Indeed, in one American study, the most severe form of sexist behaviour and reinforcement occurred in boys' schools (Lee, Marks and Byrd, 1994).

To summarise this section on the effects of coeducation on girls' achievement, the more cautious conclusion appears to be that, on average, coed schools have:

- A slight negative effect on girls' average academic achievement, with a somewhat greater impact on achievement among girls of below-average academic ability

- A more significant negative effect on girls' take-up of, and performance in, "male" subjects, such as Maths, the physical sciences and technical subjects

- Negative effects on personal and social development outcomes when attention is paid to those studies (like Bryk et al., 1993) which have adequate samples and controls and more sophisticated analyses.

There appear to be three main underlying reasons why these patterns are likely to occur:

(1) If coed schools, in their policies and practices, behave in much the same way as their environing social groups, they will reflect the conventional presumptions about female and male aptitudes, interests and role expectations in their ethos and schooling processes: in their adult role models, particularly in the senior positions in the school; in gendered teacher roles (e.g. male teachers for male subjects); in gendered biases in access to particular subjects, or in timetabling; in teacher expectations, and in pupil-teacher interaction in the classroom.

(2) The dynamics of mixed-sex small-group interaction processes in coed classrooms (between boys, girls and teachers), unless proactively managed by teachers, are more likely to lead to male dominance and female passivity in interaction processes:

in teacher-initiated interaction, in responses to teachers' questions, in student initiated interaction with the teacher and in pupil–pupil interaction.

(3) Where mixed classes are difficult to control (particularly boys), most studies show that teachers either spend disproportionate time in control behaviour or they attempt to win the consent of boys by allowing them more leeway in classroom interaction — with less disciplinary/control behaviour directed towards girls, even when misbehaving (Riddell, 1992). Girls, on average, also appear to use more indirect and subtle counter-school behaviour which increases their "invisibility" including: withdrawal from classroom interaction, greater use of body language, silent protest etc. (Wolpe, 1988; Riddell, 1992; Lees, 1993). Such classroom reactions appear to vary by ability/performance level, with high-ability girls being more assertive in classroom interaction (Wolpe, 1988). Thus, compared to a single-sex setting, mixed classes appear to reduce significantly the relative level of active participation of girls in pupil–teacher interaction. This finding is supported by some longitudinal case studies of amalgamations of boys' and girls' schools and colleges where, at least in the initial period, girls' level of classroom participation decreased as the proportion of boys in the class increased (Canada and Pringle, 1995). Nevertheless, as already indicated, this is not a universal finding in case studies of amalgamations.

2.8   COEDUCATION AND PERSONAL AND SOCIAL DEVELOPMENT

The two earliest and most influential studies of coeducational schooling and adolescent development — Coleman's (1961) American study and Dale's (1971) British study — in many respects came to different conclusions. Coleman's classic study of American adolescent peer subcultures emphasised the superficial social aspects of adolescent preoccupations while attending coed high schools, with girls, on average, feeling that social life and "rating and dating" have a higher priority than academic pursuits (1961: 52–3). Dale's (1971) British study, on the other hand, found that both boys and girls attending, or having attended, coeducational schools were more satisfied with their schooling as a preparation for life, and with the personal and social development aspects of their education than those educated in single-sex schools (op. cit.: 251). Both male and female former pupils of coed schools also considered that attitudes towards, and relationships with, the opposite sex had been healthier and less preoccupied with dating than those in single-sex schools (1971: 188–90). Girls in general were happier in coed grammar schools than in equivalent girls' schools (Dale, op. cit., Ch. 2). Dale emphasises the "normality" of girls and boys being educated and growing up together in the family-like atmosphere of the coed school, with women school-leavers reported as saying: "we were all good friends, we thought of them as if we were all one sex and not as the object of the next date as we probably thought of other boys" (1971: 190). This result is at variance with the tenor of Coleman's (1961) results.

The political and ideological context of both studies, however, was one of rapid expansion of second-level education in the United States and Britain, and one which saw single-sex education as a barrier to successful (cross-sex) adolescent socialisation. In general, there was also much less concern with schooling effectiveness in the context of the rapidly expanding economies of the time. As a result, single-sex education tended to be seen as élitist, oppressive and controlled, with coeducation seen as providing a more positive and healthy social context for adolescent development. Single-sex education was perceived as too narrowly academic, with too much emphasis on control, order and discipline and too little on adolescent developmental needs. Interestingly, all of the former characteristics are ones that have now become central to the school effectiveness debate in the changed political and economic climate of the 1990s.

In the Irish context, one large-scale study of recent school-leavers (Hannan and Shortall, 1991) found that both male and female former pupils of coed schools reported consistently higher satisfaction with the personal and social development aspects of their education than those of single-sex schools (op. cit.: 199). Of course, this study was carried out five years after young respondents had left school and may not reflect their attitudes while in school. In many American and British studies (Feather, 1974; Schneider et al., 1982, 1988; Stables, 1990), and in Dale's original studies, both boys and girls in coed schools are reported to have more positive attitudes to their schools. These results are not supported by one of the most sophisticated recent American

studies (Lee, Bryk and Holland, 1993), which found some significant social and personal development advantages to single-sex
education.

The underlying reasons why girls, rather than boys, might be
disproportionately affected by coed schooling appear to be the
result of the more complex, more ambiguous and often contradictory expectations faced by girls at the adolescent stage of development, particularly in direct contact with boys in coed classes. The
expectations of attractive femininity and active sociality with
one's peer group, of the disciplined and high-achievement schol-
arly role, and the contradictory expectations of anticipated adult
roles (in combining occupational achievement with spousal/mater-
nal roles) present adolescent girls with both more variable and
more ambiguous priorities than is true of adolescent boys (Lees,
1983; Hudson, 1984). These gender-role expectation differences —
both current and anticipated — are likely to be more obvious and
salient in the coed setting. For instance, high-achieving girls are
expected to be both "masculine" in their independence, autonomy
and work dedication and, at the same time, "feminine" in their
interaction with others, with the emphasis on gentleness, social
emotional supportiveness, and lower assertiveness (Hudson, 1984).
These mostly implicit clashes in expectations are perhaps more
easily resolved for the more academically able middle-class girl:
where potentially contradictory courtship and spousal/familial
roles can be scheduled at a much later stage of the life course. For
the high-achieving, lower-middle or working-class girl, however,
such contradictory expectations are more pronounced and more
pressing. For the lower-achieving working-class girls, as indeed for
the boys, alternative pathways to adult status may well be more
attractive options (Willis, 1977; Anyon, 1983; Hannan, Ó Riain,
1993). Coed schooling appears likely to increase the saliency of
such differential gender-role expectations. Single-sex education,
on the other hand, is posited to have many advantages for girls: a
more favourable academic climate for girls' academic achievement, strong female role models, and less distracting peer pressures, particularly in relation to dating.

In studies of the effects of coeducation, particular attention has
been paid to two specific aspects of pupils' social psychological
well-being: self-image/confidence, both general and in specific
academic-ability terms, and "locus of control" or sense of control
over one's life/fate. A number of British and American studies

(Carpenter, 1985; Mahony, 1985; Rowe, 1988) have suggested that girls are more likely to develop higher academic, and socially competent, self-images in the less competitive environment of single-sex classrooms and schools. However, these are not universal findings, with Schneider et al. (1988), for instance, finding that coed students had higher self-images of academic ability, with stronger "abasement press" in single-sex schools (where "the teacher often makes you feel like a child"). Many of these studies, however, had inadequate statistical controls for the wide social class and ability differences amongst school types.

Most studies show that, at least as measured conventionally, females have lower academic self-esteem than males, though this gender difference appears to be greater in single-sex schools than in coed schools (Foon, 1988; see also Hannan, Breen et al., 1983: 36). Both the standards/expectations used to judge performance, and the comparative status of the "significant other" to whom one compares oneself are crucial in explaining such self-image differences. Bandura's (1990) contention, that people partly judge their own capabilities through social comparison, and these social comparisons have a profound influence on self-image/confidence, expresses such membership/reference group effects succinctly. Thus, if girls in coed settings are equally likely to compare themselves to their male as to their female peers, they are as a result more likely than their counterparts in girls' schools to have lower self-images.

Research by Maccoby (1990) and Canada and Pringle (1995) indicates that the verbal and actual interaction behaviour of females is strongly influenced by the presence of males in the class. Thus, their reference groups are also likely to be affected, with girls in single-sex classes likely to have higher academic self-concepts and senses of control (Rowe, 1988). Differentially gendered self-concepts and role expectations are, in this context, likely to become amplified in the mixed-sex setting — such as boys "natural" abilities in Maths and the physical sciences, and girls' "natural" advantage in verbal/language areas (Skaalvik, 1990; Eccles et al., 1993). Skaalvik's (op. cit.) results, however, suggest that boys' self-concepts in "female domains" may not be as greatly affected as girls' concepts in "male domains". We may cautiously conclude, therefore, that, although general and academic self-concepts may be higher in single-sex schools for both sexes, gender differences in attitudes towards non-traditional subject areas and associated self-concepts are likely to be greater in coed settings.

A closely related concept to self-image is that of "locus of control": the extent to which people consider that they control events, or that events control them, because of external forces like luck, fate or "powerful others". Although conceptually distinct from self-concept, the two variables are closely inter-related, with high-achieving, high self-concept pupils generally attributing their success to their innate abilities, and those with lower self-image/ confidence more likely to attribute it to luck. In relation to academic achievement, most studies show that females, on average, have lower senses of control, or a greater likelihood to attribute life events, or success in exams, to external forces such as luck or having a good day. Males, on the other hand, are more likely to attribute such success to internal factors such as inherent ability or talent, and failure to bad luck (Phares, 1976; Fennema and Sherman, 1977a, 1977b; Wolleat et al., 1980). Cairns' (1990) study indicated higher control levels and senses of academic self-competence in single-sex settings, but only in the more academically oriented grammar schools. Contrary to earlier studies, there was no evidence that coeducation had any advantage in building up greater social competence, locus of control or general concepts of self-esteem. Indeed, single-sex education appeared to be of advantage to locus of control and specific academic self-image/concept (Lee and Bryk, 1986; Cairns, 1990). Furthermore, in Bryk, Lee and Holland's (1993) large-scale American study, controlling for pre-existing social-class differences and school selectivities, single-sex education was shown to be of significant advantage to girls, in terms of academic self-image, locus of control, level of educational aspirations and gender role stereotyping, as well as in progress in reading and Science. Thus, at the beginning of the 1990s, we end up with some significant British and American evidence that is directly at variance with Dale's (1971) conclusions and closer to Coleman's earlier (1961), more cautious, indeed partly negative, conclusions about the likely social and personal development effects of co-education.

2.9 CONCLUSIONS

Much of the research on coeducation has been concerned with comparing coed and single-sex schools or classes in relation to a number of studies, both national and international, have suggested that academic achievement, particularly among girls, is higher in single-sex than in coed schools. However, many of these studies failed to take into account differences in social class and ability intake between the school types. When these school-level variables are controlled for, much of the achievement difference disappears; although this is not the case in all studies. It appears wiser, therefore, to hypothesise that coeducational schools do disadvantage girls' academic achievements, particularly in highly gender-typed subjects.

In relation to personal and social development, the earlier view of coed schools tended to be more favourable. In contrast, more recent evidence suggests that single-sex education has some advantages concerning academic self-image and locus of control, though not necessarily for general self-image/concept. However, all of these effects, if present, are likely to be highly influenced by school policy and school-management effectiveness.

In general, however, much of the research on the effects of coeducation, particularly on academic achievement, remains somewhat inconclusive, principally because of the failure to control adequately for school differences in pupils' ability and social background. In this study we will be able to control for such differences in pupil composition in assessing the effects of coed and single-sex schools on gender differentiation in achievement.

2.10 DERIVATION OF HYPOTHESES

Three general research questions guide the research:

- Do girls in coed schools achieve poorer examination results than girls in single-sex schools, and boys in coed and single-sex schools?

- Does coeducation have a negative impact on girls' personal and social development: self-image/confidence, body-image and locus of control?

- If coeducation has such negative effects on girls' educational achievement and personal/social development, why does this occur?

Before we go on to derive hypotheses we need to specify more clearly what is involved. What we wish to test is: "all else being equal", whether the average examination grades of girls in coed schools are below the average of girls in single-sex schools; as well as of boys in coed and single-sex schools. We need to ensure, therefore, that effects which may be attributed to attending coed schools are in fact the result of their intrinsic coeducational nature — particularly the effect of girls and boys being taught the same subjects/levels in the same classroom — and are not simply consequences of differences in pupils' social class or ability levels, or of schooling processes which have no intrinsic relationship to coeducation per se.

We derive our general hypotheses from the preceding review of the research literature. If we ensure that the social/ability composition of the pupil body is statistically controlled to be the same in coed and single-sex schools, our review suggests the following main hypotheses:

(1) That, on average, girls in coed schools do not achieve as well as girls in single-sex schools, or as boys in either school type

(2) That girls, on average, have lower levels of (academic) self-confidence, body-image and senses of "control' (or higher senses of fatalism) than boys; and that this gender difference is more marked in coed school settings.

If our central hypotheses (1) and (2) are supported, the following five summary hypotheses are proposed to explain why this occurs:

(3) Coed schools provide less favourable "role model environments" for girls' academic achievement and personal and social development — in their management arrangements and roles, curricular provisions for girls' high academic achievement and organised encouragement for honours-level achievements.

(4) Since coed schools are more likely than girls' schools both to "stream" their pupil intake and to allocate their curricula accordingly, girls' of below-average academic ability are likely to be disproportionately negatively affected by coeducation.

(5) The saliency of adolescent gender-identity formation processes is greater in coed settings, thus reinforcing traditional role orientations, particularly for girls; widening alternative school/social-life options for coed girls, and reducing the relative priority of academic achievement roles. In addition, coeducation is likely to reduce self-images and senses of "control" and heighten "body-image" preoccupations.

(6) The dynamics of the cross-gender pupil–teacher interaction processes in coed classes leads to the dominance of boy–teacher interaction, in both instructional and control aspects, and to teacher under-attention to girls. Where girls appear to react more positively than boys to teacher support and encouragement, such gender-biased interaction, if present, would significantly disadvantage girls' academic achievement in coed schools.

Chapter 3 outlines the various concepts and variables which are used in our hypothesised model of educational achievement. These are summarised in a block model format at the end of the chapter. The hypotheses will be tested using statistical (multi-level) modelling techniques and the results presented in Chapters 6 to 9.

3

Research Methods

There are four noteworthy features of the research methods used in this study: large-scale, representative samples of pupils and schools; the collection of extensive information on pupils and schools; clear specifications of the variables used, and the relationships between them; and the use of sophisticated statistical techniques (Multi-Level Modelling) to test for the net effects of coeducation on pupil outcomes. This chapter is divided into three main sections: the first outlines the research procedures used in the study, the second describes the main concepts and variables used, while the third presents the method used to assess the impact of coeducation on educational achievement.

Given the objectives of the study and the necessity to generalise to the total population of schools, a large national quantitative survey appeared essential. Qualitative studies (such as classroom observation studies or case-studies of individual schools) yield rich information on the intricacies of school and classroom organisation, school ethos and interaction among teachers and pupils. However, since schools vary significantly in their composition and their organisation, one cannot generalise from studies of a small set of schools to the national population. Therefore, it appeared essential to collect data on a large representative sample of schools and pupils in order to provide an accurate and generalisable estimate of the impact of coeducation and other schooling factors on pupil outcomes.

Three main data sources were used in this study:

(1) Interviews were conducted with principals and guidance counsellors (or staff members filling the role), and questionnaires were administered to representative samples of pupils from Junior and Leaving Certificate classes in a national sample of 116 schools.

(2) Verbal Reasoning and Numerical Ability (DATS) tests were carried out by Department of Education psychologists on the Junior Certificate sample.

(3) Examination results were subsequently obtained for all Junior and Leaving Certificate pupils in the schools surveyed.

Details of the research procedures used are described in the following section.

3.1   RESEARCH PROCEDURES

Figure 3.1: Research Procedures

Tasks	Timing
*Phase 1: Research Design and Planning**	
Design of questionnaires	March–April 1993
Pilot testing of questionnaires	May 1993
Revision of questionnaires	June 1993
Sample selection: schools and classes	November–December 1993
Phase 2: Fieldwork	
Administering of pupil questionnaires	December 1993–March 1994
Interviews with principals and guidance counsellors	December 1993–March 1994
Ability testing of Junior Cert pupils	April 1994
Phase 3: Coding and Data Analysis	
Coding of questionnaires	February–April 1994
Data inputting	May–June 1994
Analysis of data (descriptive)	June–September 1994
Addition of exam results to data file	September–October 1994
Multivariate analyses of data	November 1994 onwards

* Some of the initial design and planning work was completed before the Department of Education granted funding in November 1993.

3.1.1 Questionnaire Design

An initial set of pupil, principal and guidance counsellor questionnaires was prepared by May 1993. These questionnaires drew on the relevant research literature — reviewed in the previous chapter — and incorporated a number of questions from the *Schooling and Sex Roles* (1983) study in order to provide some measures of change over time. The pupil questionnaires focused on pupils' social background, their perceptions of their schooling, and their educational and occupational aspirations. The principal and guidance counsellor questionnaires were designed to collect information on school management and organisation, along with detailed information on the nature of curricular provision and subject choice.

The initial questionnaires were tested in four large schools: a comprehensive coed school, a secondary coed school, a boys' school and a girls' school. The pupil questionnaires were subsequently revised to take account of the results of this pilot study. The final pupil questionnaires — Junior (JC) and Leaving Certificate (LC) — contain almost all of the variables suggested to be important by the research literature. A copy of the Leaving Certificate pupil questionnaire is given in Appendix 2.1; this questionnaire is equivalent in most respects to that for Junior Certificate pupils.

3.1.2 Sample Selection

Selection of Schools

The original sample was drawn using stratified random sampling. Four strata were used in order to obtain the most representative sample possible. These were:

- School Sector: Secondary
                          Vocational
                          Community/Comprehensive

- Gender Composition: Male pupils only
                          Female pupils only
                          Coeducational

- School Size: < 300 pupils
                          300–499 pupils
                          500+ pupils

- Location: Dublin city/county
                          Other.

Table 3.1: Comparison of Original Sample of Schools with Achieved Sample

School Type	Original Sample	Achieved Sample
Secondary, of which:		
Single-sex	47	44
Coeducational	22	20
Vocational	37	34
Community/Comprehensive	20	18
Total	126	116

Four schools were dropped from the original sample: three had changed over to Post Leaving Certificate colleges, while the other had just been amalgamated with two other schools and would have been impossible to extract. Six schools refused to co-operate with the study in spite of many efforts to secure their participation. Table 3.1 compares the original sample with the achieved sample. A breakdown of the actually sampled schools by the stratification criteria used is outlined below in Table 3.2 and compared to the breakdown for the total population.

Table 3.2: Percentage Breakdown of Achieved Sample and Population of Schools by Sector and Size

Size	Secondary Schools		Vocational Schools		Comm./Comp. Schools		Schools: All Sectors	
	Sample	Popu-lation	Sample	Popu-lation	Sample	Popu-lation	Sample	Popu-lation
< 300	10	16	16	15	1	0	27	31
300–499	19	19	9	9	4	2	32	30
500+	26	25	5	8	10	6	41	39
All Sizes	55	60	29	31	16	9	100	100
Total no. schools	64	473	34	249	18	69	116	791

As Table 3.2 indicates, there is greater disparity between the sample and population for the community/comprehensive sector. This occurred because a double sample was drawn in this sector to ensure sufficient numbers of "greenfield" and amalgamated schools for analysis. Where necessary, these schools are weighted to reflect their proportion in the national population.

Table 3.3: Gender Composition of Secondary Schools

School Type	Sample	National Population
	%	%
Girls Only	37.5	36.9
Boys Only	26.6	30.0
Coeducational	35.9	33.1
Total	100.0	100.0

Table 3.3 shows a breakdown of secondary schools by gender composition of the school; all but one of the vocational and community/comprehensive schools are coed. In keeping with the Department of Education statistics, a "de facto" definition of co-education is adopted for this study: that is, a school enrolling both boys and girls is classified as coeducational, regardless of the relative proportions of each gender. The achieved sample is very close to the national population in terms of gender composition. In addition, a quarter of the sampled schools are located in Dublin city or county, close to the equivalent national figure of 24 per cent. In summary, the achieved sample of schools appears to reflect the national population in almost all respects.

Sampling of Classes

The years selected for study were the Junior Cert (JC) and Leaving Cert (LC) exam years. In statistical terms, it would have been preferable to draw a simple random sample of all pupils from the relevant years within the sampled schools. However, this would have been very difficult to achieve, demanding considerable disruption of classes, timetabling schedules and allocation of rooms for the randomly selected pupils. It would, therefore, have significantly increased the refusal rate. Consequently, we decided to sample classes within schools, taking roughly half the total number of classes from the relevant years in each selected school. While this method involves somewhat higher sampling errors than simple random sampling, it also has substantive advantages, allowing us to examine the effects of being in a particular class. This is particularly relevant where schools allocate pupils to classes on the basis of their academic ability and classes differ significantly in the allocation of subjects and levels.

"Classes" were defined for the purposes of the study as the "permanent" (or "base") class to which students were assigned for school organisation purposes (generally also for Departmental roll purposes) and in which they took a number of subjects or class periods together as a group. In most schools, such a definition was unproblematic, although in some schools this definition did not conform with the Departmental roll class. A small number of schools, however, did not have any base classes in this sense — having individual subject classes only, with a considerable degree of movement between subjects and levels. In these cases we sampled those subject classes which, in the principal's view, corresponded most closely to the ability mix of the year.

Specific sampling rules for classes were devised to take account of the use of streaming, banding or mixed-ability teaching, as well as of the number of classes within the relevant years. These detailed sampling rules are outlined in Appendix 2.2. In brief, we selected all classes in schools with one or two classes in the relevant year, two classes in three- and four-class years, three classes out of five-, six- and seven-class years, and so on. This sampling procedure involves different sampling fractions for each school size with substantial oversampling of schools with one, two, three or five classes, and undersampling of other schools with an odd number of classes, within the relevant year. However, the sample has been reweighted accordingly, where appropriate, to yield generalisable results.

The sampling of classes in the 116 sampled schools was carried out by one or other member of the ESRI research team. Letters to the principal were followed by telephone calls to collect information on the school size, number and organisation of classes. Classes were then selected using the standardised sampling method (Appendix 2.2). Dates and times of interviews were then arranged with the principal and guidance counsellor.

3.1.3 Fieldwork

In total, 5,961 Junior Cert pupils and 4,813 Leaving Cert pupils completed the administered questionnaires. Pupils completed the questionnaires during class sessions supervised by members of

the ESRI research team or by experienced interviewers employed
by the ESRI. The classes were given approximately 45 minutes to
an hour to complete the questionnaires. Pupils were assured of
the complete confidentiality of their responses. Almost all of the
fieldwork was completed by mid-March 1994.

Interviews with school principals and guidance counsellors
were conducted by members of the ESRI interview team over the
period December 1993 to March 1994. Because of the very detailed nature of the information required, interviews took approximately one and a half to two hours to complete.

3.1.4 Ability Testing

A version of the Differential Aptitudes Test (DATS Tests in Verbal
Reasoning and Numerical Ability) was administered by Department of Education psychologists to Junior Cert pupils in our
sample. These two tests of verbal reasoning (VR) and numerical
ability (NA) are drawn from a battery of six tests of cognitive
skills for 15-year-old pupils developed in the United States and
adapted for Irish standards by the Educational Research Centre.
They measure two distinct aspects of pupils' cognitive abilities or
aptitudes which are very closely associated with academic
aptitude/ability and, combined in a single score (VRNA), provide
the best estimated measure of general "academic ability".[1] This
approach is consistent with the emphasis on abilities and aptitudes as multifactorial in nature (see work in the United States
carried out by Thurstone (1935, 1947) and his student Guilford
(1954)). It contrasts with the emphasis among earlier theorists on
"general intelligence" as a unidimensional phenomenon (see, for
example, Spearman, 1904, 1927). The two general academic-
ability tests used correspond closely to Gardner's (1987) proposed
measures of the logical mathematical, linguistic and logical
reasoning dimensions of intelligence, and in general are conceptu-
alised within a similar multifactorial approach to human abilities
and aptitudes.

---

[1] The other measures included in the battery of DATS tests are Abstract
    Reasoning, a non-verbal measure of reasoning ability; Mechanical
    Reasoning and Space Relation, understanding of physical forces and prin-
    ciples and the ability to visualise and manipulate concrete objects;
    Clerical Speed/Accuracy, and Spelling and Language Usage tests, dealing
    with aptitudes/abilities in language usage in office/ commercial settings.

Because of the initial oversampling of community/comprehensive schools, ability testing was not carried out in nine schools in this sector. In addition, one school refused to co-operate with the testing. Within the schools tested, there was some shortfall in the numbers caused by absenteeism on the day of testing. These tests yielded complete information on 4,696 Junior Cert pupils, 79 per cent of the total sample or 93 per cent of sampled pupils within the schools involved in the testing. Test results were matched to the anonymised pupil data file (questionnaire responses) using Department of Education pupil numbers.

3.1.5 Examination Records

Examination results for Junior Cert and Leaving Cert pupils within the sampled schools were subsequently obtained from the Department of Education in September/October 1994. These results were matched to the pupil file using the Departmental pupil numbers. For the purposes of this study, we use the grade point average achieved for all pupils taking five or more subjects in the examination, with scores assigned using an adapted version of the Central Applications Office (CAO/CAS) marking scheme (see also Breen, 1986).

3.1.6 Data Analysis

Data analysis involved three processes. Firstly, the completeness and reliability of the data were checked, and descriptive analyses were carried out on pupil, principal and guidance counsellor questionnaires. Some of this descriptive material is presented in Chapters 4 and 5 of the study. Secondly, several composite measures or scales were constructed, particularly on the attitudinal data collected. The reliability and validity of these scales were checked before analyses were carried out. More detailed information on the derivation of these scales is presented in Chapters 8 and 9. Thirdly, statistical modelling procedures, including Ordinary Least Squares regression and Multi-Level Modelling, were used to examine the impact of a variety of background and schooling factors on examination performance (Junior and Leaving Certificate) and on a range of developmental outcomes.

Multiple regression techniques have represented the most commonly used approach to statistical modelling within social research. These techniques allow us to estimate the impact of a range of independent variables (such as social-class background, gender and so on) on an outcome, such as educational performance. More recently, however, researchers have argued that, because of their restrictive assumptions, multiple regression techniques fail to reflect adequately the complexities of group processes within schools and classrooms (Burstein, 1980; Goldstein, 1987, 1995; Bryk and Raudenbush, 1988). In contrast, multi-level modelling techniques have been found to yield significant technical and substantive benefits in conducting educational research. (A more detailed description of the differences between regression and multi-level techniques is presented in Appendix 2.3.)

For the purposes of this study, initial analyses were carried out using OLS regression procedures. These analyses allowed us to explore the impact of a range of variables on pupil outcomes and to exclude a number of non-significant variables from subsequent investigations. More detailed analyses were carried out using multi-level modelling techniques[2]. These procedures provided more accurate estimates of the effects of pupil and school factors on pupil outcomes, and allowed us to investigate the differences between schools in the outcomes concerned. The results of these models are presented in Chapters 6 to 9 of the book. The conceptual framework developed to analyse the impact of coeducation on pupil outcomes is described in the following sections.

3.2 CONCEPTS AND VARIABLES USED IN THE STUDY

In the following sections we describe the approach used to assess the effect of coeducation on educational performance. Educational attainment is affected by a range of pupil background and schooling factors. Consequently, these factors need either to be statistically controlled for in examining the effects of attendance at coeducational schools, or else used to explain the way in which coeducational schools bring about their effects. These factors fall into two categories. The first are *exogenous*, ascribed variables (such as sex and social-class background), "given" factors over which the individual has no control but which significantly affect educational performance. The second are *endogenous*, or partly

---

[2] Analyses were carried out using the ML3E computer package developed by the Institute of Education, University of London.

exogenous and partly *endogenous*, variables over which the individual, family or school has varying control, or which may themselves be partly affected by schooling, but which substantially affect the nature and effectiveness of the education received by individuals. Two types of *outcome* variables will be examined: educational (exam) performance and some personal/social development outcomes. This section describes the main variables used in the study; the detailed measures used are described in Chapters 6 to 9.

3.2.1 Ascriptive Social-Background Factors

Studies of educational achievement, both international and national, have emphasised the central role played by family socio-economic and sociocultural factors (see Coleman et al., 1966; Jencks et al., 1972; Halsey, Heath and Ridge, 1980; Breen, 1986; 1995; Hannan, Ó Riain, 1993). The following variables will be used to measure variations in the socioeconomic and sociocultural backgrounds of pupils:

- Occupational status of parents; in addition, those from a farming background are distinguished because of the specific nature of the familial culture (Hannan, 1979)

- Employment status of parents

- Educational level of parents

- Number of children in the family, and birth order of the respondent

- Location in the west of Ireland.

Besides overall family social-class effects, *mother's employment status and occupational status* are included in the analyses. These factors have been found to have a very significant independent effect on daughters' educational achievement, occupational aspirations and adult gender role expectations (Carpenter, 1985; Kalmijn, 1994).

3.2.2 Academic-Ability Differences Between Pupils

Measures of "academic ability" are used to control for variation between coed and single-sex schools in the ability range of their pupil intakes. Irish second-level schools vary widely from each other in the academic-ability characteristics of their pupil intakes

and compositions. These inter-school variances appear to be relatively high by international standards — one recent study found
that 20 per cent of the variance in Mathematics achievement
among 13-year-olds in Ireland was, between schools, higher than
among schools in North America and a number of European countries (OECD, 1992). Consequently, it is essential to control for such
differences among schools in their pupil intake characteristics.

For Junior Certificate pupils, assessments of academic ability
are based on the short form of the DATS test, administered by
Department of Education psychologists to the sample of pupils
interviewed for the study. These tests were carried out during the
pupils' third year of the junior cycle, approximately three months
before sitting the Junior Cert exam. It would have been preferable
to have tested pupils on entry to second-level schooling, in order
to examine initial differences between schools (and pupils within
schools) in ability levels. However, this was not possible within the
resource and time constraints of the present study. Such an
approach would involve a more complex longitudinal study design, following pupils from entry to second-level schooling over the
three years of the junior cycle. However, it was possible to obtain
entry-test scores from a small number of schools within the
sample. This information was used to assess the implications of
using third- (as opposed to first-) year ability scores for our
analyses of Junior Cert exam performance.

Analyses comparing the impact of third-year and entry ability-
test scores on Junior Cert performance were carried out —
detailed results are presented in Appendix 2.4. These analyses
indicate that using third-year ability scores rather than entry
scores leads to some underestimation of the impact on exam
performance of social class, parental unemployment, and being in
a bottom/remedial class. There are some indications of a falling off
in ability scores over the junior cycle within coed schools, although this effect is not statistically significant. As a result, using
third-year ability scores may somewhat overestimate the positive
effects of coeducation for boys and very slightly underestimate the
negative effects of coeducation for girls. In spite of these qualifications, estimates of the impact of coeducation are not affected
substantively by using third-year scores.[3] Consequently, while
third-year ability scores should be treated with some caution as

---

[3]   This effect is similar for girls and boys.

estimates of prior ability, they do not appear to bias seriously our estimates of the effects of coeducation on pupil achievements.

At the Leaving Certificate level, achievement in the Junior Certificate exam (taken two to three years previously) is used as a measure of prior performance. This measure fully captures the effects of any prior ability differences as well as prior performance outcomes. If coed schools impact on performance, such effects are unlikely to be confined to the junior cycle, but are likely to continue to operate throughout the senior cycle. Hence, senior cycle effects can be fully assessed using prior performance/ability levels as the main control variable. Using both Junior and Leaving Certificate exam outcomes allows us, therefore, to test for consistent coed effects over the period of second-level education.

3.2.3 School Choice

Most Irish second-level schools are in multi-school catchment areas. As a result, active choice of school (secondary, vocational or community/comprehensive, or single-sex versus coed) on the part of parents is common, and may be an important predictor of educational achievement. Controlling for objective family-background factors, parental motivations in school selection for children can have substantial effects on school composition and ethos as well as on individual achievement. Parental choice may be treated in most respects as an independent exogenous variable. This measure can be based either on aggregate pupil responses to questions on choice of school, or on the actual extent to which a school is oversubscribed and discriminates in its intake.

3.2.4 School-Type and Structural Characteristics

School-type and composition characteristics are not exogenous variables in the same way as family-background characteristics since they are open to change by school management. It is important to distinguish between school-type and composition variables:

School-Type Variables
- Coeducational or single-sex
- Vocational, secondary or community/comprehensive
- Origins of the school (for example, amalgamated, greenfield, etc.)

School-Composition and Structural Characteristics

The ability of school management and staff to influence the type of pupils accepted to the school is shaped by a number of factors, namely:

- The extent to which the school is in a multi-school catchment area

- The extent to which the school selects its intake, or suffers from cream-off by other schools in the catchment area.

School selectivity plays an important role in shaping the social composition of its pupil body; relevant dimensions of school composition include:

- Average social class of the student body

- Percentage of pupils from unemployed families

- Mean ability level of pupil intake

- Gender ratio among pupils in coed schools.

3.2.5 Curricular Emphases and Differentiation in the School

In the school-effectiveness literature, school effects appear to be more pronounced in those areas of the curriculum where learning of the subject contents outside the school is less pronounced, such as in maths and science. If the school has more important effects in some subject areas than others, and if it devotes more resources to those areas, this needs to be taken into consideration: particularly if such school effects are greater for boys than girls (Rutter et al., 1979; Madaus, Airasian and Kellaghan, 1980). Relevant aspects of the school curriculum include:

- The nature of curricular provision: the number and range of subjects, the degree of subject specialisation, or degree of multi-dimensionality in provision

- Gender bias or fairness in the curriculum and in curricular allocation procedures; the number and proportion of traditional "male" or "female" subjects

- Academic emphasis in the curriculum (see Coleman et al., 1982): the extent of "educational effort" by the school in providing extra higher level courses, or maximising achievement chances for middle to lower-academic-ability pupils

- Extent of differentiation and "tracking" in the curriculum: in particular, the extent to which the school differentiates out a separate higher level, academic subject track from a "general" or "vocational/technical" track.

3.2.6 Streaming, Gender Differentiation and Other Schooling Process Variables

The managerial and administrative decisions taken by schools can influence subject take-up and academic performance. Schools can take a number of different approaches to the allocation of pupils to classes. Relevant dimensions of this allocation process include:

- Streaming of pupils and associated curricular differentiation

- Location of pupils in streamed/banded classes

- The extent of gender bias in pupil categorisation or class allocation rules.

As well as being influenced by the formal rules and procedures of the schools, pupil performance can be influenced by the informal school ethos. School ethos cannot necessarily be measured directly, but relevant dimensions include:

- The disciplinary climate of the school, including school emphasis on homework completion, homework/study rules, and so on

- The extent of *"academic press"*, that is, the degree to which the school emphasises, and encourages, educational achievement among its pupils. This relates to factors such as the level of teacher expectations, the structure of school rewards and sanctions, and the extent to which the school provides additional higher level classes. Schools with a high level of "academic press" tend to be ones where a high proportion of Leaving Cert pupils go on to third-level education.

Aspects of the school ethos can influence the personal and social development of the pupils, as well as their academic performance. Relevant aspects include:

- The level of positive and negative rewards/sanctions in pupil–teacher interaction in the classroom

- The quality of pupil–pupil interaction, particularly the extent to which pupils experience bullying.

3.2.7 Mediating Variables (Personal and Social Development)

Many studies of educational achievement have treated aspects of pupils' personal and social development as mediating variables in examining academic performance (see Sewell et al., 1970; Turritin et al., 1983; Carpenter, 1985; Hanafin, 1992). We cannot take this approach here since these factors are themselves affected by school processes and potentially by whether a school is coed or single-sex. Instead, we treat aspects of pupils' social and personal development as important outcomes of the schooling process (see below).

3.2.8 Dependent Variables

Certification and examination grades are the most important outcomes of the educational process both from the perspective of students' perceptions (Hannan and Shortall, 1991) and as predictors of subsequent educational and occupational achievement (review by Hallinan, 1992; Hannan, Ó Riain, 1993; Breen, Hannan and O'Leary, 1995). However, this study is equally concerned with the personal and social development outcomes of education.

The following dependent variables are, therefore, measured and used in the research:

Educational Performance

- Grade Point Average (GPA) score received in the Junior and Leaving Certificate examinations — scoring the grades received in exams by using a system analogous to the Central Applications Office "points" method.

- Examination grades in English and Mathematics as examples of variation in performance across subjects.

Personal and Social Development

- Level of current stress felt by pupils — measured using an adapted form of the conventionally used GHQ scale (see Hannan, Ó Riain, 1993).

- Academic Self-Image: a measure of how pupils conceptualise and evaluate their own academic abilities.

- Locus of Control: the extent to which pupils believe that they are in control of events or believe that outside forces control events and are fatalistic about things that happen to them.

- Body-Image: pupils' evaluations of the attractiveness of their own bodies and self-presentation to others.

- Adult Gender Role Expectations: expectations about the way family and work roles are to be combined.

3.3   A MODEL OF EXAMINATION PERFORMANCE

In Figure 3.2 (p. 68), we present the above sets of variables in blocks which are ordered from left to right in terms of their hypothesised "causal order": indicating the time sequence in which they occur and their likely causal relationships to each other and to the main outcome variable — grades in the Junior and Leaving Certificate examinations. The table should be read from left to right, presenting the variables already discussed in their likely causal order.

The relationships between these sets of variables are mapped out in Figure 3.3 (p. 69). Examination performance is seen to be influenced by both background and schooling factors. Pupils' social background and prior ability influence the type of second-level school they attend but also have a direct effect on how they perform in later examinations. School organisation and process partially mediate the effects of social background and prior ability, but also have an independent effect — that is, the way in which schools manage initial differences between pupils affects their subsequent educational performance.

Single-sex and coed schools differ from each other in ways that are not related to coeducation as such but to the institutional origins and development of the secondary, vocational and community/comprehensive sectors (see Chapters 4 and 5). Therefore, it is necessary to control for pupil composition and school organisational factors before assessing the impact of coeducation on educational performance. This model is presented in greater detail in Chapters 6 and 7 where the framework is applied to educational performance among Junior and Leaving Certificate pupils respectively.

Social-psychological variables (Block 4 in Figure 3.2) are not included in the assessment of the effects of coeducation on examination grades. Since these variables are at least partially influenced by the schooling process, they are regarded as outcomes

Figure 3.2: Sets of Variables Relating to Pupil Outcomes

1. Ascriptive social-background factors	2. School Characteristics: School Selection and School Composition Factors	3. Schooling Organisation, Process and Ethos factors	4. Intervening or Mediating Social Psychological and Pupil Behavioural Factors	5. Dependent Variables: Educational Achievement and Personal/Social development outcomes
Family socio-economic status: Parental occupational status Employment status of parents Education of parents Size of family Position in family Mother's employment and occupational status Location in the West of Ireland Age of pupil Measures of Academic Ability	Type of primary school attended and nature of link to second-level school Extent to which local school catchment area is multi-school Nature and extent of selectivity in intake of school Extent to which pupil/parents chose school Type of school: • Secondary; vocational; community/ comprehensive • Fee-paying or free • Single-sex or Coed Size of school	Streaming or tracking in the school Individual's location in streamed/banded classes Curriculum: • Size and characteristics • Academic/ vocational bias • Gender differences in provision • Constriction on subject choice Extent and nature of honours courses "Academic press" of the school Disciplinary climate of the school	Individual social psychological variables: • Academic self-image • Level of aspiration • Level of self-confidence • Sense of control • Body-image Subject attitudes Pupil study habits and effort Attendance record Parental expectations Teacher expectations Nature and quality of pupil–teacher interaction	• Grade Point Average (GPA): Junior Cert; Leaving Cert • Subject composition of GPA for JC and LC (e.g. Maths and English) • Academic self-image • Locus of control • Body-image • Gender role stereotyping (expectations; practice) • Current stress levels
	Average social class of pupil intake Average ability level of pupil intake; Proportion of pupils with learning problems	Pastoral Care provision in the school	Pupil–Pupil interaction: • Extent of bullying • Participation in recreation, sport and social life, including dating behaviour etc. Pupil involvement in part-time employment	

in their own right.[4] The framework used for assessing the impact of coeducation on aspects of pupils' personal and social development is slightly different from that for examination performance. The approach adopted is discussed in greater detail in Chapters 8 and 9.

Figure 3.3: "Causal Model" of Hypothesised Relationships among Blocks of Variables Predicting Junior and Leaving Cert Grades

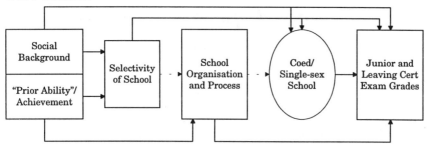

3.4 CONCLUSIONS

This chapter has outlined the research methodology used in the study. A number of aspects of the research design enhance its value as a study of coeducation in Ireland. Firstly, the large sample size means that the results are generalisable to the population of second-level schools and pupils in Ireland, and provide an accurate picture of the differences between the single-sex and coeducational sectors. Secondly, very detailed information has been collected on individual pupils as well as on the school organisation and process. This level of detail allows us to compare "like with like" and thus to provide an accurate estimate of the effects of coeducation on pupils' educational performance and personal and social development.

---

[4]   It is intended at a future date to carry out research on the effects of social-psychological variables on examination outcomes.

4

School Type and Social Composition

Second-level schools differ substantially from each other in their institutional arrangements, their intake and composition, and their schooling process. An awareness and understanding of these differences is fundamental to any attempt to measure the impact of coeducation on pupils' academic performance and social and personal development. Later in the book, we will control for these and other differences between school types, when attempting to explain variance in academic achievement.

In this chapter, we first compare and contrast the characteristics of single-sex and coed schools in terms of their size, location and origins, including a brief assessment of the impact of recent demographic change on total enrolments. We also examine the management and staffing of schools, with particular reference to the gender of teachers and principals.

Next we focus on a number of factors which combine to influence the enrolment profile of a school. Under this heading we examine the extent to which schools select their intake; the extent of choice available to prospective pupils and their parents, and the degree to which they succeed in gaining entry to the school of their choice. Other factors considered include competition and "cream off" between schools.

Finally, the chapter looks at pupil composition. We assess how school types differ in the social-class backgrounds of, and the prevalence of social problems among, their pupils. The combination of these and other factors leads to differences between school types in the average ability levels of their pupils. These differences are considered in the final section.

4.1   ENROLMENT PATTERNS

Second-level enrolments are at an all-time high. In 1993/94, more than 370,000 pupils were enrolled full-time at second-level schools and, with increasing participation rates and the introduction of a six-year cycle, an overall decline in enrolments is unlikely to be felt before 1998. Local population trends, however, have already led to a slight reduction in the total number of schools. Table 4.1 shows that over a period of 15 years, the total number of second-level schools has fallen from 823 to 782, a drop of 5 per cent.

Table 4.1: Second-Level School Numbers, 1978/79, 1993/94

	1978/79	1993/94	% Change 1979–94
Boys only	198	132	-33%
Girls only	225	168	-25%
Coed	400	482	+21%
Total	823	782	- 5%

Source: Department of Education Statistical Reports, 1978/79 and 1993/94.

As can be seen from the table, the decline is much greater for single-sex schools (down by almost 30 per cent). Many of these have been merged to form coed schools and this category has increased by over a fifth. Figure 4.1 shows that coed schools now account for more than 60 per cent of second-level schools and that almost two-thirds of boys and over half of girls now attend coed schools.[1]

Examining more closely the gender profile of coed schools, we find that, on average, girls account for about 45 per cent of pupils. There is little variance in the average figures for each type of coed school, but our survey data (Table A3.1) suggest that the

---

[1]   Department of Education Statistical Reports define coeducation on a de facto basis. The presence of pupils of both genders in a school means that the school is defined as a coed school regardless of the relative proportions or their distribution by year of course involved. Some of the growth in coeducation outlined above may be attributed to provision in single-sex schools of repeat Leaving Cert tuition to both genders. Analysis of survey data defines schools which have coed classes only at Repeat Leaving Cert level as single-sex schools.

proportion of female students varies more in secondary and vocational schools than in community and comprehensive schools. In other words, strong gender imbalance is least likely to occur in these latter schools.

Figure 4.1: Growth in Second-Level Coeducation, 1979–94

Source: Department of Education Statistical Reports, 1978/79 and 1993/94.

Second-level school size varies considerably. In general, community and comprehensive schools tend to have the highest enrolment numbers. Almost three-quarters of these schools in 1993/94 had enrolments in excess of 500 pupils compared to 47 per cent of secondary schools and 27 per cent of vocational schools.[2] This disparity is also evident from the survey results in Table 4.2.

Table 4.2: Average Enrolments, Change in Enrolments and Teacher Numbers by Type of School

	Single-Sex Sec'y	Coed Sec'y	Vocat.	Comm./ Comp.	All Types
Average Enrolment	550	410	342	721	491
Percentage of schools experiencing:					
Fall (≥ 2%) in first year enrolments from 1988/9 to 1992/3	40	20	38	22	34
Fall in staff numbers	7	—	18	11	10
No. of Schools Surveyed	44	20	34	18	116

Source: National Survey on Coeducation.

---

[2]   Source: Department of Education Statistical Report, 1993/94.

Published statistics indicate that first-year enrolment figures and aggregate staff numbers increased by 6 per cent and 9 per cent respectively in the five-year period from 1989/90 to 1993/94 (see Table A3.2). However, these figures mask regional and local variations from the national trend. Table 4.2 shows that the impact of demographic change is already being felt in some areas, with one in three schools recording a fall in pupil intake over a five-year period to 1993/94.[3] The decline has been greatest in single-sex secondary schools and in vocational schools, with almost 40 per cent of these schools experiencing a reduction. Despite the decline in pupil numbers, consequent reductions in staffing have been limited, with only one in ten schools reporting small net reductions in staff numbers. In this context, secondary schools seem to have had most success in limiting reductions in staffing.

4.2 LOCATION AND ORIGINS

Table 4.3 shows that single-sex schools are concentrated in larger towns and cities while coed schools tend to be more evenly distributed between urban and rural areas. Over 70 per cent of coed secondary and vocational schools and almost half of community and comprehensive schools surveyed are located in open country or in towns of less than 5,000 inhabitants, while the equivalent figure for single-sex schools is just 20 per cent. We shall see in section 4.4 that these distribution patterns have implications for parental choice and inter-school competition.

Within the coed sector itself, there are important differences between school types in terms of their origins. Table 4.4 below shows that the majority of coed schools were coed ab initio ("greenfield"), while about 40 per cent became coed as a result of amalgamation or through the intake of pupils of the opposite sex. Almost all vocational and most community and comprehensive schools surveyed were established as coed schools. Within the coed secondary category, the majority of schools which have expanded to include pupils of the opposite gender, were originally girls' schools. This may be partly because of the more restricted objectives or "missions" of religious orders in single-sex boys' schools, such as the Christian Brothers.

---

[3] One in ten schools experienced a fall in enrolments of at least 10 per cent.

Table 4.3: Location of Coed and Single-Sex Schools

	Single-Sex Secondary	Coed Secondary	Vocational	Comm./ Comp.	All Types
	%	%	%	%	%
Cities*	50	25	9	35	31
Other towns > 5,000	30	5	18	18	20
Towns 1,000–5,000	20	25	38	12	25
Small Town < 1,000 or Open Country	—	45	35	35	23
Total %	100	100	100	100	100
No.	44	20	34	17	115

* Cork, Dublin, Galway, Limerick, Waterford.
Source: National Survey on Coeducation.

Table 4.4: Surveyed Coed Schools: Breakdown by Origin and School Type

Origin	Present School Type			
	Coed Secondary	Vocational	Comm./ Comp.	All Types
	%	%	%	%
Greenfield	10	94	59	62
Took in Opposite Sex				
• Originally Boys Only	20	3	6	7
• Originally Girls Only	45			14
Amalgamation	25	3	35	17
Total %	100	100	100	100
No.	20	34	17	71

Source: National Survey on Coeducation.

Most amalgamations involve the merger of two pre-existing schools, but in four cases, three or more schools were involved. Relatively few of these amalgamations have occurred in recent times with just three of the twelve mergers taking place over the past decade and only two more in the previous 10 years. Similarly, the broadening of pupil intake to include pupils of the opposite

sex does not seem to be a reaction to the growing impact of demographic change on enrolments — of the 15 schools in this category,
only two changed to coed intake in the past 10 years.

The pattern of conversion to coed schools has changed significantly in recent years. Figures obtained from the Planning Section of the Department of Education show that, of 56 new coed
schools established between 1985 and 1995, 31 (55 per cent) were
formed through amalgamation, while 23 (41 per cent) were greenfield projects.[4] Similarly, among our sample, greenfield schools
represent only a minority (37 per cent) of coed schools established
in the decade prior to the survey.[5] It appears that amalgamation
has become the main basis for the establishment of new coed
schools, a trend that is not surprising given the projected decline
in second-level enrolments.

4.3 STAFFING

To some extent, staffing mirrors pupil composition in second-level
schools. Single-sex schools have staff predominantly of the same
gender, while there is more of a gender balance among staff in
coed schools. Table 4.5 shows that female teachers constitute a
majority of staff in all 26 girls' secondary schools surveyed,[6] while
a similar but somewhat less extreme gender imbalance applies in
favour of male teachers in boys' secondary schools. However, the
situation is more balanced in coed schools where female teachers,
on average, account for over half of total staff. High female representation in coed secondary schools is linked to the fact that many
of them were originally girls' secondary schools (see Table 4.4).

Although women constitute a slight majority (54 per cent)[7] of
the full-time teaching profession at second level, positions of
authority in schools remain male-dominated. Table 4.5 shows that
high female representation on staff does not automatically translate into equivalent representation at managerial levels.

---

[4]   The remaining two schools changed status from coed secondary to voca-
      tional and community/comprehensive schools.

[5]   However, the numbers are very small, with only eight of the sampled coed
      schools established after 1983.

[6]   No girls' school has fewer than 74 per cent female staff while three
      schools have all-female staffing.

[7]   Source: Department of Education, Statistical Report 1993/94, Table 3.13.

Table 4.5: Gender of Staff and Positions of Authority in Second-Level Schools

	Single-Sex Secondary		Coed			Total
	Boys-only	Girls-only	Sec'y	Vocat.	Comm./ Comp.	
	%	%	%	%	%	%
Females as proportion of total staff:						
Mean proportion of female staff	26	88	63	48	51	56
Minimum female proportion	12	74	32	19	22	12
Maximum female proportion	51	100	87	74	69	100
Females in managerial positions:						
% of principals female	0	92	50	15	12	36
(of whom % religious)	—	(67)	(80)	(0)	(50)	(61)
% of vice principals female	0	77	35	18	18	31
% of "A" post holders female	5	82	53	28	37	43
% of "B" post holders female	18	84	52	35	46	48
No. of Schools	18	26	20	34	17	115

Source: National Survey on Coeducation.

Overall, women account for just a third of principals and vice-principals, and are under-represented in proportion to their numbers on total staff in all categories except girls' secondary schools. Gender patterns tend to be reproduced in single-sex schools surveyed, with all senior managerial posts in boys' schools held by males and the vast majority of such posts held by females in girls' schools. A clear divergence is also present between the different types of coed schools. Relative to their staff presence, women are highly under-represented at principal and vice-principal level in community/comprehensive and vocational schools, accounting for just 12 per cent and 15 per cent of principals respectively. However, in coed secondary schools their under-representation is less extreme, with women accounting for 50 per cent of principal and

35 per cent of vice-principal posts. This is mainly because of the high proportion of schools in this category which originally catered only for girls.

Approximately 30 per cent of principals are religious, and the majority of these are female. More than three in five female principals are of religious status, while the equivalent figure for males is just one in five. The decline in religious vocations will continue to lead to a greater proportion of appointments of lay staff as principals. Given that a high proportion of women principals are religious, and that women account for an even smaller proportion of vice-principals, their representation at principal level is liable to decline further, particularly in girls' and coed secondary schools. In general, female representation improves at lower managerial levels ("A" and "B" post-holders), but even here women are still in a minority in relation to their teacher representation, most notably in vocational schools.

4.4 FACTORS AFFECTING ENROLMENT PROFILES

Three main factors combine to influence initial pupil intakes:

(1) School selectivity — whether and how schools act to influence their enrolment profiles

(2) Competition between schools

(3) Pupil and parental choice, including the availability of alternative schools within local catchment areas.

4.4.1 School Selectivity

More than a fifth of schools surveyed limit their pupil intake (see Table A3.3). This practice is much more common in single-sex (34 per cent), and especially boys', schools,[8] than in coed schools (14 per cent).[9] Numerous criteria are used to select pupils, with the attendance of a sibling at the school cited by almost all schools which limit entry. Three other criteria cited by a significant proportion of such schools concern the primary school attended by

---

[8] Forty-four per cent of boys' secondary schools limit entry, compared to 27 per cent of girls' secondary schools.

[9] The practice of limiting entry is virtually non-existent among vocational schools.

prospective entrants (that is, whether an applicant attended an attached school, feeder school or other local primary school). Only six schools (four of them boys' schools) surveyed claimed to use pupil ability as a selection criterion,[10] and only two of these regarded ability as "very important". The key constraint imposed by schools on parental choice, therefore, would appear to concern *prior* decisions relating to the choice of the pupil's first-level school or choice of second-level school for an older sibling, as well, of course, as contiguity of residence.

4.4.2 Competition between Schools

As well as being influenced by a school's own selection processes, pupil intake is also affected by competition between schools. We saw in section 4.2 that single-sex schools are more likely to be located in larger towns and cities, while coed schools tend to be more equally distributed between urban and rural areas. However, as Table 4.6 shows, a greater range of alternatives for prospective applicants does not necessarily result in a higher incidence of competition among schools.

Two-thirds of schools surveyed (excluding cases where principals stated that there were no alternative schools in the locality) reported the existence of competition between schools. From Table 4.6 we can see that there is no significant difference between single-sex and coed secondary schools in the proportions who perceive competition. Vocational schools, at more than 80 per cent, were most likely to note the existence of competition, while community/comprehensive schools (not surprisingly) were least likely.

How does this competition impact on pupil intakes? Table 4.6 shows that just over two in five schools claimed to suffer from "cream off" of more able students. The proportion of single-sex secondary schools suffering from cream off at one in five is not very different from the proportion for coed secondary schools (28 per cent) but well below the figures for community and comprehensive schools (45 per cent) and particularly for vocational

---

[10]   This is a surprisingly low figure when one considers that 38 per cent of schools surveyed assess pupils for ability before entry. This practice is most widespread among community and comprehensive schools (61 per cent), boys' secondary schools (44 per cent) and vocational schools (41 per cent). The proportions for girls' and coed secondary schools are lower at 31 per cent and 15 per cent respectively.

schools (77 per cent). One in seven principals asserted that they gained as a result of inter-school competition and this claim was more prevalent among secondary-school principals.

Table 4.6: Perceived Competition between Schools and "Cream Off" of More Able Pupils

	Single-Sex Secondary	Coed Secondary	Vocational	Comm./ Comp.	All Schools
	%	%	%	%	%
Percentage of principals reporting competition	60	61	81	45	65
Extent of Perceived Cream Off					
Some/great deal	20	28	77	45	42
None	61	44	23	45	45
We get the better pupils	20	28	—	9	14
Total* %	100	100	100	100	100
No.	41	18	31	11	101

* Totals may not sum exactly to 100 per cent because of rounding.
Source: National Survey on Coeducation.

In examining the factors which determine enrolment profiles, our analysis has so far been confined to school-based influences. We now turn to the other side of the equation and examine pupil and parental choices.

4.4.3 Parental Choice of School

There would appear to be a great deal of "active" selection of schools by pupils and their parents. Only half of all pupils surveyed reported that they attend their nearest or most accessible school. Since many of these do so on the basis that they had no alternative school within easy reach (10 per cent of principals surveyed indicated that there was no alternative school in the locality), the proportion actively choosing their nearest school is even lower.

Table 4.7 suggests a tendency among parents and pupils to seek out single-sex schools. The proportion of pupils in single-sex secondary schools who do not attend their nearest available school is higher (at 58 per cent) than the equivalent figures for coed secondary schools (51 per cent) or vocational schools (45 per cent). Community and comprehensive schools (30 per cent) show the lowest tendency for pupils to have rejected other schools and conversely, the highest proportion of pupils who attend their nearest available school. The very low "rejection" figure for community and comprehensive schools is partly explained by the fact that a substantial proportion of lone schools not subject to local competition fall into this category.[11]

Table 4.7: For Pupils in Each School Type:

(a) Percentage who do *not* attend their nearest* available school

(b) Percentage of parents who obtained their choice of school

	Single-Sex Secondary	Coed Secondary	Vocational	Comm./ Comp.	All Schools
	%	%	%	%	%
Do not attend nearest school	58	51	45	30	50
Parental Choice					
(a) Parents' choice and nearest available	40	45	48	65	46
(b) Parents' choice but not nearest	52	45	38	26	44
(c) Not parents' choice	7	10	15	9	10
Total %	100	100	100	100	100
No.	2,660	947	1,282	881	5,771

* Nearest includes most accessible.
Source: National Survey on Coeducation.

The table also shows that nine out of ten parents succeed in obtaining their choice of school, though the proportion of disappointed parents is somewhat higher (15 per cent) in respect of vocational schools. Closer examination of the preferences (as

---

[11]   This is mainly because of the location of community and comprehensive schools (see Table 4.3).

perceived by their children) of disappointed parents reveals further evidence of a pattern of preference for single-sex education (Table A3.4). Almost half of all disappointed parents would have opted for a single-sex secondary school, with just under 40 per cent preferring a coed secondary, or community/comprehensive school. Vocational schools, by contrast, were the preferred option for a mere 13 per cent of disappointed parents.

The tendency to choose schools actively applies irrespective of socioeconomic status, with the distribution across social classes fairly close to overall proportions (Table A3.5). However, upper middle-class pupils, almost 60 per cent of whom did not attend the nearest school, are an exception. Part of the explanation for this is that pupils from such backgrounds are more likely to attend boarding schools than children from other social classes.

4.5 PUPIL COMPOSITION

In the previous section we looked at some of the effects of school and parental choices on school intake. We now go on to examine the net impact these and other influences have on the social composition of pupil intakes.

Traditionally, Irish second-level schools have differed considerably in terms of the social background of their pupil bodies (Hannan, Breen et al., 1983; Breen, 1986). Table 4.8 confirms that secondary schools tend to be more middle class in composition than vocational or community/comprehensive schools. Almost half of pupils in secondary schools come from middle and upper middle-class backgrounds, compared to one in three for community/comprehensive schools and one in four for vocational schools. Similarly, vocational schools attract a higher proportion of pupils from manual backgrounds (55 per cent compared to 30–33 per cent for single-sex and coed secondary schools). The similarity between the figures for single-sex and coed secondary schools indicates that class polarisation is not a coed phenomenon per se. Class composition is slightly more skewed towards the middle classes at Leaving Cert level (see Table A3.6) because of higher dropout rates among pupils from lower social classes.

The extent of social problems and deprivation in a school is closely linked to the socioeconomic backgrounds of its pupils. Given the wide variance between school types in social class composition, we should also expect a high degree of variance in the frequency of reported social problems.

Table 4.8: Social-Class Composition at Junior Cert Level by School Type[12]

	Single-Sex Secondary	Coed Secondary	Vocational	Comm./ Comp.	All Schools
	%	%	%	%	%
Upper Middle Class	20	21	7	10	16
Middle Class	27	28	18	25	25
Lower Middle Class	21	20	20	21	21
Upper Working Class Skilled Manual	18	19	33	26	23
Working Class/Semi-skilled and Unskilled Manual	15	12	22	18	17
Total %	100	100	100	100	100
No.	2,642	969	1,234	862	5,707

Social-class classifications are based on the 1986 Census of Population "social-class" categories of paternal/maternal (whichever is higher) occupational status.

Source: National Survey of Coeducation.

In the course of interviewing school principals, we asked them for their assessment of the proportion of first-year students who came from homes affected by poverty and unemployment. Figure 4.2 shows that principals in single-sex and coed secondary schools tend to report the lowest levels of poverty and unemployment among their pupils' families.

The figure shows that between one in ten and one in six single-sex and coed secondary schools report a poverty rate of more than 20 per cent compared to almost half of vocational schools. Similarly, only around a fifth of secondary schools indicate an unemployment rate of more than 30 per cent, compared to half of the vocational schools. These trends to some extent reflect the social-class distinctions identified in Table 4.8. Our own

---

[12] Table excludes 254 cases (4.3 per cent) where parental occupation was not recorded by pupils. It is suspected, based on examination of other variables, that many of these cases would fall into the lower social classes.

estimates[13] of unemployment rates based on Junior Cert pupil responses indicate little variance in unemployment rates between single-sex and coed secondary schools (11–13 per cent) but confirm that unemployment is significantly higher among the families of pupils in community/comprehensive (19 per cent) and vocational (24 per cent) schools.

Figure 4.2: Extent of Perceived Poverty and Unemployment by Type of School

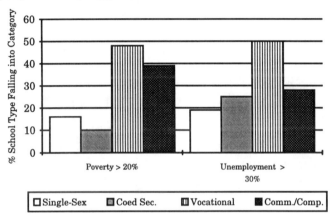

Source: Principals' Questionnaires, National Survey on Co-education. See Tables A4.7 and A4.8 for percentages.

These patterns must be interpreted with caution. Firstly, they are based on principals' perceptions and, while their best estimates, do not necessarily present an accurate picture. Although respondents endeavoured to answer as honestly and accurately as possible, they may be influenced by subjective criteria.[14] Secondly,

---

[13] See Table A3.8. The rate is taken as the proportion of pupils with at least one unemployed parent.

[14] In this context, it is interesting to note that principals of boys' secondary schools tended to report lower incidence of social problems than their counterparts in girls' or coed secondary schools. This may be partly attributable to boys' secondary schools' tendency to be more selective in their intake procedures (see Table A3.3) or might also suggest that principals in those schools may be somewhat more optimistic in their outlook. Their lower figures for alcoholism (see Table A3.9) — which, although extremely difficult to estimate with any degree of accuracy, is unlikely to vary much by social class — might provide some support for the latter view.

objective criteria on which to base estimates are more readily available in some cases (participation in free book scheme as a proxy for poverty, for example) than others (alcoholism, for example) and more available in some schools than others. Thirdly, percentages in the various categories of schools are based on a relatively small number of schools, relate only to one year of intake within those schools and may not be representative of the national population of schools or the pupil population within the sampled schools. Nevertheless, as our own estimated figures for unemployment (based on student responses) show, the perceived patterns do have some merit in providing a socioeconomic context within which later analysis may be viewed.

4.6 DIFFERENCES BETWEEN SCHOOL TYPES IN AVERAGE ACADEMIC-ABILITY LEVELS

We have already outlined how school selectivity and parental choice influence the enrolment profile of different school types and how the combination of these and other factors leads to differences in the social-class composition of pupil intakes. We now examine whether such influences also result in differences between school types in the average academic ability of their pupils.

In order to obtain a reliable and valid measure of ability, the Department of Education's Psychological Service administered Differential Aptitude Tests (DATS) to almost 5,000 of the Junior Cert students surveyed. These tests (discussed in greater detail in Chapter 3) comprised assessments of competence in verbal reasoning (VR) and numerical ability (NA). The summed score of both tests provides an indicator of general academic ability (VRNA).[15]

Table 4.9 shows that there is considerable variance between coed and single-sex schools in the average academic-ability levels of their pupils, with pupils in single-sex schools scoring on average between 3 and 8 points higher than their counterparts in coed schools. These differences are statistically highly significant ($p<.001$) for each of the three tests.

On average, boys tend to do slightly better in the tests of academic ability than girls. The equal scores for boys and girls in

---

[15] The maximum test scores are: 50 (VR), 40 (NA) and 90 (VRNA). For the purposes of this section, the original raw scores on the three tests are used.

Verbal Reasoning are surprising as girls have generally been found to do better in this area.[16] This may be related to the higher dropout rate over the junior cycle (approximately 5 per cent) amongst boys. Boys in single-sex secondary schools consistently outscore pupils in all other categories, while girls in single-sex secondary schools are, on average, of higher academic ability than pupils of either gender in coed schools. Within coed schools, the differences between genders are very slight, with girls faring as well as, or better than, boys in each of the tests. The differences between coed and single-sex schools are statistically significant for all pupils as well as for boys and girls separately.

Table 4.9: Average Scores (Raw Scores) in Tests of Academic Ability by Gender in Single-Sex and Coed Schools

	VRNA	Verbal Reasoning	Numerical Ability
All Pupils	46.6**	26.2**	20.4**
• Single Sex Schools	50.3	28.5	21.9
• Coed Schools	42.6	23.8	18.8
Boys	46.9**	26.2**	20.7**
• Single-Sex Schools	52.4	28.9	23.5
• Coed Schools	42.2	23.9	18.4
Girls	46.2**	26.2**	20.0**
• Single-Sex Schools	48.7	28.1	20.6
• Coed Schools	43.0	23.8	19.3

** p<.01, for tests of differences in average scores between single-sex and coed schools.
Source: National Survey on Coeducation.

Table 4.10 disaggregates the figures for general ability (VRNA) by type of single-sex and coed school. A number of key patterns can be seen from the table. Firstly, the distinction between school types in terms of average pupil ability would appear to be more a

---

[16] Tests of reading literacy among both 9- and 14-year olds in Ireland indicate significantly higher average scores among girls than boys (Martin and Morgan, 1994).

feature of a secondary versus non-secondary divide, rather than, as suggested by Table 4.9, a single-sex and coed phenomenon. Although boys in single-sex schools, on average, have higher scores than pupils in other school types, girls in single-sex schools have similar average levels of ability to girls in coed secondary schools. Meanwhile, pupils in community, comprehensive and vocational schools have significantly lower average-ability levels than their counterparts in secondary schools.

Table 4.10: Average VRNA Scores by Type of School[17]

| | Single-Sex Secondary | | Coed | | |
	Boys only	Girls only	Secondary	Vocational	Comm./ Comp
Mean Score					
All Pupils**	52.4	48.7	48.9	38.0	43.3
Boys**	52.4	—	50.3	37.2	44.7
Girls**	—	48.7	47.6	39.2	41.6
Less able pupils as a percentage of total enrolment*	10.2	14.0	13.7	30.8	27.0

* Defined as the proportion of pupils within each school type falling more than one standard deviation below the aggregate mean VRNA score.
** Significant, p<.01.
Source: National Survey on Coeducation.

Secondly, although pupils are, on average, of significantly lower ability in vocational and community/comprehensive schools, gender differences in academic ability scores within coed schools are slightly less marked than within the single-sex sector. Boys outscore girls by almost 4 points in single-sex schools, and by around 3 points in coed secondary and community/comprehensive schools. However, girls in vocational schools score more highly in academic ability tests than their male counterparts.

Finally, the last row of Table 4.10 shows that the concentration of less able pupils is highest in vocational and community/

---

[17] See Tables A3.10 and A3.11 for breakdown of VR and NA scores by school type.

comprehensive schools. A total of 18 per cent of pupils tested scored less than one standard deviation below the overall mean score. The proportions are lowest amongst pupils in single-sex secondary schools (10–14 per cent) compared to 27 per cent for community/comprehensive schools and 31 per cent for vocational schools. In Chapters 6 and 7 we will assess whether this high concentration of lower-ability pupils has any impact (over and above the effects of ability at an individual level) on academic achievement.

4.7 SUMMARY

The past 15 years have witnessed a growth in the prevalence of coeducation both in terms of absolute numbers of pupils and schools and also in relative importance compared to single-sex schooling. Despite this growth, the gender imbalance in coed schools in favour of boys remains intact.

Gender patterns at pupil level are to a large extent reproduced at staff level. In proportion to their representation on teaching staff, female teachers are under-represented at senior managerial level in all school types except girls' secondary schools. The situation is slightly more representative at lower levels of management. Declining religious vocations are likely to worsen this under-representation.

More than one in five schools surveyed limit their intake. This is more common in single-sex (34 per cent) than coed schools (14 per cent). Most schools report that ability is not an important criterion of selection, even though competition for pupils is reported by two-thirds of principals and over 40 per cent claim to suffer from consequent "cream-off" of more able pupils. This claim is more widespread among principals in coed (particularly vocational) schools. Active selection of schools by parents also plays an important role. Half of all pupils do not attend their nearest available school. There is some evidence of a preference for single-sex education.

The combination of these and other factors impacts on the social composition of school types. Secondary schools tend to be more middle class and vocational schools more working class. There would also appear to be a higher incidence of social problems among pupils in some types of school, particularly vocational schools.

Similarly, there are considerable differences between school types in terms of average pupil ability, as measured by DATS tests. Pupils in secondary schools (particularly single-sex boys' schools) are, on average, of higher ability than their counterparts in vocational and community/comprehensive schools, where there is a higher concentration of less able pupils. Although girls in both school types are of lower ability than girls in secondary schools, they are at least as able as boys in these schools.

In this chapter we have looked at some of the differences between different types of schools in terms of their selection processes and pupil composition. We have seen how social-class differences are linked to differences in average pupil ability between school types. Chapter 5 will now examine some of the differences *within* school types.

5

School Process, Subject Take-up and Academic Performance

The previous chapter described some of the factors which influence the enrolment profiles of different school types and outlined the extent to which coed and single-sex schools vary in terms of the social composition and average ability of pupil intakes. The focus of this chapter, however, is on internal school process: how managerial and administrative decisions taken by the schools themselves can influence subject take-up and academic performance.

The chapter considers the various ways in which schools differentiate between their pupils under two broad headings. Firstly, the different approaches taken by schools to the allocation of pupils to classes are examined. These include the use of streaming and banding as opposed to mixed-ability teaching. Secondly, the chapter focuses on gender differentiation in terms of allocation of pupils to classes, bias in the curriculum (relative provision of "male" and "female" subjects) and some of the regulations concerning subject availability.

As well as being affected by the factors outlined above, subject take-up is significantly influenced by the type of curriculum offered. The third section of the chapter describes how school types differ in the size and nature of the curriculum offered. We then examine gender bias in take-up and assess how this varies over time.

Finally, the chapter describes the variance in average academic performance at Junior and Leaving Cert levels of girls and boys in different school types. As well as describing overall performance, we take a brief look at performance levels by gender in particular subjects. Chapters 6 and 7 will then seek to determine how much of the differences in aggregate performance result from school process/organisation and compositional factors described in this and the previous chapter and whether, taking all these factors into account, coeducation has a significant impact on academic performance.

5.1 ALLOCATION OF PUPILS TO CLASSES

Schools with more than one class in a given year generally use one of three approaches to allocating pupils to classes. *Streaming* involves grouping pupils of similar levels of assessed academic ability into the same classes. Classes are then ranked in terms of average pupil ability, although the ranking order may not be made explicit by decision-makers.[1] Some form of random allocation process (such as alphabetical listing) is usually used in the case of *mixed-ability* allocation, although, in a few cases, schools specifically aim to produce a mix of ability by actively dispersing pupils of different levels of assessed ability between the various classes. *Banding* is practised in many larger schools. This entails dividing pupils into broad ability bands; each of these bands is then further subdivided into classes on the basis of mixed ability (usually some form of random allocation).

Not all schools fall neatly into one of the three categories, with some operating a combined approach. For the purposes of this analysis such schools are classified according to the dominant system used (that is, the system by which the majority of pupils are allocated to classes). For example, a school which allocates most pupils on the basis of mixed ability but also caters for a small number of students in a separate remedial class would be defined as using mixed ability. Finally, a small number of schools use gender as a criterion for allocation, and these are identified separately in Tables 5.1 and 5.2.

Table 5.1 shows that there is considerable variation in allocation systems by year within schools. At entry year, mixed-ability teaching is by far the most widely used approach, operated by more than half of the schools surveyed. This proportion falls to a third of schools at Junior Cert level, with a corresponding growth in the use of streaming (34 per cent). Many schools, therefore,

---

[1]   The measures of "ability" used vary across schools, and include a variety of standardised tests, subject exams set by the school, and teacher assessments.

postpone pupil allocation decisions until the end of first year, facilitating more informed assessment of individual ability.

Table 5.1: Extent and Nature of Differentiation in the Allocation of Pupils to Classes in Year of Entry and at Junior and Leaving Cert Levels, 1993/4

Nature of Differentiation	Year of Entry	Junior Cert	Leaving Cert
	%	%	%
Only one class/no "base" class	5.3	8.6	22.3
Mixed ability	52.6	33.6	48.2
Banding	16.7	15.5	8.0
Streaming	25.4	34.5	18.8
Combined ability and gender differentiation	**	5.2	0.9
Gendering (without regard to ability)	**	2.6	1.8
Total %	100	100	100
No.	114	116	112

** It was not possible to determine on the basis of information obtained whether and to what extent gendering takes place in the year of entry.
Source: National Survey on Coeducation

The reduction in enrolments after the Junior Cert means that in many smaller schools, pupil allocation decisions do not arise at Leaving Cert level. The wide range of subjects and levels in the Leaving Cert also leads to greater dispersal of pupils, so that base classes may cease to exist in any meaningful sense. The result of these factors is that allocation decisions at Leaving Cert level do not arise in more than a fifth of schools. Mixed ability is the most common method of allocating Leaving Cert students to classes, and is operated in almost half of schools surveyed. Excluding schools with only one class or without base classes, this proportion rises to more than 60 per cent. Streaming is practised in less than one in five schools, while the prevalence of banding (in effect, a looser form of streaming) also falls. These trends are not surprising in view of the lower enrolments and increased dispersal of students described above.

A small proportion of schools (5 per cent) combine ability and gender differentiation at Junior Cert level. These schools separate pupils firstly by gender and then according to ability within gender, resulting in a rigid system of streaming within gender. A smaller number separate pupils according to gender but allocate pupils to gendered classes on the basis of mixed ability. Both these proportions are much lower at Leaving Cert level. We will return to this subject later in the chapter when considering gender differentiation in coed schools.

How have these trends changed over time? Table 5.2 compares the results of Hannan and Boyle's (1987) analysis of data relating to schools surveyed in 1980/1 with the results of the present survey. The table excludes schools with only one class or without base classes. These accounted for a higher proportion of schools surveyed in 1980/1 and their inclusion could distort possible trends.

Taking only those schools which actively allocate pupils to classes, Table 5.2 shows that there has been a substantial increase since 1981 in the use of mixed-ability teaching at all three levels. There has been a corresponding decline in the prevalence of streaming, although at Junior Cert level there has been little change. The popularity of banding has also declined slightly while the limited use of gender differentiation at Junior and Leaving Cert levels remains unchanged.

Table 5.2: Comparison of Pupil Allocation Systems for 1980/1 and 1993/94

Proportion of Schools which Operate	Year of Entry		Inter/Junior Cert		Leaving Cert	
	1980/1	1993/4	1980/1	1993/4	1980/1	1993/4
	%	%	%	%	%	%
Mixed Ability	40	56	27	37	49	62
Banding	20	17	21	17	17	10
Streaming	40	27	42	38	32	24
Gender-related Differentiation*	**	**	10	8	2	3
Total %	100	100	100	100	100	100
No.	82	108	81	106	63	87

*   This relates to gendering either with or without additional allocation within genders by ability. Proportions for year of entry also exclude this category of school.

** No information available.

Source: National Survey on Education.

There are significant differences between school types in the prevalence of the various systems of allocation. Mixed-ability allocation of first-year pupils is most characteristic of girls' schools (64 per cent) and coed secondary schools (94 per cent), commonly those with convent-school origins (Table A4.1). Streaming is by far the most frequently used system in vocational schools (57 per cent), more than twice the propensity of community/comprehensive schools (28 per cent), though in the latter case "broad banding" is most commonly used (39 per cent).

The decline in the use of mixed-ability classes after year of entry occurs in all school types. Although the fall is greatest in respect of coed secondary schools, they are still most likely to use mixed-ability systems (Table 5.3). Girls' schools are less likely than boys' schools to allocate pupils on the basis of ability. Ability-based differentiation is most prevalent among non-secondary schools, with more than 70 per cent of vocational and community and comprehensive schools operating either banding or streaming.

Table 5.3: Allocation of Junior Cert Pupils to Classes by School Type

	Girls' Sec'y	Boys' Sec'y	Coed Sec'y	Vocational	Comm./ Comp.	Total
	%	%	%	%	%	%
Mixed Ability	50	39	65	24	28	40
Banding	33	17	6	3	33	18
Streaming	17	44	29	72	39	42
Total %	100	100	100	100	100	100
No.	26	18	17	29	18	106

Table excludes schools with one class only/no base classes. Systems involving gender segregation are included under appropriate headings (for example, within-gender streamed schools under Streaming)

Source: National Survey on Coeducation.

Mixed-ability allocation is more widespread among all school types at Leaving Cert level (Table A4.2). However, three in five community and comprehensive schools continue to operate some form of ability-based allocation while coed secondary schools (88 per cent) and girls' schools (75 per cent) tend to favour mixed ability. The proportions for boys' schools and vocational schools are somewhat lower (64 per cent and 50 per cent respectively).

5.2 GENDER DIFFERENTIATION

The previous section outlined, inter alia, how the prevalence of ability-based differentiation in allocating pupils to classes varies between school types. We now turn to the related issue of gender-based differentiation.

5.2.1 The Extent of Formal Gender Bias

Table 5.1 showed that gender differentiation plays only a limited role in the class-allocation process. Taken as a proportion of coed schools, the percentages are somewhat higher at 14 per cent (Junior Cert) and 6 per cent (Leaving Cert). Table 5.4 shows that gendered allocation is most widespread in the vocational sector where separate classes for girls and boys at Junior Cert level are established in a fifth of schools.

Table 5.4: Proportion of Coed Schools which Differentiate by Gender in Allocating Pupils to Classes

Type of Coed School	Junior Cert	Leaving Cert
Coed Secondary	12%	0%
Vocational	21%	11%
Community/Comprehensive	6%	7%
All Coed Schools	14%	6%
Total no. Schools	64	49

Table excludes schools with one class only/without base classes.

Source: National Survey on Coeducation.

Few schools use gender as a criterion for eligibility to take particular subjects. About 7 per cent of coed schools reported that the availability of certain subjects to first- and second-year students was limited by gender. In most of these cases, boys were not allowed to take Home Economics while girls were prevented from taking traditional "male" practical subjects, such as Materials Technology (Woodwork) and Technical Graphics. Similarly, the proportion of schools showing any gender bias in the provision of separate honours classes is even smaller (see Table A4.3); only one in ten coed schools show some bias and this appears to be mainly in respect of languages.

The above results would seem to indicate that explicit gender-based approaches are used only in a small proportion (less than one in ten) of schools. However, the incidence of more subtle forms of gender bias may be higher. One way in which schools may indirectly discriminate by gender concerns the rules for eligibility to take certain subjects in the Leaving Cert.

5.2.2 Gender Bias in Subject/ Level Allocation

Leaving aside the question of eligibility on the basis of allocation to a particular class, Table 5.5 shows that almost three quarters of schools surveyed impose restrictions on *individuals'* eligibility to take Maths at higher level in the Leaving Cert, while a majority also limit access to Physics, Chemistry and Accounting. In respect of all four of these subjects, boys' single-sex schools are far less likely than girls' schools to state that they impose conditions for eligibility. Just over half of boys' schools surveyed report that they limit access to higher level Maths, compared to three-quarters of girls' schools, while the differences between boys' and girls' schools are even greater in respect of Physics, Chemistry and Accounting. Coed schools tend to impose levels of restrictions similar to, or (with the exception of higher Maths) slightly lower than, girls' schools.

This pattern of lower prevalence of restrictions in boys' schools also applies to less academic-oriented subjects, although, of course, these are less likely to be taught in boys' schools. Boys' schools report much lower incidence of restrictive conditions than coed schools in respect of practical subjects, such as Technical Drawing and Construction Studies. There are no equivalent figures for girls' schools because of their much lower rate of provision of these subjects. We do not have sufficient evidence to determine why the levels of restrictions on individual choice of practical subjects should be higher in coed schools than in boys' schools. It would not seem to be the case, for example, that there are more restrictions on the basis of allocation to classes in boys' schools. In fact, there are grounds to suggest that coed schools are more likely to impose such conditions.[2]

---

[2]   Boys' schools are more likely than vocational or community/comprehensive schools (but slightly less likely than coed secondary schools) to allow

Table 5.5: Proportion of Schools within Each School Type Reporting Restriction on Individuals' Eligibility to Take Selected Subjects at Leaving Cert Level

Subject	Girls' Sec'y	Boys' Sec'y	Coed Sec'y	Vocational	Comm./ Comp.	All Schools	No. of Schools
	%	%	%	%	%	%	
Higher Maths	76	53	75	76	81	73	107
Physics	82	38	75	57	69	65	95
Chemistry	75	40	72	64	54	63	81
Accounting	65	20	61	53	62	53	88
Technical Drawing	—	18	60	43	50	44	72
Construct. Studies	—	33	43	41	47	42	57
Engineering	—	50	75	38	56	48	48

Table covers only those schools in which relevant subjects are taught.
Source: National Survey on Coeducation,

One possible explanation might be that levels of restrictions on individuals' access to practical/technical subjects are higher in coed schools because of proportionately greater demand, and the presence of girls. An alternative possibility might be that coed schools take more traditional views of the technical versus academic divide and impose higher levels of conditions on eligibility across the board in order to encourage students to take the route perceived as appropriate for them. In addition, coed schools may have less flexibility to allow open choice since they have to cater for both genders and provide a broader range of subjects; and one way of handling such constraints could be to introduce conditions for eligibility as a means of restricting choice. Demand for practical subjects may be higher in coed schools (since the average

open access to higher levels in six Leaving Cert subjects. For example, 93 per cent of boys' schools make higher level Physics available to all classes, compared to 64 per cent of vocational schools and 47 per cent of community/comprehensive schools. The equivalent figures for higher level English are 79 per cent (boys'), 60 per cent (vocational) and 33 per cent (community/comprehensive schools). See Table A4.4 for full details.

social class is lower than in single-sex schools) and there may, therefore, be more need to limit access to the subjects.

We can determine the extent to which the conditions imposed are likely to affect pupils of either gender at Leaving Cert level. The conditions fall into two main categories: the necessity to have taken a related subject (sometimes at higher level) in the Junior Cert and attainment of a minimum grade at higher level (usually grade C or higher) in a related subject in the Junior Cert.

Table 5.6 shows that restrictions are tightest in the case of higher level Maths. Just over a quarter of schools surveyed restrict higher level Maths in the Leaving Cert to pupils who have taken higher level in the Junior Cert, while a further 42 per cent require a minimum of grade C at higher level (of these, about a quarter require minimum grade B or better). Conditions for other subjects tend to focus more on take-up of a related subject in the Junior Cert, with smaller proportions requiring a minimum of grade C (at higher level) in that subject. The fourth column of Table 5.6 illustrates the impact of subject take-up conditions by gender, while the fifth column shows the additional effect of a minimum grade stipulation, using national statistics on subject take-up and grades to examine the impact. The subject take-up requirement would mean that just under a third of girls and boys who sat the Junior Cert in 1994 would be eligible to take higher-level Maths, while the inclusion of a minimum grade C would reduce the proportions eligible to less than a quarter. Interestingly, there are no gender differences in eligibility for Leaving Cert higher level Maths.

In the case of Physics (and Chemistry), girls are disadvantaged by the take-up rule, but actually fare better than boys if a minimum grade C in science is also required; provided, of course, that the subject is made available by the school. The gender imbalance is much more severe in respect of traditional "male" practical subjects, with approximately one in a hundred girls qualified under the more restrictive conditions to take Technical Drawing, Construction Studies or Engineering. Accounting is the only listed subject in which girls have a clear advantage.

The consequence of eligibility rules based on Junior Cert take-up and performance is to exclude almost all girls from many "male" subjects at Leaving Cert level and accentuate gendered take-up of subjects at Leaving Cert level. In the next section, we shall consider the nature and extent of curricular provision and shall take a closer look at take-up of subjects at both Junior and Leaving Cert levels.

Table 5.6: Potential Impact of Eligibility Criteria for Selected Subjects on Leaving Cert 1994 Students by Gender[3]

Subject	(i) Proportion of schools surveyed which impose eligibility conditions		(ii) Proportion of pupils doing 1994 JC who would meet eligibility criteria			
	Must have taken related subject/ level in JC	Must in addition have obtained minimum Grade C (higher level) in related subject	Take-up (based on col 2)		Performance (based on col 3)	
			F	M	F	M
	%	%	%	%	%	%
Higher Maths	27	42	33	32	27	25
Physics*	40	24	80	92	44	40
Accounting	39	15	74	59	44	34
Technical Drawing	35	10	5	52	1	16
Construction Studies	32	11	3	40	1	18
Engineering	42	6	1	26	0	16

* Proportions eligible for Chemistry are the same as for Physics, except cols. 2 and 3 (41 per cent and 21 per cent respectively).

Source: (i) Survey of school principals, National Survey on Coeducation,
(ii) Estimated application of criteria to pupils who sat the Junior Cert in 1994 (source: Department of Education, Statistical Report, 1993/94).

---

[3]   Table 5.6 assumes that all students would be subject to these criteria and makes no allowance for the relative prevalence of criteria in different school types. Main "related" subjects are in order: Higher Maths, Science, Business Studies, Technical Graphics, Materials Technology (Wood) and Metalwork.

The proportions eligible in Engineering and Construction Studies are probably slightly higher than shown because two schools specified take-up or minimum grades in one out of a number of subjects (for example, their definition of "related subject" includes Materials Technology, Metalwork and Technical Graphics).

5.3   CURRICULAR PROVISION AND TAKE-UP

5.3.1 Subject Provision

Subject provision is influenced by a number of factors, principally the number of pupils enrolled in a school[4]: more pupils mean more teachers and greater capacity to cater for a wide range of choice. The previous chapter (Table 4.2) showed that average enrolments vary considerably according to school type. Community and comprehensive schools have the highest mean enrolment figure (721), well ahead of single-sex schools (550). Coed secondary schools (410) and vocational schools (342) are even smaller on average.

It would be reasonable, therefore, to expect considerable variation between school types in the breadth of curriculum on offer. Table 5.7 shows that the actual variance at Junior Cert level is very small. An average of 13 subjects is taught across school types, with (as we would expect, given enrolment figures) community and comprehensive schools highest at just under 15 subjects. Single-sex schools generally provide fewer subjects than coed schools, despite their higher average enrolment. This is partially because of the need to cater for both genders in coed schools, but also the presence of a narrower, more academic focus in single-sex schools.

Table 5.7 also shows that coed schools potentially[5] offer more scope to students to take non-traditional subjects. The proportion of girls' schools offering traditional male subjects, such as Materials Technology, Metalwork and Technical Graphics, is very low (average provision is 0.04 male subjects). Similarly, provision of female subjects (Home Economics, Music) is lowest in boys' schools. The other point to emerge here is the clear divide between secondary and non-secondary schools in terms of their curricular specialisation. Provision of (mostly male-dominated) practical subjects is highest in vocational and community/comprehensive schools, while, as we shall see, there is greater emphasis in secondary schools on more academic subjects. Much the same trends in aggregate subject provision are found at Leaving Cert level, though inter-school variations are greater. However, the average number of subjects offered is lowest in vocational schools

---

[4]   Correlations between the number of exam subjects provided and total enrolments is .66 at Leaving Cert and .43 at Junior Cert.

[5]   Leaving aside limiting factors such as gendered allocation to classes and allocation of subjects.

(14), because they are smaller and suffer most from pupil dropout after the Junior Cert, having less flexibility to offer a wide range of subjects to a smaller number of students. The patterns concerning gendered provision are similar to those discussed in relation to the Junior Cert.

Table 5.7: Size and Nature of Curricular Provision at JC and LC by School Type: Mean Numbers of Exam, "Male" and "Female" Subjects by Type of School[6]

	Girls' Sec'y	Boys' Sec'y	Coed Sec'y	Vocational	Comm./ Comp.	All Schools
Junior Cert						
Mean no. of exam subjects	12.1	12.2	13.1	12.9	14.8	12.9
Mean no. of male subjects (max=3)	0.0	1.5	1.7	2.9	2.9	1.8
Mean no. of female subjects (max=2)	1.8	0.3	1.3	1.1	1.6	0.7
Leaving Cert						
Mean no. of exam subjects	15.4	15.9	16.5	13.7	18.1	15.6
Mean no. of male subjects (max=6)	1.2	3.4	3.0	3.4	4.7	3.0
Mean no. of female subjects (max=5)	3.1	1.6	2.6	2.0	2.8	2.4

Source: National Survey on Coeducation.

---

[6]   Male and female subjects are defined as those subjects where the log of the ratio of the proportions of each gender taking the subjects exceeds +/- 0.5.
    On this basis, male subjects are, in order of degree of bias:
    JC — Metalwork, Materials Technology, Technical Graphics
    LC — Construction Studies, Engineering, Technical Drawing, Applied Maths, Physics, Economics.
    Female subjects are as follows:
    JC — Home Economics, Music
    LC — Home Economics (both types), Music, Spanish, Biology
    See Tables 5.8 and 5.9 for further details.

5.3.2 Other Factors influencing Subject Take-up

Subject take-up is also affected by a whole range of other factors, a detailed examination of which could in itself form the basis for a separate study. Extensive work has been carried out in this area by Dale (1974) and Hannan, Breen et al. (1983) among others. Factors affecting subject take-up would include administrative decisions made by schools as to whether certain subjects should be made compulsory or optional; whether these regulations apply equally to all classes; and whether some classes should be precluded from taking certain subjects. Timetabling and the structure of optional packages would also have an impact, as would advice from teachers and guidance counsellors.

However, it is likely that the main influence on subject take-up would be the attitudes and expectations of individual pupils (Hannan, Breen et al., 1983). These in turn would be affected by parental, teacher and peer expectations. Academic self-image, the perceived academic difficulty level of subjects, relevant career aspirations, previous performance, gender stereotyping and tradition all affect individuals' choices (Hannan, Breen et al., 1983: 248–82). These factors impact in different ways on girls and boys, and on pupils of different levels of ability. A detailed examination of all these aspects lies outside the scope of this book and must be left for another study.

5.3.3 Gender Bias in Subject Take-up

Table 5.8 shows that take-up of many subjects at Junior Cert is heavily gender-biased. The first two columns of Table 5.8 show the proportions (based on the 1994 Junior Cert results)[7] of male and female pupils taking each subject. Column 3 computes the ratio of these proportions. A ratio of less than 1.0 indicates that a subject is female-biased (i.e. the proportion of girls taking the subject is higher than the corresponding proportion for boys), whereas a ratio greater than 1.0 shows that a subject is male-biased. The fourth column shows the log of these ratios. This allows us to compare the extent of gender bias in different subjects. A negative

---

[7] Exam-based data are used in preference to provision statistics. The latter, which refer to take-up for the entire Junior Cycle, are not disaggregated by level taken. Generally, the proportions taking subjects within the cycle would be somewhat higher than the proportion actually taking the subject in the exam.

result means that a subject is female-biased and a positive figure indicates male bias.

The highest degree of gender imbalance occurs in respect of technical subjects. Metalwork, Materials Technology (Woodwork) and Technical Graphics (Mechanical Drawing) are all male-biased while Home Economics is female-biased. Music is also taken mainly by girls. Somewhat lower levels of take-up bias are found in respect of Art, languages and Business Studies (proportionally more girls) and science (proportionally more boys).

The final column of Table 5.8 provides the equivalent figures for students sitting the Intermediate Certificate in 1980. We can immediately see that in the space of just over a decade, there has been a marked growth in the take-up of non-traditional subjects. Although the most striking change seems to occur in respect of practical/technical subjects, this is attributable mainly to the fact that minority gender representation in these subjects in 1980 was extremely low (for example, only two girls took Metalwork in 1980 compared to 423 in 1994). Recent years have seen a gradual reduction of male bias in take-up of higher level Maths in the Junior Cert, and 1994 data show that, for the first time, proportionally more girls than boys take the subject. There has also been a substantial improvement in respect of Science and Business Studies.

The absence of significant change in French is probably linked to the growth in the popularity of German. Take-up of German by both genders has increased, and although there has been a substantial reduction in the log ratio, the absolute difference in proportions remains unchanged (1980 — boys 3 per cent, girls 10 per cent; 1994 — boys 24 per cent, girls 31 per cent; see also Table A4.5). The reduction in gender imbalance in Spanish is probably also linked to increased take-up of German by girls.

The extent of gender bias increases in most of the corresponding Leaving Cert subjects (Table 5.9). In particular, higher level Maths remains heavily biased in boys' favour despite the fact that equal proportions of both genders take higher level in the Junior Cert (see Table 5.6) and that girls perform at least as well as boys in overall terms. The introduction of a new higher level syllabus (examined for the first time in 1994) should help to reduce the continuing gender imbalance. Some preliminary evidence of this is the improvement in the ratio of males to females from 1.8 in 1993 to 1.6 in 1994. This is likely to continue given the significant improvement in girls' performance in the subject in

1994 (examined later in section 5.5). Gender bias is much greater in the sciences at Leaving Cert level, although less so than in 1980. Two exceptions to the general pattern of a widening gender gap at Leaving Cert level are Home Economics (Social and Scientific) where the gap narrows (11 per cent of boys now take the subject, compared to just 4 per cent in 1980), and Art (with a slight improvement in gender balance at Leaving Cert level).

Table 5.8: Take-up of Selected Subjects for Junior Cert 1994, by Gender

Subject	% Pupils Taking Subject		Ratio	Log of Ratios	
	M	F	M — F	1994	1980
Languages					
French	62	78	.80	- .22	- .22
German	24	31	.79	- .24	-1.11
Spanish	3	3	.84	- .17	- .31
Arts and Humanities					
Art/Craft/Design	30	42	.70	- .36	- .56
Music	5	20	.27	-1.32	-1.27
Practical / Technical					
Home Economics	6	58	.10	-2.30	-4.61
Materials Technology	40	3	13.01	2.57	6.06
Metalwork	26	1	20.56	3.02	7.95
Technical Graphics	52	5	10.24	2.33	5.08
Other					
Higher Maths	32	33	.98	- .02	.24
Science	92	80	1.14	.13	.46
Business Studies	59	74	.80	-.22	- .31

Source: Department of Education, Statistical Report, 1993/94, Tables 5.3 to 5.14; Hannan, Breen et al. (1983), p. 116, slightly amended to ensure consistency with 1994 data as follows: Science (1994) = A & E (1980); Music (1994) = A & B (1980).

Table 5.9: Take-up of Selected Subjects for Leaving Cert 1994, by Gender[8]

Subject	% Pupils Taking Subject		Ratio	Log of Ratios	
	M	F	M — F	1994	1980
Languages					
French	47	68	.69	- .37	-.27
German	15	22	.68	- .38	- .92
Spanish	2	3	.58	- .54	- .45
Arts and Humanities					
History	30	25	1.20	.18	.10
Geography	45	35	1.28	.25	.19
Art	14	20	.71	- .35	- .54
Music (A & B)	1	3	.21	-1.55	-1.64
Practical / Technical					
Home Econ. (Gen)	0	1	.09	-2.39	-4.61
Home Econ. (S&S)	11	56	.20	-1.59	-2.12
Construction Studies	23	1	33.40	3.51	6.89
Engineering	18	1	30.54	3.42	7.51
Technical Drawing	28	1	27.21	3.30	5.39
Sciences					
Higher Maths	17	11	1.58	.46	1.33
Applied Maths	4	1	7.81	2.06	3.38
Physics	29	9	3.22	1.17	2.11
Chemistry	14	12	1.19	.17	1.04
Biology	33	62	.53	- .63	- .43
Business					
Accounting	20	21	.92	- .09	.03
Business Organisation	36	40	.89	- .11	- .14
Economics	14	6	2.23	.80	. 68

Sources: Department of Education, Statistical Report, 1993/94, Tables 5.15
to 5.26; Hannan, Breen et al. (1983), p. 116 (slightly amended).

---

[8]   The inclusion of VTOS candidates, many of whom would take only a few
subjects, in the Department of Education's 1994 exam data, leads to a
reduction in the take-up proportions for most subjects.

One interesting distinction between the two tables is that gender imbalance has increased since 1980 in quite a few Leaving Cert subjects. Girls increasingly dominate languages (though not in German) and Biology, and have taken a very slight advantage in Accounting. Conversely, the relative bias towards boys has grown in History, Geography and Economics. Increasing participation by less able boys may account for some of the growth in History and Geography, which appear to be linked to lower levels of ability among Leaving Cert boys (see Table 5.11).

5.3.4 Ability Differences in Subject Take-up

So far the analysis has considered take-up in general terms, without any reference to academic ability. However, it is likely that within each gender there may be some tendency for pupils of different levels of academic ability to treat subjects in different ways. For example, one might expect that higher-ability boys would tend to be allocated or choose a language, whereas boys of lesser ability might tend to take practical subjects instead. More limited provision and take-up of practical subjects means this is less likely to happen among girls. Consequently, one might expect to find, in respect of languages, a higher proportion of more able boys and, by implication, a higher average level of ability (relative to girls taking the subject). Section 5.5 will consider the relative performance of girls and boys within subjects and it is important as a prelude to that analysis that we attempt to assess the relative average academic-ability levels of pupils of each gender taking those subjects.

Table 5.10 outlines the correlations between academic ability (as measured by VRNA) and each Junior Cert subject for both genders. A high positive correlation indicates that those taking that subject tend to be the more able students within their gender. Conversely, a high negative correlation indicates a concentration of less able students. A very low correlation means that there is no significant relationship between take-up and ability. Take-up of English and Maths is virtually universal at Junior Cert level, so a correlation with ability should not arise. Low take-up by both genders in respect of Spanish, Italian, Classical Studies and Music also means that correlations with ability are not significant. These six subjects are omitted from the table.

Low take-up of "male" practical subjects (see Table 5.8) and Latin/Greek explains the absence for girls of a significant correlation between these subjects and academic ability. Interestingly, the only subject in which there is a significant correlation for girls and none for boys is Technology. This occurs even though take-up in 1994 was slightly higher for boys (5.8 per cent as against 2.5 per cent for girls).

Table 5.10: Correlations between VRNA and Subject Take-up for 1994 Junior Cert Pupils, by Gender

Subject	Girls	Boys
Languages		
Irish	.06**	.13**
French	.12**	.26**
German	.16**	.23**
Latin/Greek	.03	.15**
Practical / Technical		
Home Economics	-.17**	-.11**
Technical Graphics	.01	.07**
Materials Technology	-.04	-.24**
Metalwork	-.03	-.24**
Technology	.09**	-.03
Arts and Humanities		
History	.08**	.13**
Geography	.05**	.12**
Art	-.13**	-.16**
Other		
Science	.13**	.16**
Business Studies	.08**	.17**

** Significant, $p < .01$.
Source: National Survey on Coeducation.

In general, there appears to be a stronger relationship between academic ability and take-up for boys than for girls. This is not surprising given that the availability of practical subjects is generally very limited for girls. Less academically able girls tend to be concentrated in Home Economics and Art, while their more able colleagues tend to take languages. The larger range of alternatives for less able boys leads to greater polarisation between subjects. More able boys generally tend to take languages, History, Geography, Science and Business Studies, while their less able colleagues predominate in practical subjects and Art.

It is more difficult to assess the relationship at Leaving Cert level. We have no equivalent test of prior ability and therefore have to rely on Junior Cert performance (GPA) as a proxy for ability. Table 5.11 shows relationships between take-up and previous performance similar to those found at Junior Cert level.

Table 5.11: Correlations between Junior Cert Performance and Subject Take-up for Leaving Cert 1994 Pupils, by Gender

Subject	Girls	Boys
Languages		
French	.21**	.32**
German	.24**	.18**
Maths/Science		
Physics	.28**	.34**
Chemistry	.26**	.27**
Physics & Chemistry	.13**	.05*
Applied Maths	.00	.18**
Business		
Economics	.07**	.10**
Business Organisation	-.19**	-.13**
Accounting	.18**	.16**
Practical		
Home Economics S & S	-.30**	-.16**
Home Economics General	-.19**	-.06**
Engineering	-.05**	-.19**
Construction Studies	-.01	-.25**
Arts and Humanities		
Art	-.22**	-.19**
Music	.05*	-.03
History	.03	-.10**
Geography	-.07**	-.17**
Classical Studies	.05**	.00
Other		
Agricultural Science	-.07*	-.14**
Agricultural Economics	.05*	.02

* Significant, p<.05
** Significant, p<.01.
Source: National Survey on Coeducation.

Languages, some science subjects (especially Physics and Chemistry) and Accounting tend to be taken by higher-performing pupils of both genders. Lower-performing pupils tend to predominate in Art, Business Organisation, Home Economics and technical/practical subjects.[9] Schools and pupils, therefore, do distinguish clearly amongst subjects in terms of their expected academic "difficulty" and make choices accordingly.

5.4   AVERAGE ACADEMIC PERFORMANCE BY GENDER AND SCHOOL TYPE

The preceding sections have shown how schools differentiate between pupils in allocation to classes and subject provision and have suggested ways in which such differentiation impacts on subject take-up by pupils of different genders and levels of ability. Chapter 4 also showed how various factors combine to influence the social-class composition of schools and how this in turn results in substantial differences between school types in average pupil ability.

This section assesses the extent to which these differences in average ability and subject take-up translate into exam performance. The measure used to compare academic performance is the grade point average (GPA). This is calculated by allocating points to pupils according to the exam grades obtained, and then dividing by the total number of subjects taken. Only those students who sat at least five subjects in the Junior or Leaving Cert[10] are included. Points are allocated to all subjects in accordance with Tables 5.12 and 5.13.

No points are allotted for grades below grade D. A change of one unit in the Junior Cert grade point average (Table 5.12) is the equivalent of an increase of one grade per subject taken. The allocation of Leaving Cert points is adapted from the CAO/CAS common points scale (see Table 5.13). Here the situation is

---

[9]   English, Irish and Maths were not included in the table as these subjects are taken by the vast majority of Leaving Cert pupils. No significant correlations were found for either gender for Spanish, Biology, Mechanics, Technical Drawing, Economic History, Latin/Greek and Italian. Consequently, these are omitted from the table.

[10]   Five thousand nine hundred and four (99 per cent) Junior Cert and 4,770 (99 per cent) Leaving Cert students surveyed.

slightly more complicated because of the number of sub-divisions within grades and a change of one unit in the GPA represents an increase of one subdivision of a grade per subject.[11]

Table 5.12: Allocation of Points to Junior Cert Subject Grades

Grade	Higher Level	Ordinary Level	Foundation Level
A	10	7	4
B	9	6	3
C	8	5	2
D	7	4	1

Maximum of 12 subjects counted.

Table 5.13: Allocation of Points to Leaving Cert Subject Grades

Grade	Higher Level	Ordinary Level
A1	20	12
A2	18	10
B1	17	9
B2	16	8
B3	15	7
C1	14	6
C2	13	5
C3	12	4
D1	11	3
D2	10	2
D3	9	1

Maximum of eight subjects counted.

Table 5.14 shows that the average grade obtained by pupils surveyed approximated to Ordinary Level, Grade B in the Junior

---

[11]   For example, an increase in the LC GPA from 13 to 14 would indicate an increase in the average grade obtained from higher level C2 to C1.

Cert and Ordinary Level Grade B2 in the Leaving Cert. A gender difference is evident at both levels, with girls on average out-scoring boys by more than half a grade at Junior Cert level and by almost a full subdivision at Leaving Cert level.[12]

Table 5.14: Junior and Leaving Cert GPA by Gender, Broad School Type

	Junior Cert GPA	Leaving Cert GPA
All Girls	6.6	8.1
All Boys	6.0	7.3
Single-Sex Pupils	6.6	8.3
Coed Pupils	6.0	7.2
All Pupils	6.3	7.7

Source: National Survey on Coeducation.

Chapter 4 showed that, because of a combination of factors, coed schools have a higher concentration of less able pupils and pupils from lower social classes. It might be expected, therefore, that pupils in coed schools would not perform as well as their single-sex counterparts. Table 5.14 confirms that this is indeed the case, with pupils in single-sex schools on average outscoring coed pupils by 0.6 grades (9 per cent) in the Junior Cert and 0.9 sub-grades (5 per cent) in the Leaving Cert.

Do these differences hold within the various types of single-sex and coed schools? Table 5.15 sets out GPA figures for Junior and Leaving Cert pupils in each of the five school types. A number of interesting patterns emerge from this table. Firstly, the clear divide between coed and single-sex schools identified earlier masks considerable variance within different types of coed schools. As we saw in Chapter 4, polarisation in class and ability composition is more a secondary and non-secondary divide than a purely single-sex *v.* coed phenomenon, and, in fact, it is clear that

---

[12]   The existence of a substantial gender gap in Leaving Cert exam perfor-mance is confirmed by a recent analysis of 1994 results (Kellaghan and Dwan, 1995a). By allocating points in respect of candidates' six best sub-jects, it was shown that the median score for girls (275) was significantly higher than the equivalent score for boys (235).

the variance within types of coed schools is greater than the overall divergence between coed and single-sex schools.

Table 5.15: Junior and Leaving Cert GPA by School Type

| | Single-Sex Secondary | | Coed | | |
	Girls Only	Boys Only	Secondary	Vocational	Comm./ Comp
Junior Cert GPA					
All JC Pupils	6.9	6.4	6.6	5.5	6.0
All Girls	6.9	—	6.8	5.7	6.3
All Boys	—	6.4	6.3	5.3	5.7
Leaving Cert GPA					
All LC Pupils	8.5	8.0	8.3	6.0	7.4
All Girls	8.5	—	8.9	5.9	7.6
All Boys	—	8.0	7.6	6.0	7.2

All differences for each category of pupils by school type are statistically
significant, p<.01.
Source: National Survey on Coeducation.

In view of the differences in ability by school type (see Table 4.10),
it is not surprising to find that Junior Cert pupils in coed secondary schools (GPA 6.6) clearly do better than pupils in community
and comprehensive schools (6.0) and especially pupils in vocational schools (5.5). The difference between secondary and vocational pupils is considerable, amounting to the equivalent of an
entire grade per subject on average. Similar, but less extreme,
variance is also found at Leaving Cert level.

The second point to emerge is that the gender divide noted earlier holds within all school types and at both levels, with the exception of Leaving Cert results in vocational schools. Here, boys appear
to have closed the gender gap which existed at Junior Cert level;
however, this may merely indicate the higher dropout rate among
less able boys in vocational schools prior to the Leaving Cert.

Finally, it is important to note that not all categories of coed
pupils score lower than single-sex students. At Leaving Cert
level, girls in coed secondary schools do slightly better than

their counterparts in single-sex schools while outperforming boys in coed and single-sex schools at both Junior and Leaving Cert levels.

5.5 ACADEMIC PERFORMANCE WITHIN SUBJECTS

The previous section examined relative performance in terms of aggregate grade point average across all subjects. Although a useful indicator, GPA provides no information on performance within particular subjects. The Department of Education's Statistical Reports provide breakdowns of results for each subject by gender (but not by school type).

A number of factors should be considered when making gender-based comparisons of performance in individual subjects. Firstly, in order to ensure reliability of comparison, there should be substantial numbers of both genders taking the subjects in question. Secondly, it is necessary to ensure as far as possible that a comparison does not involve an ability bias for either gender. Table 5.10 showed that most Junior Cert subjects involve some element of gender bias in terms of ability. Excluding minority subjects, only English and Maths showed no gender ability bias in take-up for either gender. Since these subjects are taken by almost all students, we can compare relative performance by each gender with some confidence.

Relative performance in Science and languages have been the focus of recent attention (Martin, Hickey and Murchan, 1992; Drudy and Lynch, 1993) and it might be useful to assess performance for 1994 Junior Cert candidates in these subjects. It would seem sensible to exclude European languages other than French because of lower take-up figures. Although both French and science have fairly high take-up rates for both genders,[13] it is important to remember that both subjects are significantly positively correlated with ability (see Table 5.10) and that pupils of both genders who take these subjects generally tend to be more able academically.

The final point to remember, in respect of students actually taking the subjects in Table 5.16, is that the proportions for each

---

[13]   Science — males 92 per cent, females 79 per cent; French — males 61 per cent, females 78 per cent.

gender taking the subject at each level will vary. For example, equivalent proportions of boys and girls take English, but the proportion of girls taking higher level English is considerably larger than for boys. This would suggest, all other things being equal, that boys should perform better at higher level, since it is likely that they represent a more élite group within their gender.

Bearing these points in mind, what patterns emerge from Table 5.16? Girls' performance in English is superior to boys' at all three levels. Girls obtain more "A" grades and a considerably higher proportion of honours grades ("C" or higher) and have a slightly lower failure rate. The gender gap is most acute at higher level and this is particularly surprising when the lower proportion of male candidates sitting higher level papers is taken into account.

This performance differential is reproduced in respect of French. We saw in Table 5.10 that boys' take-up of French is more highly correlated with academic ability, with a higher proportion of less able boys tending to take practical subjects such as Materials Technology and Metalwork. Moreover, as in the case of English, the proportion of boys taking higher level is lower than for girls. Despite these advantages, boys are consistently outperformed by girls at both higher and ordinary levels.

Previous research indicates a gradual decline in boys' advantage over girls in Maths attainment (Lynch, Close and Oldham, 1994). Table 5.16 shows that, in respect of Junior Cert pupils, the situation concerning Maths is more balanced than in languages and that overall gender differences are slight. The proportions taking each level are roughly similar, with just under a third of boys and girls taking higher level Maths.[14] Boys seem more likely than girls to excel in the subject with a slightly larger proportion obtaining "A" grades at higher level. However, girls' overall performance at higher level is marginally better, with proportionally more girls obtaining honours grades and fewer girls failing the subject. Girls hold their own at ordinary and foundation levels in respect of "A" grades and, as in the case of higher Maths, tend to outperform boys in aggregate terms.

Previous research also suggests a slight male advantage in respect of performance in science. More than 90 per cent of boys and 80 per cent of girls take Science in the Junior Cert and (as

---

[14] For the first time, the proportion of girls sitting higher level Maths is slightly higher than for boys.

Table 5.10 showed) the subject is positively correlated with ability for both genders. Despite previous evidence to the contrary, girls appear to perform at least as well as, if not better than, boys although the gender differences are very slight.[15]

Table 5.16: Junior Cert Performance in Four Selected Subjects by Gender, 1994

Subject	% obtaining Grade A		% obtaining at least Grade C		% failing		Total No. (thousands)		Subject take-up (% all JC candidates for each gender)	
Gender	F	M	F	M	F	M	F	M	F	M
English										
Higher	5	3	72	55	1	5	21.6	16.7	63	49
Ordinary	7	3	82	67	1	3	11.1	14.3	33	42
Foundation	11	3	80	68	2	6	1.1	2.5	3	7
Maths										
Higher	15	18	81	78	3	5	11.2	11.0	33	32
Ordinary	8	6	67	60	9	14	18.0	16.8	53	50
Foundation	5	6	63	59	10	12	4.3	5.6	13	17
French										
Higher	10	6	73	62	4	7	20.3	13.8	60	41
Ordinary	0	0	51	40	9	14	6.3	7.4	19	22
Science										
Higher	15	11	73	67	6	9	20.6	20.1	61	59
Ordinary	3	3	61	60	10	11	6.7	11.0	20	32

Source: Department of Education Statistical Report, 1993/94.

There are difficulties in assessing whether gender differences in performance hold at Leaving Cert level. Firstly, dropout rates are highest among less able pupils, so we are dealing with a more select pupil body than at Junior Cert level. Higher dropout rates for boys mean that, in relative terms, their average ability level

---

[15] Relative performance of both genders, but especially of boys, in Science seems to have weakened compared to results for 1993.

rises compared to that of girls. A second problem is that the greater choice of subjects available and the reduction in the average number taken per student at Leaving Cert level mean greater dispersal of students between subjects, so that in many subjects take-up rates are much lower than at Junior Cert level. The final factor to bear in mind is that we do not have a general measure of ability like VRNA for Leaving Cert students and our control measure therefore is based on Junior Cert average performance (GPA). Since GPA will reflect girls' superior performance in Junior Cert exams, we would expect gender differences to be somewhat lower at Leaving Cert level.

We have seen that girls' performance in languages at Junior Cert level was substantially better than boys' and Table 5.17 shows that this gender differential is reproduced at Leaving Cert level. Boys are less likely than girls to take higher level English in the Leaving Cert but their relative performance improves slightly. However, at ordinary level, boys' aggregate performance relative to girls' is worse than in the Junior Cert, with a significantly higher proportion of failures recorded for boys.

Girls' performance in French is substantially better than boys' at higher level, even though the latter have a significant advantage in terms of the correlation between take-up and high ability (as measured by Junior/Inter Cert GPA — see Table 5.11). However, there appears to be little divergence in performance at ordinary level.

The introduction of a new syllabus for higher level Maths, first examined in 1994, already seems to have had an impact on performance. Total numbers sitting higher level are up substantially (about 1,000 additional candidates of each gender) on 1993. Aggregate performance has also improved with a sharp rise in the proportion of "A" and honours grades and a slight reduction in the failure rate at higher level.[16] Boys still score proportionally more "A" grades at higher level, but girls' overall performance in the subject is better. At ordinary level, girls now outperform boys not alone in overall terms, but also (and this is a reversal of the 1993 situation) in terms of numbers of "A" grades obtained. It is likely that the performance gap in respect of higher level Maths will

---

[16]   Corresponding 1993 figures for lines 3 and 4 of Table 5.17 are from left to right:
Higher Maths — 9%, 13%; 79%, 76%; 3%, 4%; 2.3, 3.9; 8%, 14%.
Ordinary Maths — 16%, 18%; 73%, 72%; 9%, 10%; 23.3, 20.8; 80%, 74%.

narrow further as the effects of the new syllabus filter down through the educational system.

Table 5.17: Leaving Cert Performance in Four Selected Subjects by Gender, 1994

Subject	% obtaining Grades A1, A2		% obtaining at least Grade C3		% failing		Total No. (thousands)		% all LC candidates for each gender	
Gender	F	M	F	M	F	M	F	M	F	M
English										
Higher	6	4	69	59	2	4	16.9	13.0	51	42
Ordinary	2	1	66	49	3	9	13.0	15.4	39	50
Maths										
Higher	15	18	86	82	1	2	3.3	4.9	10	16
Ordinary	23	19	74	68	10	13	23.2	20.4	70	66
French										
Higher	6	5	65	57	3	5	10.6	6.1	32	20
Ordinary	0	0	45	42	12	14	10.3	7.5	31	24
Chemistry										
Higher	8	12	63	64	10	11	3.1	3.2	9	10
Ordinary	9	4	66	54	12	20	0.7	1.1	2	3
Physics										
Higher	8	10	61	60	10	11	2.3	5.2	7	17
Ordinary	4	3	50	46	16	21	0.5	3.3	2	11

Source: Department of Education Statistical Report, 1993/94.

We saw earlier that take-up of Chemistry is linked to higher general ability but that this bias is roughly equivalent for both genders. Table 5.17 shows that girls' performance is about the same as boys' at higher level and better at ordinary level. The high failure rate for boys at ordinary level (20 per cent) represents a sharp increase over 1993 rates, whereas there has been no significant change in respect of girls. However, these trends should be interpreted with caution because of the relatively small numbers of students involved. Performance in Physics follows a similar pattern.

Overall then, it would appear that girls' performance in

languages is substantially better than boys' at both Junior and Leaving Cert while they appear to fare at least as well as boys in respect of traditional male strongholds such as Science and Maths.

5.6 SUMMARY AND CONCLUSIONS

There is considerable variation by year of course in the systems used to allocate pupils to classes. Mixed ability is the most widespread approach in year of entry, while the use of streaming increases prior to the Junior Cert. At Leaving Cert level, however, mixed ability is again the most popular method. Comparison with earlier research shows that there has been a substantial increase in the use of mixed-ability allocation in entry year and in the senior cycle, though there has been little change in the second and third year. The use of streaming/banding in all years is most prevalent in non-secondary schools. Coed secondary schools are most likely to use mixed-ability classes.

Formal gender differentiation in terms of allocation to separate girls' and boys' classes or provision of subjects at higher level is reported by only a small proportion of schools. In general, gender differentiation is more common in the Junior Cert year than in the Leaving Cert year. Less formal gender differentiation is more prevalent.

Gendered provision appears to be a very important cause of gender bias in take-up of practical subjects. Most schools surveyed in addition require individuals to meet preconditions (generally concerning take-up and performance in related Junior Cert subjects) in order to qualify to take certain subjects in the Leaving Cert. Boys' single-sex schools report the lowest prevalence of restrictions. The more restrictive conditions in girls' and coed schools effectively accentuate the degree of gender bias in take-up of traditional "male" subjects such as Technical Drawing, Engineering and Construction Studies. However, girls are not disadvantaged in respect of higher level Maths (where the restrictions are tightest), Physics or Chemistry since their overall performance in related subjects at Junior Cert level is at least as good as that of boys.

Despite substantial improvement over the past decade, take-up of many Junior Cert subjects remains heavily gender-biased. Practical subjects are most biased while somewhat less bias is found in respect of languages and Business Studies (proportionately more girls) and Science (more boys). The gender gap in higher level Maths in the Junior Cert has disappeared. At Leaving Cert level, the extent of bias in take-up generally increases compared to Junior Cert. There has also been increased polarisation in take-up of some subjects since 1980.

There would seem to be a stronger relationship between academic ability and subject take-up for boys than for girls. Less academically able pupils of both genders dominate practical subjects and Art, while their more able colleagues tend to take languages, Science and Business Studies. Similar patterns are found at Leaving Cert level. The relationship between ability and take-up is important when comparing relative performance of girls and boys in particular subjects.

In terms of mean performance across all subjects, girls clearly outperform boys in both the Junior and (slightly less so because of dropout of less able boys) Leaving Cert exams. Social class and composition differences lead to variation between school types in average pupil ability. It is not surprising, therefore, to find that there are significant differences between school types in average performance. These reflect a secondary/non-secondary divide rather than a single-sex and coed divide. Junior Cert pupils in secondary schools on average outscore their counterparts in vocational and community and comprehensive schools by between a half and one grade per subject. Girls in coed secondary schools outscore not only boys in coed schools, but also boys in single-sex schools and, in the Leaving Cert, girls in single-sex schools. Girls' average performance in languages is superior to boys'. The gender gap in boys' favour in Maths and Science in the Junior Cert seems to have closed.

Chapter 4 outlined some of the differences between coed and single-sex schools, and between different types of coed schools, in terms of their composition, particularly the social class and ability levels of their pupils. Chapter 5 has shown that there is substantial variation between school types in the extent to which they differentiate between pupils of different genders and levels of ability. These composition and process differences (along with other factors) in turn result in differences between school types in subject take-up and average exam performance.

Academic performance might generally be lower in coed schools, but this may result mainly from the fact that pupils in coed schools are on average of lower academic ability (as a consequence of social class and other selectivity differences) rather than some element of coeducation per se. Similarly, it would be simplistic to claim that all coed schools are homogenous. In many cases, as we have seen, the extent of variation between different types of coed schools is at least as great as the difference between single-sex and coed schools.

In order to determine whether "coeducation" has an impact on academic performance and on personal and social development, we will first need to control for these differences in social composition and school processes. This approach will be explained in greater detail in the following chapters.

6

Junior Certificate Examination Performance: The Impact of Coeducation

This chapter analyses the impact of a range of factors on the examination performance of Junior Certificate pupils. Existing research on the impact of coeducation on educational achievement has been outlined in Chapter 2. While a number of studies, both national and international (for example, Hanafin, 1992; Bryk et al., 1993), have indicated that coeducation tends to disadvantage girls in terms of their academic performance, there are good reasons for treating these findings with caution. Firstly, many studies have failed to control adequately for social background and ability differences in pupil intake. Given the marked differences in the nature of pupil intake across school types in the Irish context (see Chapter 4), these factors must be controlled for in any analysis of school differences in exam performance.

Secondly, these studies have tended to use statistical techniques which may not accurately reflect the impact of schooling processes. Earlier studies of educational performance tended to adopt ordinary least squares (OLS) regression approaches (see Chapter 2); however, these models have been criticised for failing to reflect adequately the complexities of group processes within education (Burstein, 1980; Goldstein, 1987, 1995; Bryk and Raudenbush, 1988). Consequently, multi-level modelling has increasingly been adopted both in studies of school effectiveness (Nuttall et al., 1990; Goldstein et al., 1993) and of coeducation (Bryk et al., 1993). Unlike OLS regression, multi-level models assume that pupils in the same school are more likely to have similar characteristics than a sample drawn from the student population at random. In addition, OLS regression techniques can overestimate the significance of school-level factors, thus yielding less precise estimates of the impact of factors operating at both the pupil and school level. This study attempts to overcome some of these limitations by employing multi-level modelling techniques to assess the impact of background and schooling factors on exam performance.

This chapter analyses the impact of a range of factors on the examination performance of Junior Certificate pupils. The initial sections of the chapter focus on the factors influencing aggregate exam performance (Grade Point Average), in particular assessing whether aggregate performance differs between coed and single-sex pupils. Later sections explore whether the factors shaping exam performance differ for girls and boys, for different ability groups and for different exam subjects (using English and Mathematics as examples).

6.1 MODELLING JUNIOR CERT EXAM PERFORMANCE

The following sections of the chapter present the findings of a series of multi-level models assessing the impact of a variety of factors on the examination performance of Junior Certificate pupils. In particular, the discussion focuses on whether exam performance among girls and boys differs between coed and single-sex schools. A two-level model, with pupils at level 1 nested within schools at level 2, is specified. A number of educational research studies have conducted analyses at three levels — pupils within classes within schools (see Gamoran, 1991; Rowe and Hill, 1994). While this is an important element in assessing school effectiveness, the meaning of class is not unproblematic. Some schools have no base classes in any meaningful sense, while in other schools pupils take very few subjects together — among our sample of schools, for instance, one-third of Junior Cert classes were together for only three (or fewer) subjects. Since the relevance of class allocation varies within and between schools and since the substantive focus of the study is on school-level characteristics, a two-level model is used in the following analyses. The models described are random intercepts models, that is, these models allow us to test whether average exam performance varies between schools[1].

The models described in this chapter test and cumulatively control for five blocks of variables:

(1) Personal and family background characteristics

(2) Selectivity at the school and pupil level

(3) School type, whether coeducational or single-sex

(4) School process and organisation factors

(5) Ability, a combined measure of performance in verbal reasoning and numerical ability tests.

These variables are described in greater detail in Table 6.1.

Table 6.2 presents a series of multi-level models which test for the impact of a set of variables on Junior Certificate Grade Point Average (GPA). These models are based on information concerning 4,587 pupils within 106 schools[2]. Model 1 presents the null model, a baseline against which the contribution of the explanatory variables can be assessed. In this model, the grade point average for all pupils across the sampled schools is 6.4 — that is, the average grade is just over a B on an ordinary level paper. The variance terms allow us to partition the variance in grade point average into: (a) the variance between schools, and (b) the variance between pupils within schools. These terms indicate that average exam performance differs significantly between schools, and between pupils within schools. Over a fifth of the total variance in GPA is at the school level, highlighting the significant difference between schools in exam performance.

---

[1] A two-level random intercepts model can be specified as follows:

$$Y_{ij} = \beta_0 + \sum_{k=1}^{K} \beta_k x_{ijk} + \sum_{l=1}^{L} \alpha_l W_{jl} + (\mu_j + \varepsilon_{ij})$$

where Y_{ij} is the grade point average (GPA) of pupil i in school j

β_0 is the constant

$\beta_k x_{ijk}$ is a set of k pupil-level explanatory variables

$\alpha_l W_{jl}$ is a set of l school-level explanatory variables

μ_j is the differential (or unexplained variance) in GPA for school j

ε_{ij} is the differential in grade point average (GPA) for pupil i in school j.

[2] Pupils and schools are included in the model only when complete information is available for all of the variables.

Table 6.1: Variables Used in the Analysis of Junior Cert Exam Performance

Variable	Description
Outcome:	
Junior Cert Grade Point Average (GPA)	The average grade received per subject for those taking at least 5 subjects. Grade scoring is based on a modified version of the CAO method (see also, Breen, 1986): Higher Level: A=10, B=9, C=8, D=7; Ordinary Level: A=7, B=6, C=5, D=4; Foundation Level: A=4, B=3, C=2, D=1.
Family Background:	
Gender	Dummy variable where 1 = Girl.
Social Class	Census Social Class scale ranging from 0 (Higher Professional) to 5 (Unskilled manual worker) based on the occupational status of parents.
Father Unemployed	Dummy variable where 1 = Unemployed.
Mother Unemployed	Dummy variable where 1 = Unemployed.
Mother's Education	Highest level of mother's education ranging from 0 (Primary education) to 4 (University degree).
Mother in Professional Job	Dummy variable where 1 = Mother employed in higher or lower professional occupation.
No. of Siblings	Number of siblings; only child is coded as 0.
Birth Order	Position in family (no. of older siblings as a proportion of siblings); values range from 0 (only/eldest child) to 1 (youngest).
Farm Daughter	Dummy variable where 1 = daughter of farmer.
West of Ireland	Dummy variable where 1 = school located in west of Ireland.
Age	Age at 1 January 1994; recoded into 4 categories: under 14½; 14½–15; 15½–16; 16 and over; contrasted against those aged 15 to 15½ years of age.
Selectivity:	
Parental Choice	Extent to which parents actively chose the present school; values range from 0 (no choice) to 5 (active choice).
School Cream-off	Level of cream-off experienced by school: from 0 (low) to 3 (high).
School Type:	
Coeducation	Dummy variable where 1 = attendance at a coeducational or co-institutional school.
School Process / Organisation:	
Streaming	Extent of streaming and associated curricular differentiation in the school; Guttman scale with values ranging from 0 (low differentiation) to 4 (high differentiation).
Class Position:	
Top Class Middle Class Bottom Class	Set of dummy variables where 1 defines membership of top, middle and bottom/ remedial classes respectively; contrasted against being in mixed-ability class.
Average Social Class	Social class of Junior Cert pupils averaged over the school; centred on its mean value.
Homework Rules	Extent to which the school has and enforces rules on the setting, doing and checking of homework; values range from 0 (few rules) to 2 (a no. of rules which are enforced).
Academic Ability:	
VRNA	Combined verbal reasoning and numerical ability scores (in DATS tests); centred on its mean value.

Table 6.2: Multi-level Models of Grade Point Average (GPA) for Junior Cert Pupils (N = 4,587)

Fixed Effects	Model 1	Model 2	Model 3	Model 4	Model 5	Model 6
Intercept	6.397*	6.873*	7.011*	7.059*	6.639*	6.239*
Family Background Variables:						
Gender (Girls = 1)		.448*	.431*	.434*	.506*	.719*
Social Class		-.202*	-.197*	-.197*	-.133*	-.070*
Father Unemployed		-.357*	-.353*	-.354*	-.296*	-.145*
Mother Unemployed		-.307*	-.302*	-.302*	-.207*	-.077
Mother's Education		.086*	.082*	.082*	.051*	.003
Mother in Professional Job		.208*	.214*	.213*	.133*	.033
No. of Siblings		-.068*	-.067*	-.066*	-.039*	-.021*
Birth Order		-.230*	-.236*	-.238*	-.190	-.074
Farm Daughter		.275*	.275*	.276*	.217*	.185*
West of Ireland		.372*	.310*	.311*	.329*	.193*
Under 14½ Years		.099	.092	.090	.013	.026
14½–15 Years		.128*	.127*	.126*	.078	.048
15½–16 Years		-.506*	-.485*	-.486*	-.265*	-.065
16 Years and Over		-1.324*	-1.296*	-1.294*	-.932*	-.425*
Selectivity:						
Parental Choice			.070*	.068*	.057*	.035*
School Cream-off			-.288*	-.256*	-.120	-.005
School Type:						
Coed School				-.161	-.035	.156
Coed-Gender Interaction				-.010	-.254	-.275*
School Process / Organisation:						
Streaming					-.117	-.105*
Class Position:						
Top Class					1.004*	.454*
Middle Class					-.238	-.008
Bottom/Remedial Class					-1.275*	-.315*
Average Social Class					-.523*	-.250*
Homework Rules					.267*	.149
VRNA						.151*
VRNA Squared						-.001*
Random Effects:						
Variance at School Level	0.691*	0.295*	0.226*	0.220*	0.215*	0.105*
Variance at Pupil Level	2.555*	2.220*	2.211*	2.211*	1.645*	0.945*
% Variance Explained:						
School Level	—	57.3	67.3	68.2	68.9	84.7
Pupil Level	—	13.1	13.5	13.5	35.6	63.0
Proportion of Remaining Variance at:						
School Level	21.3	11.7	9.3	9.0	11.6	10.0
Pupil Level	78.7	88.3	90.7	91.0	88.4	90.0
Deviance	17581.9	16871.4	16831.5	16829.3	15496.6	12937.8
Reduction in Deviance	—	<.001	<.001	n.s.	<.001	<.001

* Approximates to statistical significance at the <.05 level.

6.2   FAMILY AND PERSONAL BACKGROUND FACTORS

Model 2 examines the impact of personal and family-background characteristics on exam performance. The coefficients given provide an estimate of the change in the value of grade point average caused by a unit change in each independent variable, controlling for the effects of all other independent variables.[3] Since there is a substantial difference in the range of values for each variable, the magnitude of the coefficient is not an estimate of the relative contribution of each variable.

The intercept term (6.873) is different from that in model 1 because it now represents the average performance for the "baseline" pupil — in this case, a pupil with values of zero on all variables included in the model, that is, a boy of average age (15–15½ years) who is an only child from a higher professional background, whose mother has a primary education, and so on.

Controlling for other background variables, girls do significantly better (by almost half a grade) in the Junior Cert exams than boys. Therefore, the average grade for girls is over an A on an ordinary level paper or a D on a higher level paper, compared with an ordinary level B for their male counterparts. Age also has a significant impact on average grades. Those in the very youngest age group (those under 14½ years on 1 January 1994) do not differ significantly from those of average age, while those aged 14½–15 do slightly better in the Junior Cert. In contrast, those in the older age groups, particularly those aged 16 or over, have significantly lower achievement levels than the average. This association should not be seen as causal since the pattern is most likely to reflect the lower academic ability of pupils whose entry to post-primary school has been delayed or who have been "kept back" during the junior cycle.

A number of measures of parental socioeconomic status have a significant impact on grade point average. Pupils from lower social classes have a lower grade point average than those from the higher classes. Thus, controlling for other factors, those from a higher professional background differ, on average, from those from an unskilled manual background by just over one grade. In addition,

---

[3]   Thus, for example, for each extra sibling, GPA is predicted to decrease by 0.07 grades when all other background variables are controlled for (Model 2, Table 6.2).

mother's employment in a professional occupation has a positive effect on GPA, over and above the impact of family social class.

Pupils from households where either the father or mother is unemployed tend to have lower exam grades than other pupils; the effect of father's unemployment has a slightly stronger negative effect than mother's unemployment. Parental education also has a strong and positive effect. Because of the high intercorrelation between father's and mother's education, only mother's education (which has a somewhat stronger effect) is included in the model. Controlling for other factors, pupils whose mothers have a university education score over a third of a grade per subject higher than those whose mothers have a primary education only.

Other sociocultural factors are seen to have a significant effect on grade point average. GPA decreases with increasing family size while only or eldest children do better, on average, in the Junior Cert than younger siblings. Daughters of farmers have a higher GPA than others, even controlling for other measures of socioeconomic status. This pattern reflects the persistent impact of patriarchal inheritance patterns on the educational expectations and attainment of farmers' daughters (Rhodes, 1986; Hannan, Ó Riain, 1993). In contrast, being the son of a farmer has no significant effect. Attending school in the west of Ireland also has a significant and positive effect on exam performance. The specific cultural characteristics of rural communities in Connaught and West Munster have been the subject of much sociohistorical debate (Hannan and Hardiman, 1978; Hannan, 1979). These characteristics have resulted in a distinctive profile of educational participation and attainment in the west of Ireland (see Higher Education Authority, 1995).

Controlling for family background factors explains 57 per cent of the variance between schools — that is, over half of the difference in average performance between schools is a result of the differing social backgrounds of their pupils. Family background factors explain 13 per cent of the variance between pupils within schools. The reduction in the deviance term (from 17582 to 16871) indicates that this set of variables adds significantly to the explanatory power of the model.

6.3 PUPIL AND SCHOOL SELECTIVITY

Model 3 examines the additional effects of pupil and school selectivity on grade point average. Pupils whose parents actively chose their present school do significantly better than those whose parents wanted them to go to another school, although the difference in terms of grades is relatively small. Selectivity on the part of the school also has a significant impact: pupils in schools which are suffering from cream-off have a lower grade point average than those in other schools. The addition of these selectivity variables does not substantially change the effects of the preceding explanatory variables.

6.4 SCHOOL PROCESS AND ORGANISATION

Model 5 indicates that the way in which schools organise and manage the educational process impacts significantly on the Junior Cert performance of pupils. Streaming is found to have a negative (but statistically insignificant) impact on the average performance of pupils — that is, controlling for other factors, pupils in schools where classes are mixed ability score just under half a grade higher than pupils in rigidly streamed schools.

Over and above the impact on average performance, being placed in a particular class within a streamed/banded school has a significant impact. These effects should be interpreted with caution since the class location variables in model 5 reflect both the effect on Junior Cert performance of being in a particular class, and the assessed academic ability of pupils on entry.[4] All other things being equal, those in the top class do better by around a grade than those in mixed-ability classes, while the GPA of those in the bottom/remedial class is over a grade and a quarter lower.

Another aspect of school organisation, the supervision and monitoring of homework, has a positive impact on performance. Pupils tend to do better in schools where there are clear rules about the carrying out and checking of homework, and where these rules are backed up by sanctions. Interestingly, a number of other aspects of school process and organisation were found to have no clear impact on Junior Cert performance. These factors included the allocation of boys and girls to separate base classes, the degree of separation between higher level ("honours") and ordinary level ("pass") classes, and the gender ratio of the teaching staff.

---

[4] Among our sample, 81 per cent of schools with streamed/banded classes allocate pupils on the basis of pre-entry tests.

An advantage of multi-level modelling is that it allows us to separate the effects of context from those of composition. A number of contextual effects were considered but could not be included in the model simultaneously because of high intercorrelations between the variables. One aggregate variable — the average social class of pupils within the school — has a significant and negative effect on GPA, that is, pupils in schools where a high percentage of their peers are from an unskilled manual background have substantially lower average grades than those in schools with a concentration of pupils from a professional background.[5] This effect operates over and above the individual level effect of being from a particular social class. The impact of school cream-off lessens when average social class is added to the model, indicating that the negative effects of cream-off occur through the concentration of pupils of lower socioeconomic background. Average unemployment operates in a similar direction, with the concentration of pupils from "deprived" backgrounds in a school having a negative impact on academic performance, controlling for background and schooling factors. Contrary to other studies (for example, Rutter et al, 1979), the average ability level of pupils in the school does not impact significantly on individual exam performance, when individual ability is controlled. A further measure of aggregate ability was investigated. Data had been collected by the Department of Education on whether pupils had ever received remedial assistance. This variable operated in the expected direction, with a negative effect on grade point average. However, it could not be taken as a reliable and valid indicator since its values reflect not only the proportion of less able pupils within a school but also the school management's decisions in relation to the provision of remedial education.[6] Problems with the aggregate measure of remedial assistance cast doubt on the usefulness of the individual-level variable since access by less able pupils to remedial help is in large part determined by the particular school (or type of school) they attend.

---

[5]   This measure may, however, conflate neighbourhood and school effects because of the overlap between neighbourhoods and school catchment areas.

[6]   For example, among those schools which report no pupils ever receiving remedial education, the proportion of pupils with low VRNA scores varies from 0 to 47.9 per cent.

6.5   ACADEMIC ABILITY

Model 6 examines the impact of a composite measure of verbal and numerical ability (VRNA) on performance in the Junior Cert. VRNA scores are derived from DATS tests conducted by the Department of Education approximately three months before the pupils sat the Junior Certificate exam. These ability scores are treated as partly endogenous in the multi-level model — that is, as partly influenced by the schooling process over the junior cycle. Chapter 3 has indicated that using third-year ability scores leads to a slight underestimation of social-background and class-allocation effects relative to using measures of ability on entry. However, estimates of the impact of coeducation on exam performance do not vary substantially when models using third-year scores are compared with models using measures of ability on entry (see Chapter 3).[7]

As expected, "academic ability" (VRNA) has a positive and significant association with Junior Cert grade point average. The VRNA squared term indicates that the relationship between VRNA and GPA flattens somewhat for those with higher ability scores.

The addition of VRNA affects the contribution of a number of social background factors. The magnitude of the effects is reduced for all variables and the effects of mother's education, mother's unemployment, mother's professional employment and birth order are no longer significant. Thus, the effects of social background variables are, for the most part, mediated through the "ability" measure. It is interesting to note, however, that some aspects of socioeconomic background (such as social class, father's unemployment, and number of siblings) continue to have a direct effect on exam performance, even controlling for ability. When ability is controlled for, the difference in grade point average between boys and girls increases from 0.5 to 0.7 grades. The addition of VRNA to the model contributes to a substantial reduction in variance at both the school and the pupil level.

Streaming becomes statistically significant when academic ability is entered into the model. Location in a streamed/banded class reduces in effect but remains significant. Thus, allocation to streamed/banded classes increases GPA for those in the top class

---

[7]   However, the positive effect of coeducation for boys is somewhat weaker, and one negative effect for girls slightly stronger, when first-year scores are used.

but depresses GPA for those in the bottom class, even when the pupils are of similar ability. There are several possible explanations for this pattern. Firstly, bottom classes are more likely to be allocated ordinary (or foundation) level subjects which will, in turn, impact on pupils' GPA. Secondly, a slower pace of instruction in bottom/remedial classes may result in a less complete coverage of the required curriculum (see Pallas et al., 1994). Thirdly, a peer culture opposed to the academic ethos may emerge within a class labelled as "less able" (see, for example, Willis, 1977).

The final model provides a good fit to the data, explaining 85 per cent of the school-level variance and 63 per cent of the pupil-level variance.

6.6   THE IMPACT OF COEDUCATION

Model 4 incorporates school type into the model. The coed term represents the effect on the grade point average for boys of attending a coed school. It is found to have a slightly negative but statistically insignificant effect. The coed-gender interaction term represents the difference between boys and girls in the effect of coed schooling: this term is found to be very slightly negative and insignificant. Thus, controlling for gender, social background and selectivity factors, being in a coed school does not significantly affect Junior Cert exam performance, and the terms add only 1 per cent to the proportion of school-level variance explained. When school process variables and ability measures are included in the model (Model 6), the coed term becomes slightly positive while the coed-gender term becomes statistically significant and negative — that is, the effect of coeducation on exam performance is slightly positive for boys and slightly negative for girls.[8]

The impact of coeducation on grade point average can best be understood by examining the predicted exam score for "baseline" pupils within each school type. Using the predicted scores allows us to estimate the average grades of different pupil categories, controlling for the impact of social background, ability, selectivity and school process factors. Thus, predicted scores provide a more

---

[8]   Because of the inclusion of the farm-daughter variable, not all of the gender-coed interaction effect is captured. When an interaction between farm daughter and coed is tested, the coefficient is found to be negative (-.22) but insignificant.

accurate picture of the net differences between coed and single-sex pupils, in contrast to "raw" scores (actual exam grades) which fail to compare "like with like". Table 6.3 indicates that Junior Cert GPA is highest for girls in single-sex schools and lowest for boys in single-sex schools. Within both coed and single-sex schools, girls attain higher grades than their male counterparts. The effect of being in a coed school is to narrow this gender differential slightly, a pattern resulting from a slight reduction (-.2 grades) in girls' performance, and a slight increase (+.2 grades) in boys' performance.

Table 6.3: Predicted Junior Cert Grade Point Average by School Type and Gender

School Type	Boys	Girls
Single-Sex Secondary	6.2	7.0
Coeducational, of which:	6.4	6.8
Secondary	6.2	6.7
Vocational	6.6	6.9
Community/Comprehensive	6.4	6.9

Source: Calculated from Model 6 in Table 6.2 and Table A5.1.[9]

Many of the differences between schools reflect a secondary/non-secondary, rather than a single-sex/coed, divide (see Chapters 4 and 5). The model presented in Table 6.2 can be developed to disaggregate the coeducational sector by school type: secondary, vocational and community/comprehensive (see Table A5.1). When school type is considered, the impact on exam performance of being in a coed school appears somewhat less clear-cut. The coed effect found in the aggregate model appears to result almost wholly from being in a vocational school — boys in vocational schools are found to have significantly higher average grades than

[9] Thus, the predicted score for single-sex boys is equal to the intercept (6.2) in Model 6 (Table 6.2); the score for single-sex girls is equal to the intercept plus the gender coefficient; the score for coed boys is equal to the intercept plus the coed coefficient, while the score for coed girls is equal to the intercept plus the gender coefficient plus the coed and coed-gender interaction terms. The predicted scores for pupils in different school types are calculated in a similar manner.

their counterparts in single-sex schools,[10] and gender differentials are narrower than for other school types (Table 6.3; see also Table A5.1). Thus, the findings cannot be regarded as "pure" coed effects — that is, effects related to being educated with pupils of the opposite sex, but rather are related to other dimensions of school type.

Secondary schools differ considerably from other school types on a range of measures (see Chapters 4 and 5). In order to isolate the impact of being in a coed school from the impact of school type, a separate analysis of secondary schools was carried out to compare "like with like". If coeducation is expected to have a negative effect on Junior Cert exam performance among girls, this effect should operate within the secondary-school sector. The results of this analysis are presented in Table A5.2. Being in a coed secondary school is found to have a slightly negative effect on grade point average. However, neither the coed term nor the gender-coed interaction term are statistically significant, and the coefficients are slightly smaller than in the full model. Therefore, even if using third-year ability results in a slight downward bias in the estimate of the coed effect, the substantive impact of being in a coed school is very small indeed.

In summary, coeducation has a slight positive effect on the Junior Cert exam performance of boys, and a slight negative effect on that of girls. However, this effect appears to be related as much to type of school as to coeducation per se, with boys in vocational schools having higher exam scores than their single-sex counterparts.

Other aspects of school type were found to have no significant impact on exam performance;[11] these include school size, whether the school is fee-paying, type of primary school attended (coed v. single-sex, linked or not), and whether the school originated from a recent amalgamation.

---

[10] It should be emphasised that predicted scores control for all variability caused by other factors, such as streaming. Since a majority (72 per cent) of vocational schools stream Junior Cert pupils, boys in "bottom" classes within vocational schools will, in fact, have lower exam scores than the predicted score for all vocational pupils.

[11] There are differences between school types in the proportion of pupils who "drop out" over the junior cycle (see Hannan, Boyle, 1987). However, the proportion of drop-outs within a school does not appear to impact on exam performance.

6.7 GENDER DIFFERENCES

Table 6.2 above presents a multi-level model for all Junior Certificate pupils in the sample. The final model indicates that, controlling for a range of background and school factors, girls do better than boys on average. This model can be elaborated to test whether variance in Junior Cert exam performance differs by gender. Boys are found to be significantly more variable in their exam performance than girls (Table A5.3), a finding which is consistent with a number of international studies (see, for example, Coleman, 1961: 252–254). However, the models presented in Table 6.2 assume that the relationship between the explanatory variables and exam performance operates in a similar manner for girls and boys. Since there are substantive reasons why the relationships may differ, Tables 6.4 and 6.5 present exam performance modelled separately for girls and boys.

In general, the models for girls and boys are similar. However, several important differences are worth highlighting. In particular, social background factors appear to have a stronger influence on the exam performance of girls than of boys. The strength of the relationship between background characteristics and grade point average is stronger for girls, and in the case of father's unemployment, the relationship is statistically significant for girls but not for boys. The stronger relationship between social background and GPA for girls holds even when ability is controlled for. Only location in the west of Ireland and birth order have a more marked effect on boys than on girls. It was hypothesised that mother's employment in a higher-status (professional) occupation would act as a positive role model for girls' educational performance; however, the pattern for mother's professional employment is contrary to that hypothesised with a weaker effect on girls than on boys.

At the level of school process, streaming is statistically significant for girls but not for boys. However, the effect of allocation to a streamed or banded class appears to differ slightly, with allocation to the top class inflating grade point average to a somewhat greater extent for boys. Rules concerning homework setting and checking, while positive for both boys and girls, are significant only for girls.

Controlling for background and selectivity factors, coeducation is found to have a negative but statistically insignificant impact on girls' grade point average (Model 4, Table 6.4). When school process and context variables are entered into the model, the coed

Table 6.4: Multi-level Models of Grade Point Average for Junior Cert Girls (N = 2,357)

Fixed Effects	Model 1	Model 2	Model 3	Model 4	Model 5	Model 6
Intercept	6.578*	7.415*	7.488*	7.564*	7.159*	6.969*
Family Background Variables:						
Social Class		-.222*	-.217*	-.218*	-.168*	-.089*
Father Unemployed		-.618*	-.605*	-.605*	-.503*	-.300*
Mother Unemployed		-.284*	-.288*	-.287*	-.176	.014
Mother's Education		.095*	.089*	.089*	.056*	.001
Mother in Professional Job		.140	.144	.144	.076	-.031
No. of Siblings		-.088*	-.086*	-.086*	-.057*	-.032*
Birth Order		-.228*	-.234*	-.236*	-.174*	-.032
Farm Daughter		.303*	.302*	.304*	.256*	.205*
West of Ireland		.328*	.256	.246	.257	.126
Under 14½ Years		.140	.132	.131	.100	.027
14½–15 Years		.136	.137	.136	.138*	.076
15½–16 Years		-.378*	-.354*	-.356*	-.160	-.016
16 Years and Over		-1.310*	-1.280*	-1.279*	-1.005*	-.499*
Selectivity:						
Parental Choice			.061*	.060*	.058*	.035*
School Cream-off			-.221*	-.189*	-.031	.013
School Type:						
Coed School				-.182	-.292*	-.119
School Process / Organisation:						
Streaming					-.148	-.138*
Class Position:						
Top Class					1.005*	.426*
Middle Class					-.251	.046
Bottom/Remedial Class					-1.079*	-.221
Average Social Class					-.508*	-.214*
Homework Rules					.271*	.195*
VRNA						.169*
VRNA Squared						-.001*
Random Effects:						
Variance at School Level	0.636*	0.287*	0.247*	0.241*	0.207*	0.090*
Variance at Pupil Level	2.365*	1.997*	1.991*	1.991*	1.569*	0.862*
% Variance Explained:						
School Level	—	54.9	61.1	62.2	67.5	85.8
Pupil Level	—	15.6	15.8	15.8	33.7	63.6
Proportion of Remaining Variance at:						
School Level	21.2	12.6	11.1	10.8	11.7	9.5
Pupil Level	78.8	87.4	88.9	89.2	88.3	90.5
Deviance	8885.3	8444.9	8428.9	8427.2	7871.2	6443.8
Reduction in Deviance	—	<.001	<.001	n.s.	<.001	<.001

* Approximates to statistical significance at the <.05 level.

Table 6.5: Multi-level Models of Grade Point Average for Junior Cert Boys (N = 2,230)

Fixed Effects	Model 1	Model 2	Model 3	Model 4	Model 5	Model 6
Intercept	6.065*	6.716*	6.891*	6.961*	6.598*	6.206*
Family Background Variables:						
Social Class		-.192*	-.182*	-.181*	-.090*	-.044*
Father Unemployed		-.116	-.112	-.113	-.093	.023
Mother Unemployed		-.337*	-.318*	-.319*	-.242*	-.165
Mother's Education		.087*	.087*	.087*	.051	.013
Mother in Professional Job		.248*	.257*	.257*	.162	.079
No. of Siblings		-.044*	-.041*	-.041*	-.022*	-.012
Birth Order		-.217*	-.227*	-.229*	-.197*	-.119*
Farm Son		-.085	-.075	-.069	.032	.066
West of Ireland		.443*	.369*	.383*	.413*	.244*
Under 14½ Years		.038	.028	.027	-.104	.008
14½–15 Years		.100	.096	.095	-.017	.004
15½–16 Years		-.638*	-.620*	-.619*	-.353*	-.108
16 Years and Over		-1.366*	-1.324*	-1.320*	-.840*	-.374*
Selectivity:						
Parental Choice			.074*	.074*	.055*	.034*
School Cream-off			-.317*	-.293*	-.192*	-.032
School Type:						
Coed School				-.151	-.048	.176
School Process / Organisation:						
Streaming					-.127	-.110
Class Position:						
Top Class					1.064*	.555*
Middle Class					-.173	.091
Bottom/Remedial Class					-1.423*	-.323*
Average Social Class					-.528*	-.264*
Homework Rules					.359*	.136
VRNA						.134*
VRNA Squared						-.001*
Random Effects:						
Variance at School Level	0.656*	0.321*	0.230*	0.224*	0.245*	0.120*
Variance at Pupil Level	2.678*	2.409*	2.399*	2.399*	1.672*	1.008*
% Variance Explained:						
School Level	—	51.0	64.9	65.8	62.6	81.7
Pupil Level	—	10.0	10.4	10.4	37.6	62.4
Proportion of Remaining Variance at:						
School Level	19.7	11.8	8.7	8.6	12.8	10.6
Pupil Level	80.3	88.2	91.3	91.4	87.2	89.4
Deviance	8679.1	8404.2	8376.8	8375.8	7595.8	6455.2
Reduction in Deviance	—	<.001	<.001	n.s.	<.001	<.001

* Approximates to statistical significance at the <.05 level.

effect becomes stronger and attains significance[12] (Model 5). However, this effect is no longer significant when current ability is controlled for (Model 6). Even allowing for the fact that "current ability" partly reflects the schooling process over the junior cycle[13] (see Chapter 3), the net impact of coeducation on girls' exam performance is slightly negative but not substantive.

The effect of coeducation on boys' grade point average is found to be positive but insignificant.[14] When the effects of coeducation are disaggregated by school type (Table A5.1), boys in vocational schools are found to have a significantly higher GPA than their single-sex counterparts.

6.8   ACADEMIC-ABILITY DIFFERENCES AMONG JUNIOR CERT PUPILS

Section 6.6 has described the effects on average performance of being in a coeducational school. However, the effects may differ according to the ability levels of pupils; for example, coed may be good for low-ability girls and bad for high-ability girls, or vice versa. In order to test this variation, the sample was divided into three equal groups based on VRNA scores and each group was modelled separately (see Tables 6.6 and A5.5 to A5.7).

Among lower-ability pupils, the coed term is significant and positive, while the coed-gender interaction term is significant and negative, indicating that coeducation has different effects on lower-ability boys and girls. Thus, being in a coed school boosts Junior Cert exam performance among lower-ability boys and slightly reduces that of girls, thereby reducing the gender differential in average grades (Table 6.6). When the effects of coed are disaggregated by school type, being in a vocational or community/comprehensive school significantly boosts male exam performance while all types of coed school significantly reduce the gender differential (Table A5.8).

---

[12]   However, when the different types of coed school are modelled separately, none of the school types has a significant impact on girls' exam performance.

[13]   However, changes in academic ability scores over the junior cycle are the same for boys and girls.

[14]   This finding highlights the greater precision obtained using multi-level modelling techniques since OLS regression models using the same data indicate significant differences between coed and single-sex schools for both boys and girls (see Appendix, Table A5.4 for OLS estimates).

Table 6.6: Predicted Junior Cert Grade Point Average by School Type, Gender and Academic Ability

	Lower Ability		Middle Ability		Higher Ability	
	Boys	Girls	Boys	Girls	Boys	Girls
Single-Sex Secondary	4.5	5.6	6.2	7.1	7.5	7.9
Coed, of which:	5.1	5.4	6.3	7.0	7.5	7.9
Secondary	4.8	5.3	6.0	6.9	7.3	7.8
Vocational	5.3	5.6	6.6	7.0	7.6	8.0
Community/Comp.	5.1	5.3	6.2	7.1	7.7	8.2

Source: Calculated from Model 6, Tables A5.5 to A5.7, and Table A5.8.

This effect may reflect curricular and pedagogical differences between secondary and non-secondary schools. Greater access to, and take-up of, technical/practical subjects among lower-ability boys in vocational and community/comprehensive schools may help to boost their Junior Cert performance. Conversely, the more "academic" focus of many secondary schools may have the opposite effect for lower-ability boys. In contrast, lower-ability girls have fewer opportunities to boost their performance through increased take-up of practical subjects: Home Economics is the only "female" practical subject, and take-up of other practical subjects is traditionally low (see Chapter 5).

Among pupils of average ability, being in a coed school has no significant impact on Junior Cert performance and, when broken down by school type, only being in a vocational school has a significant impact on boys' performance. Among pupils of higher ability, coed has no significant impact on grade point average with no significant variation by school type.

Interestingly, gender differences are greatest among lower-ability pupils, with a "gender gap" of one grade compared with under half a grade among higher-ability pupils (see Tables A5.5 to A5.7).

In addition to the impact of coeducation varying by pupil ability, the relationship between ability and performance differs between schools — that is, some schools maximise the differences between high- and low-ability pupils while other schools serve to minimise this initial difference (see Table A5.9). While an investigation of the factors shaping these differences is outside the scope of the present study, it does highlight the way in which the different policies adopted by individual schools (irrespective of school type) can impact significantly on pupil performance.

6.9 VARIATION IN PERFORMANCE ACROSS SUBJECTS

The focus of this chapter has been on assessing the impact of a range of factors on grade point average in the Junior Certificate exam. Thus, grades are averaged across all subjects, however diverse. A number of studies have suggested that school effects, in particular coeducation effects, may impact differently across different subjects. In this respect, the performance of boys and girls in "male" academic subjects, such as Maths and Science, has been a focus of attention (see, for example, Dale, 1974). While an investigation of exam performance in different subject areas will form the basis for future research, a brief analysis of Junior Cert performance in English and Maths should provide some insight into performance variation across subjects. These subjects provide a particularly useful basis for comparison, since almost all pupils in the survey sat these subjects in the Junior Cert. In contrast, those taking other subjects, such as Science, are a more selective group within the overall population, and this selectivity effect would have to be taken into account in any analysis of performance (see Chapter 5).

Tables 6.7 and 6.8 present the findings for English and Maths performance respectively. The model for English strongly resembles that for grade point average across all subjects. Controlling for other factors, girls do significantly better than boys, while those from a lower socioeconomic background, from larger families and over 16 years of age tend to do worse in the English exam. Performance in the verbal reasoning test is closely associated with performance in the Junior Cert English exam. Controlling for ability, those in top-streamed/banded classes do better, and those in middle or bottom classes do significantly worse, than their counterparts in mixed-ability classes.

The effects of background and schooling factors on English performance do not vary substantially by gender, although social class tends to have a stronger effect for girls than for boys (see Table A5.10). Being in a coed school does not significantly affect English performance for either girls or boys, with no significant variation by school type (see Tables A5.10 and A5.11).

Table 6.7: Multi-level Models of English Performance for Junior Cert Pupils (N = 4,587)

Fixed Effects	Model 1	Model 2	Model 3	Model 4	Model 5	Model 6
Intercept	6.344*	6.570*	6.878*	7.139*	6.862*	6.497*
Family Background Variables:						
Gender (Girls = 1)		.954*	.933*	.619*	.765*	.873*
Social Class		-.183*	-.176*	-.176*	-.102*	-.044*
Father Unemployed		-.279*	-.270*	-.273*	-.198*	-.056
Mother Unemployed		-.374*	-.370*	-.370*	-.276*	-.163
Mother's Education		.088*	.085*	.086*	.048	.001
Mother in Professional Job		.329*	.332*	.331*	.244*	.120
No. of Siblings		-.089*	-.086*	-.087*	-.055*	-.036*
Birth Order		-.140	-.144*	-.147*	-.100	.030
Farm Daughter		.245	.247	.248	.180	.189
West of Ireland		.399*	.330*	.356*	.268	.207
Under 14½ Years		-.014	-.019	-.021	-.111	-.108
14½–15 Years		.124	.122	.119	.069	.050
15½–16 Years		-.648*	-.633*	-.631*	-.386*	-.164*
16 Years and Over		-1.594*	-1.569*	-1.563*	-1.151*	-.722*
Selectivity:						
Parental Choice			.039	.038	.028	.011
School Cream-off			-.325*	-.269	-.106	-.015
School Type:						
Coed School				-.480*	-.322	-.230
Coed * Girls				.355	.013	.115
School Process / Organisation:						
Streaming					-.051	-.038
Class Position:						
Top Class					.976*	.514*
Middle Class					-.649*	-.425*
Bottom/Remedial Class					-1.567*	-.849*
Average Social Class					-.551*	-.342*
Homework Rules					-.074	-.135
VRA						.176*
VRA Squared						-.001*
Random Effects:						
Variance at School Level	1.001*	0.422*	0.341*	0.311*	0.309*	0.214*
Variance at Pupil Level	3.774*	3.297*	3.292*	3.293*	2.567*	1.997*
% Variance Explained:						
School Level	—	57.8	65.9	68.9	69.1	78.7
Pupil Level	—	12.6	12.8	12.8	32.0	47.1
Proportion of Remaining Variance at:						
School Level	21.0	11.4	9.4	8.6	10.7	9.7
Pupil Level	79.0	88.6	90.6	91.4	89.3	90.3
Deviance	19368.9	18681.6	18657.6	18650.5	17528.4	16366.3
Reduction in Deviance	—	<.001	<.001	<.05	<.001	<.001

* Approximates to statistical significance at the <.05 level.

Table 6.8: Multi-level Models of Maths Performance for Junior Cert Pupils (N = 4,586)

Fixed Effects	Model 1	Model 2	Model 3	Model 4	Model 5	Model 6
Intercept	5.341*	6.160*	6.483*	6.859*	6.286*	5.645*
Family Background Variables						
Gender (Girls = 1)		.217*	.186	-.137	-.000	.562*
Social Class		-.304*	-.195*	-.295*	-.199*	-.107*
Father Unemployed		-.383*	-.374*	-.381*	-.289*	-.104
Mother Unemployed		-.524*	-.518*	-.518*	-.393*	-.277*
Mother's Education		.175*	.170*	.172*	.123*	.046
Mother in Professional Job		.345*	.352*	.350*	.233*	.053
No. of Siblings		-.096*	-.093*	-.092*	-.052*	-.033*
Birth Order		-.257*	-.264*	-.272*	-.205*	-.074
Farm Daughter		.385*	.385*	.389*	.297	.202
West of Ireland		.378	.278	.310	.309	.035
Under 14½ Years		.148	.138	.131	.013	.045
14½–15 years		.200*	.198*	.193*	.127	.056
15½–16 years		-.809*	-.783*	-.781*	-.451*	-.257*
16 Years and Over		-1.817*	-1.776*	-1.766*	-1.221*	-.543*
Selectivity:						
Parental Choice			.083*	.081*	.069*	.040*
School Cream-off			-.459*	-.327*	-.097	.070
School Type:						
Coed School				-.854*	-.659*	-.119
Coed-Gender Interaction				.347	-.048	-.421*
School Process/Organisation:						
Streaming					-.159	-.175*
Class Position:						
Top Class					1.470*	.644*
Middle Class					-.276	-.373*
Bottom/Remedial Class					-1.942*	-.465*
Average Social Class					-.775*	-.296*
Homework Rules					.240	.056
Numerical Ability						.247*
Numerical Ability Squared						-.001*
Random Effects:						
Variance at School Level	1.599*	0.808*	0.633*	0.528*	0.486*	0.180*
Variance at Pupil Level	6.449*	5.756*	5.744*	5.744*	4.486*	2.411*
% Variance Explained:						
School Level	—	49.5	60.4	67.0	69.6	88.7
Pupil Level	—	10.9	10.9	10.9	30.4	62.6
Proportion of Remaining Variance at:						
School Level	19.9	12.3	9.9	8.4	9.8	7.0
Pupil Level	80.1	87.7	90.1	91.6	90.2	93.0
Deviance	21814.9	21241.8	21210.7	21196.0	20076.3	17197.9
Reduction in Deviance	—	<.001	<.001	<.001	<.001	<.001

* Approximates to statistical significance at the <.05 level.

The pattern for Maths performance is broadly similar. However, the gender differential is somewhat narrower for Maths than for English (0.56 compared with 0.87 grades). Numerical ability is more strongly related to Maths performance than is verbal ability to English performance. Being in a coed school has significant and substantial negative effects on Maths performance among girls, a difference of over half a grade from their single-sex counterparts. This effect appears to be a "pure" coed effect as girls in all types of coed schools have lower grade scores than their single-sex counterparts[15] (Table 6.9 and Table A5.12). Preliminary analyses indicate that this effect cannot be explained in terms of differential take-up patterns for higher level Maths among coed and single-sex girls. However, further research is needed to trace the complex relationships between gender, school type, curricular allocation polices and subject/level take-up. The coed/single-sex difference in girls' Maths grades is consistent with findings from international research (Dale, 1974; Stables, 1990; Lee and Lockheed,

Table 6.9: Predicted Grade Point Average Scores in English and Maths by Gender and School Type

School Type	Boys	Girls
English		
Single-Sex Secondary	6.5	7.4
Coed, of which:	6.3	7.3
Secondary	6.4	7.2
Vocational	6.2	7.3
Community/Comprehensive	6.3	7.3
Maths		
Single-Sex Secondary	5.6	6.2
Coed, of which:	5.5	5.7
Secondary	5.4	5.6
Vocational	5.7	5.8
Community/ Comprehensive	5.4	5.5

Source: Calculated from Model 6, Tables 6.7 and 6.8, and Tables A5.11 and A5.12.

---

[15] The effect is also fairly consistent across pupil categories; within lower- and middle- (numerical) ability groups, coed girls do worse than their single-sex counterparts, although there is no significant difference for the higher-ability group. Girls in both mixed and segregated base classes within coed schools have lower grades than those in single-sex schools.

1990) which suggest that the gender-typing of subjects tends to be more pronounced in coed schools, a process which results in girls' underachievement in traditionally male subjects, such as Maths and Science.

6.10 CONCLUSIONS

In summary, the main effects on pupil performance in the Junior Certificate come from social and personal-background factors. However, schools are found to differ significantly in terms of the average performance of their pupils. While much of this difference is caused by differences in pupil composition, some of the variation results from school organisation and process.

Although coeducation does not impact substantially on Junior Cert exam performance, girls have slightly higher achievements in girls only schools. Contrary to findings from a number of studies both national and international, however, girls in coed schools still outperform their male counterparts, and any differences in exam performance between girls in coed and single-sex schools are very small in magnitude. This negative coed effect for girls is limited to those of below-average academic ability. There is some evidence that coeducation narrows the performance gap between girls and boys in coed schools. However, on closer examination, this appears to be mainly due to the "boost" in performance for boys, particularly lower-ability boys, in vocational schools.[16]

The coed effect for Maths is more clear-cut. Girls in coed schools are found to underperform in Maths relative to their counterparts in single-sex schools. Further investigation of take-up and performance in a variety of subjects would be necessary in order to examine the impact of coeducation on the gender-typing of subjects.

Previous studies have indicated that girls' educational performance relative to boys declines over the period of second-level schooling. The extent to which gender and school type impact on Leaving Certificate performance will be examined in the next chapter.

---

[16]   It must be noted, however, that a relatively high proportion of vocational schools operate streaming within the junior cycle; this effect is controlled for in assessing the impact of vocational schools on the exam performance of lower-ability boys.

7

Leaving Certificate Examination Performance: The Impact of Coeducation

Chapter 6 examined the impact of a range of factors on pupil performance in the Junior Certificate examination. This chapter examines whether similar factors impact on Leaving Certificate performance. In particular, the analyses focus on whether girls' grade point advantage over boys persists to the Leaving Cert level, and whether, controlling for Junior Cert performance, attendance at a coeducational school influences exam performance at the senior level. If, as hypothesised, coeducation has a negative impact on girls' achievement, this effect should continue to operate at the senior-cycle level.

There are, however, several differences between analysing Junior Cert and Leaving Cert exam performance. Firstly, over a fifth of students drop out of the second-level system before sitting the Leaving Certificate.[1] Dropout rates are higher among lower-ability/performance pupils, particularly among males. Thus, those taking the Leaving Cert are a more selective group than their Junior Cert counterparts (see Chapter 4).

Secondly, Junior Cert and Leaving Cert performance are highly correlated $(.75)$[2] because the two sets of exams tend to measure the same kind of qualities in pupils, and since performance in

---

[1]   This figure is based on a cohort comparison of 12-year-olds in 1988 and 17-year-olds in 1993 (Department of Education Statistical Report, 1987/88 and 1992/93).

[2]   This relationship is similar to that found among a sample of pupils who sat their Leaving Cert in 1981 (0.77) (Breen, 1986).

both exams is likely to be influenced by the same factors —in terms of both social background and school effects (see Breen, 1986). One approach to this issue involves analysing "senior-cycle performance", that is, the difference between standardised measures of a pupil's Leaving Certificate and Junior/Intermediate Certificate exam performance (see Breen, 1986). This approach focuses on the analysis of the factors (both social background and schooling) which influence change in academic performance over the senior cycle.

Some difficulties arise in applying such an approach to our sample of pupils, primarily because about a tenth of the sample sat the Intermediate rather than the Junior Cert, and hence junior-cycle exam scores differ for this group. An alternative strategy has been adopted in the following analyses: Junior/Inter Cert grade point average is entered into the model predicting Leaving Cert performance; however, the relationship between Junior Cert GPA and Leaving Cert GPA is seen as predictive rather than explanatory. Such a strategy allows us to interpret the effects of the other independent variables as representing their impact on Leaving Cert performance over and above their impact at the Junior Cert level.

The initial sections of this chapter present the findings from a series of multi-level models assessing the impact of a variety of factors on Leaving Cert exam performance. Later sections explore whether the factors shaping Leaving Cert grade point average differ for girls and boys, for different ability groups, and for different exam subjects.

7.1 EXPLANATORY VARIABLES

A definition of the variables used in the Leaving Cert multi-level model is presented in Table 7.1, while Table 7.2 presents the results from the multi-level analyses.

7.2 FAMILY AND PERSONAL BACKGROUND FACTORS

The null model presents a baseline against which the contribution of the explanatory variables can be assessed (see Table 7.2). The average Leaving Certificate grade across all pupils and schools is seen to be approximately 8, that is, a B2 on an Ordinary Level paper.

Schools differ significantly from each other in terms of average performance, with over a fifth of the variance in GPA attributable to the school level, roughly the same as at Junior Cert level.

Table 7.1: Variables Used in the Analysis of Leaving Cert Exam Performance

Variable	Description
Outcome:	
Leaving Cert Grade Point Average (GPA)	Performance in Leaving Cert scored as in Table A6.1
Family Background:	
Gender	Dummy variable where 1 = Girl.
Social Class	Census Social Class scale ranging from 0 (Higher Professional) to 5 (Unskilled manual worker) based on the occupational status of parents.
Father Unemployed	Dummy variable where 1 = Unemployed.
Mother Unemployed	Dummy variable where 1 = Unemployed.
Mother's Education	Highest level of mother's education ranging from 0 (Primary education) to 4 (University degree).
Mother in Professional Job	Dummy variable where 1 = Mother employed in higher or lower professional occupation.
No. of Siblings	Number of siblings; only child is coded as 0.
Birth Order	Position in family (no. of older siblings as a proportion of siblings); values range from 0 (only/eldest child) to 1 (youngest).
Farm Daughter	Dummy variable where 1 = daughter of farmer.
West of Ireland	Dummy variable where 1 = school located in west of Ireland.
Age	Age at 1 January 1994; recoded into 2 categories: 16 years and under; 18 years and over; contrasted against those aged 17 years.
Educational Background:	
Junior/Inter Cert Grade Point Average	Performance in junior-cycle exam scored as in Table A6.2; centred on its mean value.
Inter Cert	Dummy variable where 1 = sat Intermediate rather than Junior Cert
Repeating Leaving Cert	Dummy variable where 1 = repeat student.
School Type:	
Coeducation	Dummy variable where 1 = attendance at a coeducational or co-institutional school.
Selectivity:	
School Cream-off	Level of cream-off experienced by school: from 0 (low) to 3 (high).
School Process / Organisation:	
Streaming	Extent of streaming and associated curricular differentiation in the school; Guttman scale with values ranging from 0 (low differentiation) to 4 (high differentiation).
Class Position:	
Top Class	Set of dummy variables where 1 defines membership of top,
Middle Class	middle and bottom/remedial classes respectively; contrasted
Bottom Class	against being in mixed-ability class.
Average Social Class	Social class of Leaving Cert pupils averaged over the school; centred on its mean value.

Table 7.2: Multi-level Models of Grade Point Average for Leaving Cert Pupils (N = 4,434)

Fixed Effects	Model 1	Model 2	Model 3	Model 4	Model 5	Model 6
Intercept	7.971*	8.190*	7.749*	7.769*	7.986*	7.900*
Family Background Variables:						
Gender (Girls = 1)		.863*	.289*	.438	.416	.447
Social Class		-.446*	-.111*	-.110*	-.108*	-.093*
Father Unemployed		-.479*	-.128	-.125	-.125	-.099
Mother Unemployed		-.784*	-.345	-.345	-.339	-.325
Mother's Education		.331*	.179*	.178*	.176*	.166*
Mother in Professional Job		.691*	.335*	.336*	.335*	.314*
No. of Siblings		-.063*	.021	.021	.022	.022
Birth Order		-.303*	.072	.071	.076	.096
Farm Daughter		.350	.127	.134	.131	.110
West of Ireland		.478	-.287	-.296	-.379	-.379
16 Years and Under		.372*	.026	.026	.027	.018
18 Years and Over		-.609*	.085	.086	.082	.112
Educational Background:						
Junior/ Inter Cert GPA			1.804*	1.803*	1.798*	1.728*
Inter Cert			1.424*	1.413*	1.426*	1.233*
Repeating Leaving Cert			2.017*	2.026*	2.031*	2.039*
School Type:						
Coed School				-.083	.063	.193
Coed-Gender Interaction				-.169	-.152	-.232
Selectivity:						
School Cream-off					-.284*	-.147
School Process / Organisation:						
Streaming						.135
Class Position:						
Top Class						-.312
Middle Class						-1.058*
Bottom/Remedial Class						-1.365*
Average Social Class						-.765*
Random Effects:						
Variance at School Level	3.832*	2.190*	0.989*	0.982*	0.898*	0.699*
Variance at Pupil Level	14.840*	13.840*	6.166*	6.165*	6.164*	6.084*
% Variance Explained:						
School Level	—	42.8	74.2	74.4	76.6	81.8
Pupil Level	—	6.7	58.5	58.5	58.5	59.0
Proportion of Remaining Variance at:						
School Level	20.5	13.7	13.8	13.7	12.7	10.3
Pupil Level	79.5	86.3	86.2	86.3	87.3	89.7
Deviance	24803.1	24445.0	20862.7	20861.7	20852.6	20773.5
Reduction in Deviance	—	<.001	<.001	n.s.	<.01	<.001

* Approximates to statistical significance at the <.05 level.

Model 2 introduces a number of family background variables. The intercept changes slightly as it now represents the average performance of the "baseline" pupil: a boy aged 17 years from a higher professional background, who is an only child, and so on. As in the junior cycle, girls significantly outperform boys, with a difference of over three-quarters of a grade. A number of socio-economic factors impact on performance. Pupils from a higher professional background do over two grades better than their counterparts from an unskilled manual background. Having a mother currently in professional employment has an additional positive impact, over and above the parental social-class measure. Parental unemployment has a negative impact on average grades, with the effect of mother's unemployment being somewhat stronger. Mother's education has a positive and substantial impact on grade point average — pupils whose mothers had only a primary education score over one grade lower than those whose mothers had a university education.

Number of siblings and position in the family operate in the expected direction with only or eldest children doing better in the Leaving Certificate than younger siblings. Age also has a significant impact with younger pupils (those aged 16 years on 1 January) doing slightly better, and their older counterparts somewhat worse, than those of average age. Unlike the pattern for the Junior Certificate, being a farmer's daughter or coming from the West of Ireland do not confer significant gains in grade point average, although the relationships operate in the expected direction[3].

The addition of family background variables explains 43 per cent of the differences in GPA at the school level — that is, almost half the variance in exam performance between schools is caused by differences in the social background and gender of their pupils. In contrast, these social background variables explain less than 7 per cent of the variation between pupils within schools.

7.3 JUNIOR-CYCLE EXAM PERFORMANCE

The addition of measures of Junior Cert performance adds significantly to the explanatory power of the model. As might be expected, those who do well in the Junior (or Inter) Cert tend to

---

[3]   These groups may, of course, have advantages relating to lower drop-out rates in the senior cycle rather than higher performance.

do well in the Leaving Certificate: for each extra grade point in the junior-cycle exam, pupils score almost two grades higher in the Leaving Cert.[4] However, it is important to stress that this is not a causal relationship — rather, performance in both exams is likely to be influenced by the same underlying factors.

Most of the pupils sampled sat for the Junior Cert exam in 1992. However, about 10 per cent of the sample sat the Inter Cert in an earlier year, because they had either done a transition year[5] or were repeating the Leaving Certificate. Grading structures differ somewhat between the Inter and Junior Certs because of the introduction of a foundation level for Irish, English and Maths, and separate higher and ordinary level courses in other subjects, in the Junior Cert. The Inter Cert term in the model corrects for these grading differences but cannot be interpreted in substantive terms.

Controlling for other background variables and junior-cycle performance, those who are repeating the Leaving Cert exam score, on average, two grades higher per subject than those sitting the exam for the first time.

The impact of family-background variables is affected by the addition of Junior Cert exam results. Only social class, mother in professional employment and mother's education remain significant. This implies that the effects of parental unemployment and family size operate indirectly through junior-cycle performance. However, it is noteworthy that a number of socioeconomic factors continue to have a direct impact on Leaving Cert performance.

Age no longer has a significant effect on average grades when prior performance is controlled for; so the effect of being older than the average operates through Junior Cert performance (see also Chapter 6) rather than directly. The size of the gender difference is reduced to a quarter of a grade point when prior performance is controlled for; nevertheless, this still remains a substantial advantage to girls. Almost three-quarters of the variance at the school level is explained by a combination of family-

---

[4]   It is important to note that the grading system for the Leaving Certificate is more finely differentiated (e.g., A1, A2, B1, etc.) than the Junior Certificate system (A, B, C, etc.).

[5]   Unfortunately, because of multicollinearity problems, the effects of having taken Transition Year cannot be assessed from this model.

background and performance measures, and this model explains over half of the variation between pupils.

7.4 PUPIL AND SCHOOL SELECTIVITY

Unlike the pattern for the Junior Cert, parental choice does not impact significantly on grade point average, and so is not included in the model. In any case, it is likely that any effects from such parental choice would operate indirectly through performance in the Junior Certificate. In contrast, the impact of school selectivity is direct and negative: being in a school which suffers a great deal from cream-off has a dampening effect on Leaving Certificate results, by almost one grade point per subject taken.

7.5 SCHOOL PROCESS AND ORGANISATION

In contrast to the findings for the Junior Certificate, streaming does not have a significant impact on average performance in the Leaving Certificate. This may occur because streaming processes tend to be less rigid at the Leaving Cert level (see Chapter 5) and/or because the effect of streaming may operate indirectly through Junior Cert performance. It does, however, impact on pupil performance through placement in streamed/banded classes. Pupils in middle and bottom/remedial classes score over a grade lower than their counterparts in mixed-ability classes, even controlling for their performance in the Junior Cert.

Contextual effects also impact significantly on Leaving Cert grade point average. Average social class has a significant and negative effect over and above the impact of individual social-class background, with a drop of one point in the average class of pupils within a school associated with a decline of three-quarters of a grade. It is difficult to disentangle this effect from the impact of a number of other contextual factors. Firstly, average social class is highly correlated with whether the school is fee-paying or not. Thus, the effect of average socioeconomic status may in part reflect the impact of a high concentration of upper middle-class pupils in boarding and other fee-paying schools. Secondly, average social class is also highly correlated with dimensions of school ethos, such as orientation towards third-level education. Hence, it may reflect higher performance among pupils in schools where they are expected to do well in their exams and go on to third-level education.

Other school-level variables, such as homework rules, and the proportion of separate classes provided at higher level, do not have a significant effect on Leaving Cert performance.

The final model provides a good fit to the data, explaining over 80 per cent of the variance at the school level and 59 per cent of the variance between pupils within schools.

7.6 THE IMPACT OF COEDUCATION

Controlling for gender, social background and prior performance, both coeducation and the coed-gender interaction terms are slightly negative but insignificant. Thus, boys and girls in coed schools do not perform significantly worse in the Leaving Certificate than their counterparts in single-sex schools, once family background and Junior Cert results are controlled for. These terms do not add significantly to the model — in fact, type of school only explains 0.2 per cent of the variance in grade point average between schools.

When school selectivity, process and organisation are entered into the model, the coed term becomes slightly positive, while the coed-gender interaction term becomes more strongly negative. This pattern is similar to the direction of effects found among Junior Cert pupils; however, neither coefficient is statistically significant. Looking at these effects in terms of predicted grade point average (Table 7.3), the highest exam scores are found among girls (regardless of the coed/single-sex distinction) while boys in single-sex schools score marginally (0.2 grades) lower than their coed counterparts.

Table 7.3: Predicted Leaving Cert Grade Point Average by Gender and School Type

School Type	Boys	Girls
Single-Sex Secondary	7.9	8.3
Coeducational, of which:	8.1	8.3
Secondary	8.1	8.7
Vocational	8.1	8.2
Community/Comprehensive	8.0	8.0

Source: Calculated from Model 6, Table 7.2, and Table A6.3.

When these effects are broken down by school type (Tables 7.3 and A6.3), there is a slight positive effect for boys in all types of coed school. Among girls, there is a slight negative effect for those in a vocational or community/comprehensive school. However, none of these effects are statistically significant and any differences are extremely small in magnitude.

In summary, being in a coed school does not have a significant impact on the Leaving Cert performance of either girls or boys, when background, prior performance and school process factors are controlled. In order to compare "like with like", a separate analysis was conducted on secondary schools only (see Table A6.4). The absence of a significant coed effect is also evident within the secondary sector. Compared to single-sex secondary schools, being in a coed secondary school is positively related to Leaving Cert performance, with slightly stronger effects for girls than for boys (Table A6.4). However, neither of the coed terms are significant so coeducation per se cannot be seen as securing advantage or disadvantage in exam results.

7.7 GENDER DIFFERENCES

Table 7.2 indicates that, on average, girls outperform their male counterparts in the Leaving Certificate.[6] Chapter 6 indicated that, in addition to gender differences in average exam results, the relationships between background factors and Junior Cert exam performance differ somewhat for boys and girls. These differences are also apparent at the Leaving Certificate level (see Tables 7.4 and 7.5).

In particular, family-background variables impact more strongly on girls' exam performance than for their male counterparts. Family background factors explain almost 10 per cent of the variance in girls' performance but under 4 per cent in the case of boys. This effect persists even when girls' junior-cycle exam performance is controlled for.[7] In addition, the relationship between

---

[6]   As among the Junior Cert group, boys' exam results are significantly more variable than those of girls (see Table A6.5).

[7]   This effect is likely to be, at least partly, related to the greater variation in social-class background among girls taking the Leaving Cert; working-class boys have a disproportionate tendency to drop out of school before the Leaving Cert.

Table 7.4: Multi-level Models of Grade Point Average for Leaving Cert Girls (N = 2,382)

Fixed Effects	Model 1	Model 2	Model 3	Model 4	Model 5	Model 6
Intercept	8.216*	9.389*	8.470*	8.574*	8.719*	8.581*
Family Background Variables:						
Social Class		-.535*	-.155*	-.154*	-.151*	-.132*
Father Unemployed		-.677*	-.043	-.040	-.040	-.023
Mother Unemployed		-1.061*	-.321	-.320	-.315	-.290
Mother's Education		.484*	.249*	.248*	.245*	.236*
Mother in Professional Job		.502*	.284	285	.283	.287
No. of Siblings		-1.317*	.013	.014	.015	.017
Birth Order		-.303	.036	.036	.036	.070
Farm Daughter		.259	.048	.052	.050	.033
West of Ireland		.379	-.433	-.441	-.498	-.484
16 Years and Under		.304	-.056	-.055	-.048	-.052
18 Years and Over		-.950	.083	.084	.074	.086
Educational Background:						
Junior/ Inter Cert GPA			1.949*	1.948*	1.943*	1.890*
Inter Cert			1.734*	1.723*	1.709*	1.486*
Repeating Leaving Cert			1.906*	1.916*	1.940*	1.956*
School Type:						
Coed School				-.155	-.040	.013
Selectivity:						
School Cream-off					-.211	-.038
School Process/Organisation:						
Streaming						.217
Class Position:						
Top Class						-.664
Middle Class						-.764
Bottom/Remedial Class						-1.528*
Average Social Class						-.841*
Random Effects:						
Variance at School Level	4.151*	1.995*	0.987*	0.984*	0.950*	0.789*
Variance at Pupil Level	15.150*	13.700*	5.574*	5.573*	5.570*	5.506*
% Variance Explained:						
School Level	—	51.9	76.2	76.3	77.1	81.0
Pupil Level	—	9.6	63.2	63.2	63.2	63.7
Proportion of Remaining Variance at:						
School Level	21.5	12.7	15.0	15.0	14.5	12.5
Pupil Level	78.5	87.3	85.0	85.0	85.5	87.5
Deviance	13411.5	13127.1	10997.8	10997.5	10993.6	10954.3
Reduction in Deviance	—	<.001	<.001	n.s.	<.05	<.001

* Approximates to statistical significance at the <.05 level.

Table 7.5: Multi-level Models of Grade Point Average for Leaving Cert Boys (N = 2,052)

Fixed Effects	Model 1	Model 2	Model 3	Model 4	Model 5	Model 6
Intercept	7.395*	7.765*	7.264*	7.391*	7.691*	7.590*
Family Background Variables:						
Gender (Girls = 1)		-.372*	-.072	-.071	-.066	-.044
Father Unemployed		-.215	-.161	-.160	-.164	-.093
Mother Unemployed		-.531	-.356	-.359	-.344	-.360
Mother's Education		.159	.083	.082	.080	.063
Mother in Professional Job		.946*	.408*	.409*	.406*	.329
No. of Siblings		.021	.035	.036	.037	.036
Birth Order		-.324	.114	.114	.130	.143
Farm Daughter		-.053	-.006	-.005	-.016	-.021
West of Ireland		.474	-.165	-.166	-.298	-.324
16 Years and Under		.398	.073	.071	.063	.072
18 Years and Over		-.224	.140	.141	.142	.199
Educational Background:						
Junior/ Inter Cert GPA			1.668*	1.668*	1.659*	1.555*
Inter Cert			1.090*	1.086*	1.147*	0.897*
Repeating Leaving Cert			2.142*	2.144*	2.134*	2.199*
School Type:						
Coed School				-.169	.031	.211
Selectivity:						
School Cream-off					-.399*	-.219
School Process / Organisation:						
Streaming						.021
Class Position:						
Top Class						.198
Middle Class						-1.470*
Bottom/Remedial Class						-1.221*
Average Social Class						-.923*
Random Effects:						
Variance at School Level	3.530*	2.583*	1.358*	1.355*	1.161*	0.869*
Variance at Pupil Level	14.230*	13.720*	6.512*	6.512*	6.512*	6.339*
% Variance Explained:						
School Level	—	26.8	61.5	61.6	67.1	75.4
Pupil Level	—	3.6	54.2	54.2	54.2	55.5
Proportion of Remaining Variance at:						
School Level	19.9	15.8	17.3	17.2	15.1	12.0
Pupil Level	80.1	84.2	82.7	82.8	84.9	88.0
Deviance	11425.0	11332.6	9809.6	9809.4	9799.4	9727.5
Reduction in Deviance	—	<.001	<.001	n.s.	<.01	<.001

* Approximates to statistical significance at the <.05 level.

Junior Cert performance and Leaving Cert performance appears to be somewhat stronger for girls than for boys.

Among other school-level variables, school cream-off has a negative and significant impact on boys but not on girls. this effect does not entirely disappear when average social class is controlled for.

The impact of coeducation is not significant for either girls or boys. In other words, being in a single-sex school does not significantly advantage either male or female pupils, once background factors, prior performance and schooling process are controlled for.

7.8 ABILITY DIFFERENCES AMONG LEAVING CERT PUPILS

Chapter 6 examined potential variation in the impact of co-education across ability groups. This analysis has been repeated for the Leaving Cert cohort, dividing pupils into three "ability" groups on the basis of their junior-cycle exam performance (Tables A6.6 to A6.8).

Among the lower-ability group, being in a coed school is associated with slightly higher (0.2–0.4 grades) Leaving Cert exam scores for both girls and boys, although the differences are not statistically significant. The effects on girls differ by school type, with coed secondary schools securing the greatest advantage; boys' predicted exam scores are slightly higher in all types of coed school, although none of the differences are significant (Table A6.9). Among lower-ability pupils, the performance of girls does not differ significantly from that of boys (Table A6.6).

Table 7.6: Predicted Leaving Cert Grade Point Average by Gender, School Type and Prior Performance

	Lower Ability		Middle Ability		Higher Ability	
	Boys	Girls	Boys	Girls	Boys	Girls
Single-Sex Secondary	4.7	4.5	7.0	7.3	11.6	12.3
Coed, of which:	5.0	4.9	7.2	7.2	11.9	12.2
Secondary	5.0	5.3	7.3	7.4	11.8	12.1
Vocational	5.0	4.8	7.2	7.5	12.1	12.4
Community/Comp.	5.0	4.6	7.1	6.7	11.9	12.3

Source: Calculated from Model 6, Tables A6.6 to A6.8, and A6.9.

Being in a coed school does not have a significant impact on Leaving Cert performance for middle- and high-ability pupils either (Tables A6.7 and A6.8). Middle- and high-ability boys do slightly better in all types of coed school, while the effects of co-education vary by school type for girls, though none of these differences are statistically significant (Table A6.9). Girls do better than boys within both ability groups, although the difference is greatest for those of higher ability.

In summary, the impact of coeducation does not vary substantially across ability groups. Within ability groups, the impact of coed varies by type of school; however, none of these differences are statistically or substantively significant.

7.9   VARIATION IN PERFORMANCE ACROSS SUBJECTS

In addition to examining the impact of coeducation on aggregate exam performance among Junior Cert pupils, Chapter 6 analysed the impact of a range of factors on performance in English and maths. The findings suggested that being in a coed school had no appreciable impact on English performance but was associated with underperformance in Maths among girls. These analyses were repeated for the Leaving Cert sample.

Table 7.7 presents the findings for performance in English in the Leaving Certificate. In overall terms, the pattern for English results is fairly similar to the pattern for overall grade point average. The gender differences are more marked, however — controlling for social-background factors, girls do better in English by over two grades than their male counterparts. This gender difference is reduced somewhat when Junior Cert English grade is controlled for, and is no longer significant when school-level measures are entered into the model.

Coeducation does not have a significant impact on English performance once background characteristics are controlled for. Similarly, there is little variation in English grades across school types, although there is a slight tendency towards lower scores for vocational pupils (Tables 7.9 and A6.10). Other school process/composition variables operate in the expected direction, with average social class and being in a bottom/remedial class having a negative impact on performance.

Table 7.7: Multi-level Models of English Performance for Leaving Cert Pupils (N = 4,395)

Fixed Effects	Model 1	Model 2	Model 3	Model 4	Model 5	Model 6
Intercept	8.011*	7.891*	8.166*	8.588*	8.855*	8.636*
Family Background Variables:						
Gender (Girls = 1)		2.162*	.869*	.617	.588	.705
Social Class		-.519*	-.279*	-.277*	-.272*	-.237*
Father Unemployed		-.232	-.099	-.094	-.096	-.030
Mother Unemployed		-.638	-.238	-.245	-.236	-.197
Mother's Education		.394*	.172*	.171*	.166*	.148*
Mother in Professional Job		.880*	.550*	.554*	.550*	.512*
No. of Siblings		-.130*	.024	-.023	-.021	-.021
Birth Order		-.193	-.127	-.126	-.118	-.040
Farm Daughter		.126	.215	.224	.220	.173
West of Ireland		-.241	-.254	-.266	-.372	-.355
16 Years and Under		.529*	.307*	.301*	.303*	.270*
18 Years and Over		-.753*	-.579*	-.575*	-.581*	-.466*
Educational Background:						
Jun./Inter Cert English Grade			1.521*	1.518*	1.513*	1.412*
Inter Cert			.280	.260	.283	.024
Repeating Leaving Cert			1.029*	1.039*	1.050*	1.120*
School Type:						
Coed School				-.618	-.438	-.275
Coed-Gender Interaction				.269	.293	.130
Selectivity:						
School Cream-off					-.354*	-.183
School Process/Organisation:						
Streaming						.055
Class Position:						
Top Class						.645
Middle Class						-.776
Bottom/Remedial Class						-1.884*
Average Social Class						-.981*
Random Effects:						
Variance at School Level	5.408*	3.182*	1.409*	1.364*	1.247*	1.177*
Variance at Pupil Level	21.510*	19.670*	12.430*	12.430*	12.430*	11.970*
% Variance Explained:						
School Level	—	41.2	73.9	74.8	76.9	78.2
Pupil Level	—	8.5	42.2	42.2	42.2	44.4
Proportion of Remaining Variance at:						
School Level	20.1	13.9	10.2	9.9	9.1	8.9
Pupil Level	79.9	86.1	89.8	90.1	90.9	91.1
Deviance	26215.6	25780.5	23731.1	23727.6	23718.1	23550.4
Reduction in Deviance	—	<.001	<.001	n.s.	<.001	<.001

* Approximates to statistical significance at the <.05 level.

Table 7.8: Multi-level Models of Maths Performance for Leaving Cert Pupils (N = 4,357)

Fixed Effects	Model 1	Model 2	Model 3	Model 4	Model 5	Model 6
Intercept	7.277*	7.476*	7.240*	7.747*	7.916*	7.595*
Family Background Variables:						
Gender (Girls = 1)		.088	.208	.013	-.005	.008
Social Class		-.360*	-.156*	-.153*	-.148*	-.123*
Father Unemployed		-.181	.156	.167	.168	.193
Mother Unemployed		-.350	.096	.086	.091	.102
Mother's Education		.279*	.154*	.152*	.147*	.133*
Mother in Professional Job		.753*	.277*	.284	.282	.263
No. of Siblings		.009	.038	.041	.042	.047
Birth Order		-.181	.060	.059	.064	.073
Farm Daughter		.067	-.030	.012	-.015	-.018
West of Ireland		.218	-.150	-.171	-.240	-.172
16 Years and Under		.659*	.432*	.423*	.426*	.426*
18 Years and Over		-.847*	-.345*	-.339*	-.347*	-.324*
Educational Background:						
Jun./Inter Cert Maths Grade			1.193*	1.194*	1.188*	1.153*
Inter Cert			-.922*	-.957*	-.945*	-1.144*
Repeating Leaving Cert			.754*	.779*	.801*	.876*
School Type:						
Coed School				-.782*	-.662*	-.578
Coed-Gender Interaction				.193	.201	.116
Selectivity:						
School Cream-off					-.231*	-.078
School Process / Organisation:						
Streaming						.354*
Class Position:						
Top Class						-.517
Middle Class						-1.052*
Bottom/Remedial Class						-1.307*
Average Social Class						-.806*
Random Effects:						
Variance at School Level	3.632*	2.683*	1.032*	0.931*	0.885*	0.754*
Variance at Pupil Level	18.580*	17.840*	11.300*	11.300*	11.300*	11.240*
% Variance Explained:						
School Level	—	26.1	71.6	74.4	75.6	79.3
Pupil Level	—	4.0	39.2	39.2	39.2	39.5
Proportion of Remaining Variance at:						
School Level	16.4	13.1	8.4	7.6	7.3	6.3
Pupil Level	83.6	86.9	91.6	92.4	92.6	93.7
Deviance	25326.2	25124.6	23093.5	26084.3	23078.9	23042.9
Reduction in Deviance	—	<.001	<.001	<.05	<.05	<.001

* Approximates to statistical significance at the <.05 level.

Table 7.9: Predicted Leaving Cert Grade in English and Maths by Gender and School Type

School Type	Boys	Girls
English		
Single-Sex Secondary	8.6	9.3
Coed, of which:	8.4	9.2
Secondary	8.3	9.6
Vocational	8.0	8.6
Community/ Comprehensive	8.8	9.3
Maths		
Single-Sex Secondary	7.6	7.6
Coed, of which:	7.0	7.1
Secondary	7.2	7.4
Vocational	6.9	7.2
Community/ Comprehensive	6.9	6.8

Source: Calculated from Model 6, Tables 7.7 and 7.8, and Tables A6.10 and A6.11.

The pattern for Maths performance is quite different from that for English or overall grade point average (see Table 7.8). Interestingly, schools account for less of the variance in Maths grades than in the case of English grades. The gender effect differs considerably from the pattern for English: controlling for other background factors, there is no significant difference between girls and boys in Leaving Cert Maths grade. Social-background factors account for less of the difference in Maths than in English. This pattern is consistent with international findings which indicate that results in Maths are less likely to be influenced by the social and cultural resources provided by parents.

Controlling for background factors, Junior Cert Maths grade and school organisation, pupils in coed schools perform slightly worse than their counterparts in single-sex schools. However, the effect is not statistically significant.[8] The pattern varies somewhat with girls in vocational and community/comprehensive

---

[8]   When girls and boys are considered separately, coeducation has a negative, but non-significant effect, for both groups (see Table A6.12).

schools reporting much lower Maths grades than their counterparts in single-sex schools, the community/comprehensive school effect being statistically significant (Table A6.11). In the case of boys, lower Maths performance appears to be the result of a lower take-up of higher level Maths in coed schools: only 10 per cent of boys in coed schools take higher level Maths for the Leaving Cert, compared with 29 per cent of their counterparts in single-sex schools.[9] However, in the case of girls, there is little difference between coed and single-sex schools in the take-up of higher level Maths, when other factors are taken into account. Consequently, Leaving Cert girls in coed schools appear to show a tendency towards underperformance in Maths similar to, though less pronounced than, their Junior Cert counterparts. However, further research is needed in order to explore the complex relationship between provision, allocation and choice of subjects and levels within coed and single-sex schools.

7.10 CONCLUSIONS

In summary, performance in the Leaving Cert is found to be closely related to performance in junior-cycle exams. However, socioeconomic factors are found to have a direct effect on Leaving Cert grade point average over and above the effect of earlier performance. There is also evidence of gender differences in Leaving Cert performance, with girls outperforming boys, when background and prior performance are controlled for. Thus, boys do not appear to "catch up" with their female counterparts in the way some international studies have suggested, although the gender gap is narrower than among Junior Cert pupils (0.4 on a finely differentiated grade scheme, compared with 0.7 grades on a broader scheme).

Perhaps the most significant finding is the lack of impact of coeducational schooling on overall Leaving Cert performance. With somewhat clearer results than the Junior Cert pattern, there is no significant difference between single-sex and coed pupils in overall grade point average, and no evidence that co-education disadvantages girls in terms of overall academic

---

[9] Preliminary analyses indicate that the coed/single-sex difference persists when background, prior performance and schooling process are taken into account.

achievement. Thus, the differences in raw exam scores discussed in Chapter 5 are seen to reflect differences in school composition rather than a coed effect per se. The effect of being in a coed school differs slightly with type of school and ability level of pupils; however, none of these differences are significant or substantive. For Maths performance, however, the results are less clear-cut with some evidence that coed schools disadvantage both girls and boys.

This is not to discount the impact of school policy on overall exam performance, however. School process and organisation — in particular streaming or banding — impact on average grades at the Leaving Cert level as well as at the Junior Cert level. However, the impact of school policy on exam performance appears to occur within, rather than between, school types.

Chapters 6 and 7 have focused on an analysis of the impact of schooling and other factors on exam performance. However, exam performance is only one of a number of outcomes of the educational process. The following chapter assesses the impact of schools on a range of social-developmental outcomes.

8

Social- and Personal-Development Outcomes of Education

Chapters 6 and 7 focused on the impact of coeducation on examination performance. While this issue has been the subject of much controversy, both nationally and internationally, research findings on the impact of coeducation on personal and social development have been equally contentious. Earlier research (for example, Dale, 1969, 1971, 1974) found that the more positive and "natural" social interaction between the sexes in coed schools resulted in clear social-developmental advantages for both girls and boys. However, more recent work (Bryk, Lee and Holland, 1993) has shown advantages for girls in single-sex schools in terms of self-concept, locus of control and gender role stereotyping.

This chapter examines social- and personal-development outcomes of the schooling process for both Junior and Leaving Certificate pupils. The first section examines pupils' own views of their schooling and its benefits. Later sections examine the impact of educational factors on a range of developmental outcomes, namely, academic self-image, locus of control, body-image and gender role stereotyping. These measures provide a broad indication of how young people evaluate important aspects of their own development, and give a more complete account of the impact of schooling on the lives of pupils than focusing on examination performance alone.

8.1 PUPILS' PERCEPTIONS OF THEIR EDUCATION

Pupils were asked whether they would prefer to be in a single-sex school rather than a coeducational school. Figure 8.1 indicates

that only a small minority (5–6 per cent) of pupils in coed schools
would rather be in a single-sex school. In contrast, with the exception of Leaving Cert girls, the majority of pupils in single-sex
schools would prefer to be in coed schools. It is interesting to note,
however, that girls in single-sex schools show a stronger sense of
attachment to single-sex schooling than their male counterparts.

**Figure 8.1: Pupils' Preferences for Coeducational
Schooling**

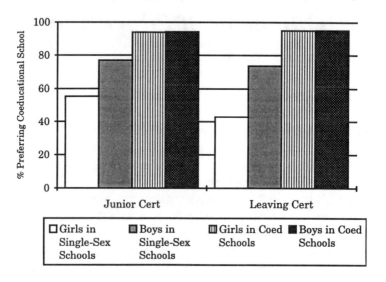

Pupils were asked about the impact of their second-level schooling
on a range of social/personal-development outcomes. Among both
girls and boys, those in coed schools were more likely to report
that their education had been "a lot" of benefit in relation to:
increasing their self-confidence, helping them to develop into a
well-balanced person, building good relations with friends of the
opposite sex, being able to talk and communicate well with others,
and helping them to make new friends.[1] Girls were somewhat
more likely than their male counterparts to report a positive
evaluation of their schooling (Figures 8.2 and 8.3).

---

[1] This pattern of coed/single-sex differences is similar to that found among
     a sample of ex-pupils interviewed at 22–24 years of age (see Hannan and
     Shortall, 1991).

Figure 8.2: Junior Cert Pupils' Perceptions of the Personal- and Social-Development Aspects of Their Second-Level Education[2]

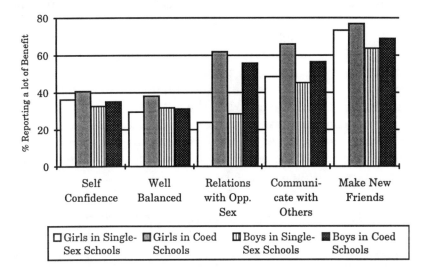

Figure 8.3: Leaving Cert Pupils' Perceptions of the Personal- and Social-Development Aspects of Their Second-Level Education

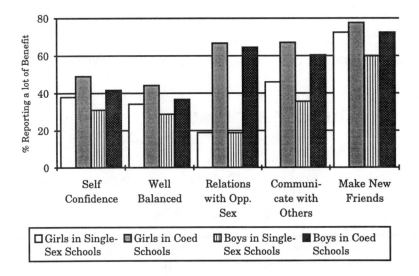

---

[2]   Data for Figures 8.2 and 8.3 are presented in Appendix Table A7.1.

While pupils' own views of the benefits of their education are of obvious importance, a number of more "objective" measures of personal and social development outcomes can also be derived from the survey data. The following sections examine: (i) pupils' academic self-confidence (or self-image); (ii) their locus of control, that is, the extent of their perceived sense of control over their lives and ability to cope with problems; (iii) their body image, that is, their evaluations of, and feelings about, the attractiveness of themselves and their body; and (iv) the degree of stereotyping in gender role expectations. With the exception of academic self-image and control, these measures are not, however, highly inter-correlated (see Table 8.1). Therefore, they appear to reflect quite different aspects of adolescents' self-development and to be formed from different influences (see Bryk et al., 1993).

Table 8.1: Correlations among Measures of Social and Personal Development, Junior Cert Pupils (Leaving Cert Pupils in Parentheses)

	Academic Self-Image	Control	Body Image	Gender Role Expectations
Academic Self-Image	1.00 (1.00)	.45 (.46)	.17 (.19)	.02 (.02)
Control		1.00 (1.00)	.16 (.20)	.01 (.02)
Body Image			1.00 (1.00)	.004 (-.03)
Gender Role Expectations				1.00 (1.00)

Note: Detailed descriptions of the variables are presented in Appendix A7.2.

8.2 ACADEMIC SELF-IMAGE

"Self-esteem" can be seen in terms of global self concept, "the individual's positive or negative attitude towards the self as a totality" (Rosenberg et al., 1995: 141), or in terms of specific felt competence in particular roles or tasks, such as academic per-formance. Earlier studies have highlighted the importance of global self-concept in a successful transition from adolescence to adulthood — low self-esteem has been associated with many types of adolescent problems (Rosenberg, Schooler and Schoenbach, 1989; Smelser, 1989; Covington, 1992), while high self-esteem has reduced the incidence of such problems (Owens, 1994: 391). In this research, however, we consider specific (academic) self-image — pupils' belief in and evaluation of their academic competence. This measure is more restricted in that it does not cover, for instance, pupils' sense of moral worth or virtue.

Academic self-image may reflect objective social circumstances, such as social-class background (Rosenberg, 1985; Pearlin, 1989). In addition, the performance expectations and the supportiveness of parents are likely to be particularly important. Academic self-concept is partly reflective of performance evaluations by parents, teachers and schools. These evaluations impact on pupils' sense of self-worth, which in turn fosters further academic success (Owens, 1994: 401). Positive feedback and support from teachers can, however, moderate the relationship between performance and academic self-confidence (Dreeben, 1968; Gamoran and Dreeben, 1985; Bidwell and Friedkin, 1986; Covington, 1992). Given the reciprocal effects between actual performance and academic self-image, this measure is likely to be subject to change with progress through the educational system. In summary, family background, teacher support and school-process factors are expected to have a pronounced effect on academic self-concept. These relationships are tested in Tables 8.2 and 8.3 below.[3]

Among pupils in the sample, a number of background factors are found to impact on academic self-image. Social class has a slight negative effect on self-image among Junior Cert pupils, with middle-class pupils having higher scores (Table 8.2), but the effect is not statistically significant among their Leaving Cert counterparts (Table 8.3).[4] Other measures of socioeconomic status have an impact: pupils whose mothers are more highly educated have higher academic self-images, while those from larger families tend to have lower self-images. Girls have somewhat lower academic self-images than boys at both Junior and Leaving Cert levels, even when ability/prior performance is controlled for, and their self-images are somewhat less variable than those of boys (Table A7.4).

---

[3]   Detailed descriptions of the variables used to measure these developmental outcomes are presented in Table A7.2 while the explanatory variables are described in Table A7.3.

[4]   Tables 8.2 and 8.3 present the final models for each of the personal and social development outcomes. Where the effects of variables change as subsequent variables are added, this is indicated in the text.

Table 8.2: Social Psychological Outcomes among Junior Cert Pupils (N = 3,706)

Fixed Effects	Academic Self-Image + = High	Control + = High	Body Image + = Good	Gender Role Expectations + = Non-traditional	Involvement in Domestic Labour + = High involvement
Intercept	-1.399	-.743	-.617	-1.185	-1.029
Family Background					
Gender	-.249*	-.174*	-.531*	.113*	.348*
Social Class	-.041*	-.005	-.048*	-.024	-.016
Mother's Education	.026	-.011	-.009	.015	.022
Mother's Employment	-.022	.027	-.001	.076*	.108*
No. of Siblings	-.019*	-.011	.009	.016*	.030*
Ability	.015*	.007*	-.005*	.003*	-.002
School Type					
Coed School	-.157*	-.117*	-.181*	.035	-.076
Coed-Gender Interaction	.187*	-.004	.135	-.019	.330*
Educational Expectations					
Own Expectations	.400*	.287*	.222*	-.013	.024
Parents' Expectations	.013	.011	.015	.061*	.005
Parental Pressure	.056*	.042*	.021	-.006	-.005
Lack of Parental Support	-.072*	-.127*	-.053	.166*	-.181*
Teachers' Expectations	.107*	-.053	-.011	-.037	-.010
Mother's Gender Role Expectations	.021	.010	.012	.481*	.011
Hours of Study	-.009	-.024	-.009	.047*	.069*
Part-time Employment	.020	-.005	.029	.016	.028
Domestic Labour	-.021	.003	-.036*	-.006	—
School Interaction					
Bullying	-.025	-.403*	-.375*	-.039	.291*
Positive Teacher Interaction	.527*	.219*	.154*	.014	.131*
Negative Teacher Interaction	-.127*	-.189*	.004	.056	-.083*
School Process/Context					
Homework Rules	-.074	.035	.075	.087*	.010
Class Position:					
Top Class	-.139*	-.034	-.022	-.035	.028
Middle Class	.012	.058	-.047	-.051	-.016
Bottom Class	.081	-.091	-.033	-.046	.040
Average Social Class	.172*	.068	-.082*	.040	-.006
Mediating Variables					
Pastoral-Care Provision	.011	.017	-.009	-.009	-.006
Recreation	.021*	.032*	.016	.016	.043*
Social Life	-.013	.023*	.106*	.001	.033*
Social Skills Development	.014*	.067*	.038*	.002	.031*
Random Effects					
Variance at School Level	0.020*	0.014*	0.008*	0.005	0.013*
Variance at Pupil Level	0.615*	0.796*	0.826*	0.761*	0.828*
% Variance Explained:					
School Level	49.6	51.6	84.0	65.3	69.3
Pupil Level	35.9	18.0	13.0	22.8	13.5

Note: Explanatory variables are described in Appendix Table A7.3; outcomes are standardised to have a mean of zero and a standard deviation of one.
* Approximates to statistical significance at the <.05 level.

Table 8.3: Social Psychological Outcomes among Leaving Cert Pupils (N = 3,852)

	Academic Self-Image	Control	Body Image	Gender Role Expectations	Involvement in Domestic Labour
Fixed Effects					
Intercept	-2.142	-1.316	-.925	-1.120	-.546
Family Background					
Gender	-.288*	-.184*	-.533*	.091	.596*
Social Class	-.022	-.001	-.010	.009	-.014
Mother's Education	.028*	-.006	.033*	-.017	-.001
Mother's Employment	-.015	.008	.028	.001	.098*
No. of Siblings	-.028*	-.017*	.003	-.002	.009
Junior Cert GPA	.108*	.012	-.020	.024*	-.027*
Inter Cert	.169*	.077	-.035	-.005	.022
School Type					
Coed School	-.013	-.108	-.265*	.210*	.120
Coed Gender Interaction	.083	-.010	.284*	-.155*	.008
Educational Expectations					
Own Expectations	.387*	.304*	.180*	.002	-.012
Educational Aspirations	.101*	.102*	.022	.072*	.005
Parents' Expectations	.134*	.050	.033	.045	.018
Parental Pressure	.015	.041	-.029	.015	-.070*
Lack of Parental Support	.049	-.049	-.057	.138*	-.161*
Teachers' Expectations	.155*	-.027	-.028	-.045	-.078*
Mother's Gender Role Expectations	-.001	.023	-.025	.460*	-.013
Hours of Study	-.007	-.017	.012	.019	.053*
Part-time Employment	-.009	.043	.010	-.006	-.007
Domestic Labour	-.032*	-.020	-.059*	.002	—
School Interaction					
Bullying	-.070	-.405*	-.331*	.003	.124*
Positive Teacher Interaction	.433*	.234*	.178*	.018	.126*
Negative Teacher Interaction	-.097*	-.209*	.060	.068*	-.025
School Process / Context					
Homework Rules	.072	.060	.034	-.005	-.016
Class Position:					
Top Class	-.041	.060	-.052	-.032	-.032
Middle Class	.014	.046	-.028	.068	-.171
Bottom Class	-.002	.075	-.140*	-.031	-.054
Average Social Class	.079*	.024	-.045	.008	-.013
Mediating Variables					
Pastoral-Care Provision	.009	.001	-.007	.004	-.014
Recreation	.006	.024*	-.009	.012	.065*
Social Life	.013	.033*	.153*	-.009	.050*
Social-Skills Development	.009	.060*	.054*	-.012	.006
Random Effects					
Variance at School Level	0.010*	0.015*	0.007	0.011*	0.025*
Variance at Pupil Level	0.627*	0.798*	0.824*	0.806*	0.843*
% Variance Explained:					
School Level	68.4	45.6	85.1	45.7	64.8
Pupil Level	35.1	17.9	13.5	17.9	9.1

* Approximates to statistical significance at the <.05 level.

As hypothesised, pupils with higher verbal/numerical ability or who have performed better in their junior-cycle exam tend to have higher academic self-images. This indicates that prior performance tends to boost self-confidence which is likely to have a positive impact on subsequent academic performance.

Also as hypothesised, academic self-image is influenced by parents' and teachers' expectations. Those who expect to do well or very well in the forthcoming exam have a higher self-image, as do Leaving Cert pupils who hope to go to third-level education. Among Junior Cert pupils, parental educational pressures — that is, high parental expectations coupled with high study hours and participation in grinds/outside tuition — tends to increase academic self-image slightly, while lack of parental support has the opposite effect. Among Leaving Cert pupils, parental expectations concerning exam performance have a stronger effect. There is some indication that parental expectations relating to involvement in domestic labour have a negative impact on academic self-image; the effect is slight but is statistically significant for Leaving Cert girls (Table A7.8).

At both Junior and Leaving Cert levels, pupils have higher self-images where teachers expect them to do well or very well in their exams. Positive interaction with teachers has an even stronger impact than teacher expectations, boosting academic self-image by half a standard deviation for each one point increase in the positive interaction scale. As expected, negative teacher interaction has a negative impact, although the effect is relatively small in magnitude. Thus, the more open and positive interaction is with teachers, the higher the self-confidence, while the higher the level of negative sanctioning, the lower the level of self-confidence. Interestingly, the quality of interaction with peers, as measured by the bullying scale, has no appreciable impact on academic self-image.

School-process variables have relatively little effect on academic self-image. Being in a top class within a streamed/banded school appears to lower academic self-image among Junior Cert pupils (Table 8.2). This may relate to the reference group used by pupils: the more academically competitive the nature of classroom interaction is, the higher the standards used to judge one's own performance — hence, even average to above-average ability pupils in "top" classes may feel academically inadequate. This effect does not hold for Leaving Cert pupils, most likely because of the lower levels of rigidity in streaming and banding practices within the senior cycle (see Chapter 5). In addition, lower average social class within a school appears to boost academic self-image. This may also be the result of reference group effects, where pupils in high socioeconomic status schools are subject to a greater competitive ethos.

The mediating variables have little effect on academic self-image. A high involvement in sports/recreational activities and a positive evaluation of the school's impact on personal development tend to boost academic self-image among Junior Cert pupils. However, the effects are extremely small in magnitude and do not hold for Leaving Cert pupils.

The impact of type of school is present but slight. Table 8.4 shows the predicted differences in academic self-image between pupils in coed and in single-sex schools, using boys in single-sex schools as a reference group. Among both Junior and Leaving Cert pupils, boys in single-sex schools have the highest, and girls in single-sex schools the lowest, academic self-images. There is some evidence that academic self-image is slightly lower among Junior Cert pupils in coed schools than among their counterparts in single-sex schools (see also Table 8.2). However, this effect holds only for boys, is relatively small in magnitude (one-fifth of a standard deviation) and does not occur among Leaving Cert pupils.

Table 8.4: Predicted Academic Self-Image by Gender and School Type

	Junior Cert		Leaving Cert	
Type of School	**Boys**	**Girls**	**Boys**	**Girls**
Single-Sex Secondary	0	-.3	0	-.3
Coed, of which:	-.2	-.2	-.01	-.2
Secondary	-.2	-.3	-.05	-.2
Vocational	-.1	-.2	+.02	-.1
Community/Comprehensive	-.03	-.4	-.02	-.3

Source: Coefficients are calculated from Tables 8.4, 8.5, A7.5 and A7.9 using boys in single-sex schools as a reference group.

There is some variation by type of coed school: academic self-image appears to be slightly higher among girls in vocational schools than among their counterparts in secondary schools, while self-image appears to be lowest for Junior Cert girls in community/comprehensive schools. The negative effect of being in a coed school is greatest among Junior Cert boys in coed secondary schools. However, none of these differences is statistically significant.

Other aspects of school type, such as previous attendance at a coed primary school, have no significant impact on academic self-image.

In summary, academic self-image tends to be most closely related to the nature of the parental and teacher feedback given to pupils and to the set of expectations with which they are confronted. Even controlling for these factors, however, girls tend to have lower academic self-images than their male counterparts. Coeducation has a slight negative impact on academic self-image among Junior Cert boys, but no appreciable impact on girls.

8.3 LOCUS OF CONTROL

Locus of control refers to the extent of pupils' perceived sense of control over their lives and ability to cope with problems. The factors shaping sense of control appear to differ from those shaping academic self-image. In overall terms, control is less predictable in terms of background and schooling factors — the final model accounts for 18 per cent of the variance among pupils, compared with 35 per cent of the variance in the case of academic self-image (Tables 8.2 and 8.3). Locus of control does not appear to be influenced by objective background factors, such as social class, parental education or family size. Girls are found to have somewhat lower senses of control than boys, although the difference is comparatively small (around one-sixth of a standard deviation). Among Junior Cert pupils, higher ability levels tend to increase feelings of control (Table 8.2). However, junior-cycle exam performance has no appreciable effect on control among Leaving Cert pupils (Table 8.3).

Pupils who expect to do well in their exams exhibit higher levels of control, as do those who plan to go on to third-level education. Parental pressure appears to increase sense of control slightly, while lack of parental support has the opposite effect, at least for Junior Cert pupils.

The quality of interaction with teachers also has an impact, with positive interaction increasing sense of control, while negative interaction has the opposite effect. Bullying has a significant negative effect on control levels. The effect here is likely to be reciprocal, with negative peer interaction reducing control and more passive pupils more likely to experience bullying. School process and organisation factors have no appreciable impact on pupils' sense of control.

The effects of background and schooling factors on sense of control are mediated through personal resources or coping strategies. At both the Junior and Leaving Cert level, pupils' favourable evaluations of the school's impact on personal/social development are associated with higher levels of control. Activities outside schools, such as sports/recreation and dating, also have a positive impact.

Being in a coeducational school has no significant impact on locus of control when background and schooling factors are controlled. However, the pattern changes when the mediating variables are entered into the model: the effect of coeducation becomes negative, significantly so for Junior Cert pupils. Coed pupils tend to report higher levels of recreation, social life and social skills development than their counterparts in single-sex schools. When these mediating variables are included in the model, however, these higher levels do not appear to "translate" into comparably high levels of control.

In summary, while control is not easily explicable in terms of objective background factors, the quality of interaction with parents, peers and teachers appears to have a significant impact on the development of feelings of control over one's own life. Being in a coed school does not have a consistent negative impact on locus of control.

8.4 BODY-IMAGE

Pupils were asked to evaluate their personal appearance in terms of being good-looking, attractive, graceful and fat/thin. The perception and evaluation of one's own physical attractiveness appears to be less subject to schooling influences and experiences than other measures of social and personal development. There is a whole series of personal and interpersonal factors affecting body-image, which are outside the remit of this study. However, the study does allow us to explore the interaction of gender and schooling in shaping the body-image of girls and boys.

The impact of social-background factors on body image is somewhat unclear. Among Junior Cert pupils, higher social class has a slight positive effect on body-image — a difference of a quarter of a standard deviation between pupils from an unskilled manual background and those from a higher professional background (Table 8.2). At the Leaving Cert level, mother's education appears to have a positive effect on body-image, though again the effect is very slight (Table 8.3). The relationship with ability and performance is quite complex. At the Junior Cert level, pupils with higher verbal/numerical ability tend to have lower body-images, a pattern that holds for both girls and boys. Among Leaving Cert pupils, girls (but not boys) who had a higher grade point average in their junior-cycle exam also have a lower body-image (Table A7.8). This may be related to being stereotyped as "swots" by their peers.

Girls have consistently lower body-images than boys, at both Junior and Leaving Cert levels.[5] This pattern holds even when background and schooling factors are controlled. This gendered pattern can be seen in terms of different sets of cultural expectations for girls and boys in relation to appearance, weight, and so on (Orbach, 1986; MacSween, 1993).

Parental expectations have little appreciable effect on body-image. Pupils who expect to do well in their exams have more positive body-images — this effect is likely to reflect an underlying sense of global self-esteem rather than being causal in nature. Among Leaving Cert pupils, those with a high level of involvement in domestic labour tend to have lower body-images.

Positive interaction with teachers is associated with higher body-image. However, the impact of negative teacher interaction is less clear-cut: it has no appreciable effect on girls' body-image but actually has a positive impact on the body-image of boys (Tables A7.6 and A7.9). This pattern is difficult to explain but may be related to the development of a counter-school culture within which positive body-images are associated with a "macho" identity (Willis, 1977; Mac an Ghaill, 1994). Bullying has a strong negative effect on body-image. This is likely to reflect the type of bullying involved, especially students being jeered/mocked or upset by things said about them/their appearance (see Lees, 1993).

---

[5] While girls' body images are consistently more negative than boys', they are significantly more variable (Table A7.4).

As might be expected, school-process variables have little effect on body-image. However, Leaving Cert pupils in a bottom/ remedial class appear to have lower body-images than those in mixed-ability or higher classes — this may relate to a greater emphasis on appearance, especially among lower-ability/stream girls (see Wolpe, 1988; McRobbie, 1991; Riddell, 1992).

Formal pastoral-care provision in schools has no effect on body image. In contrast, pupils who feel that school has benefited their social/personal development tend to have higher body-images. Those with a more active social life have more positive body-images — thus, having a boy/girlfriend appears to act as a positive reinforcement to pupils' evaluations of their appearance.

Table 8.5: Body Image by Gender and School Type

Type of School	Junior Cert		Leaving Cert	
	Boys	Girls	Boys	Girls
Single-Sex Secondary	0	-.5	0	-.5
Coed, of which:	-.2	-.6	-.3	-.5
Secondary	-.2	-.6	-.4	-.6
Vocational	-.1	-.6	-.1	-.4
Community/Comprehensive	-.2	-.5	-.3	-.5

Source: Coefficients are calculated from Tables 8.2, 8.3, A7.7 and A7.10 using boys in single-sex schools as a reference group.

Coeducation has a significant and negative impact on body-image for boys but not for girls. This effect is somewhat surprising given international case-study evidence that coeducation leads to a greater emphasis on physical appearance, particularly for girls (Lees, 1993). It may be that the effects on girls' body-image are more diffuse, coming from a wide range of cultural arenas (for example, the media, popular culture and so on), while the negative effects for boys only occur in the context of day-to-day interaction with girls in schools. Thus, the closer interaction with pupils of the opposite sex characteristic of coed schools appears to make boys more aware of, and self-conscious about, their appearance. The impact on boys appears to be a "pure" coed effect, since it occurs across all types of coed school (Table 8.5, A7.11 and A7.12). The negative effects of coeducation are weakest in vocational schools, a pattern which may be related to the lower proportion of female pupils.

In summary, while only a small proportion (13 per cent) of the variance in body-image can be explained by background and schooling factors, both gender and coeducation are found to have highly significant effects on body-image. Girls have significantly lower body-images, a pattern which appears to be as much related to general cultural messages/evaluations regarding female appearance as to specific contexts or situations. In addition, being in a coed school has an appreciable negative effect on how boys evaluate their personal appearance and attractiveness.

8.5 GENDER ROLE EXPECTATIONS

Respondents were asked to choose from five alternative arrangements of employment and child-care roles as the one they would be most likely to adopt in the future. For girls, the alternatives range from (1) "You would give up your job to mind your children on a full-time basis" to (5) "You would work full-time; your spouse would mind the children full-time". The scoring is reversed for males. Thus, the scale ranges from a score of 1 "most traditional" to 5 "most non-traditional". Boys at both Junior and Leaving Cert levels are more likely than girls to select the most traditional option. At the other extreme, boys were more likely than girls to consider "non-traditional" arrangements as more likely in the future. It is important to stress that these represent the options that respondents consider "most likely" rather than their preference. While there are clear gender differences in gender role expectations, it is important to control for other variables which might affect these expectations.

Table 8.6: Gender Role Expectations by Gender and Stage

Scale	Junior Cert Sample		Leaving Cert Sample	
	Male	Female	Male	Female
	%	%	%	%
1 ("Traditional")	16.8	9.1	12.6	5.2
2	39.9	50.9	42.5	53.3
3 ("Dual Career")	39.6	33.5	36.0	37.1
4	10.6	5.5	6.9	3.8
5 ("Non-traditional")	3.1	1.0	2.0	0.6
N	2,811	2,956	2,198	2,475

Controlling for other background factors, Junior Cert girls have less traditional expectations than their male counterparts (Table 8.2). However, at the Leaving Cert level there is no appreciable gender difference when other factors are controlled for (Table 8.3). There are no significant social-class differences in gender role expectations. However, mothers with higher levels of education and those in paid employment tend to have less traditional expectations of their children — these less traditional expectations influence their children's expectations, in turn. In addition, mother's employment has a direct effect on the gender role expectations of Junior Cert pupils — this effect operates over and above the effects of mothers' expectations and appears to reflect the impact of having a "non-traditional" role model. Pupils (both girls and boys) with higher numerical/verbal ability tend to have less traditional expectations, as do girls who do well in the junior-cycle exam.

Mothers' gender role expectations (as perceived by the pupil) have a strong impact on pupils' own expectations at both the Junior and the Leaving Cert level. Among Junior Cert pupils, parents' educational expectations have a positive impact, as do higher levels of educational aspirations at the Leaving Cert level. Girls with a stronger commitment to the study role (with longer hours of study) tend to have less traditional expectations. Surprisingly, lack of parental support in relation to education/career decisions is associated with less traditional expectations among pupils. This pattern is difficult to interpret but may be related to a greater independence among those who do not rely on parental advice or support. Among Junior Cert girls, greater current involvement in domestic labour is associated with more traditional expectations, perhaps because this influences what girls see as "likely" in the future (Table A7.5). Conversely, among Junior Cert boys greater involvement in domestic labour is associated with non-traditional expectations (Table A7.6).

School interaction and process have little impact on gender role expectations. However, among Junior Cert girls, homework rules appear to be associated with less traditional expectations. This is likely to reflect an underlying dimension of school ethos, rather than being a direct effect. None of the mediating variables affect gender role expectations.

Among Junior Cert pupils, there are no differences in gender role expectations between those in coed and those in single-sex schools. However, by the Leaving Cert stage, being in a coed school tends to be associated with less traditional expectations on the part of boys (but not girls). This pattern applies across all types of coed school but is statistically significant only for boys in coed secondary and vocational schools (Table A7.12).

In summary, the strongest influence on gender role expectations captured by the survey appears to be notions of appropriate gender roles learned from parents. To a large extent, mother's gender role expectations mediate the effects of more "objective" background factors. Being in a coeducational school does not appear to heighten gender stereotyping for girls, while for boys there is tentative support for the hypothesis that coeducation reduces stereotyping in gender role expectations, at least among Leaving Cert pupils.

8.6   INVOLVEMENT IN DOMESTIC LABOUR

The previous section examined the extent to which pupils' expectations of their future roles are gender stereotyped. This section presents additional information on pupils' current involvement in household labour, in order to investigate the extent to which work roles in the pupils' own family situation are stereotyped.

A Likert scale was constructed from responses on the extent of involvement in household labour over the previous two weeks. Table 8.7 indicates that there are substantial gender differences in the level of involvement in domestic labour. Boys are much less likely to help with household labour, and the nature of their involvement is quite gendered, focusing on "outside" work. This pattern appears to indicate that the gendered division of labour among adolescents mirrors that of the adult population (see Berk, 1985; Delphy and Leonard, 1992). Interestingly, the extent of involvement in housework does not appear to be reduced among Leaving Cert pupils to take account of additional study pressures.

As one would expect from Table 8.7, girls are significantly more involved in domestic labour than their male counterparts, controlling for all other background factors (Tables 8.2 and 8.3). Mother's employment tends to increase housework load for both girls and boys, thus involving some reallocation of tasks within the household. In addition, having more siblings increases the workload for Junior Cert girls[6]. Interestingly, social class has no impact, with the allocation of household labour relatively evenly spread across the social spectrum. For Junior Cert boys, mother's education tends to have a positive impact on domestic involvement, perhaps indirectly through attitudinal differences (Table A7.6).

Table 8.7: Percentage of Respondents with High Levels of Domestic Labour Involvement

Did the following 6 or more times in preceding 2 weeks	Junior Cert Sample		Leaving Cert Sample	
	Male	**Female**	**Male**	**Female**
	%	%	%	%
Made Own Bed	35.5	55.4	39.6	57.4
Swept up/Vacuumed	11.2	21.1	9.2	19.3
Set Table for Meals	16.0	31.6	16.5	32.8
Cleaned up After Meals	19.3	38.7	21.0	39.9
Prepared Meals	6.5	11.9	9.1	15.5
Did Ironing	2.7	6.5	3.1	6.9
Cleaned up Rubbish/Yard	20.2	4.1	19.1	4.0
N	2,917	2,995	2,267	2,512

Pupils who did well in their Junior/Inter Cert tend to have less involvement in household labour, a pattern which indicates some adjustment of household labour to study commitments. This is further supported by the finding that pupils whose parents and teachers have higher expectations for them, and those who spend more hours studying, do less housework. Contrary to expectations, lack of parental support tends to decrease housework involvement — perhaps parental disinterest in a pupil's education reflects the quality of the relationship, with these adolescents spending less time with their parents and being less involved in the household.

---

[6]   This may, in effect, underestimate the impact of number of siblings on workload since respondents were not questioned about babysitting/ looking after younger siblings. It is possible that if such a measure were included, gender differentiation would appear even more marked.

Bullying tends to be associated with higher levels of involvement in domestic labour, especially among Junior Cert pupils. It may be that boys who have greater interaction or involvement with their parents are labelled as "sissies" by their peers. However, the pattern also applies to girls, so it may, in fact, reflect a withdrawal into the home because of poor relations with peers. Unexpectedly, positive teacher interaction is associated with higher levels of housework involvement. This may indicate an underlying (over)conformity and reliance on the expectations/ support of authority figures on the part of pupils: "good" pupils get on with teachers and are conscientious at home. As might be expected, school process and organisation have little appreciable impact on involvement in domestic labour.

Both recreation and social life mediate the impact of other factors on housework workload. It appears that pupils who have an active life outside school (through sports, discos, dating, and so on) are also more involved in their own household.

Being in a coeducational school tends to be associated with increased involvement in domestic labour among girls. At Junior Cert level, there are higher levels of involvement in domestic labour among girls in all types of coed school (Table A7.11). The pattern among Leaving Cert pupils is less clear-cut. Being in a coed secondary school is associated with higher work loads for both girls and boys (Table A7.12), but there is no significant relationship with coeducation overall (Table 8.3).

In summary, girls are considerably more involved in household labour than their male counterparts. There appears to be some adjustment between study and household roles, with higher study commitment and parental expectations resulting in a lighter housework load. Coeducation tends to be associated with increased domestic labour for Junior Cert girls, although patterns at the Leaving Cert level do not appear to indicate a clear-cut polarisation of such gender roles among coed pupils.

8.7 CONCLUSIONS

This chapter has examined a range of social- and personal-development outcomes among Junior and Leaving Cert pupils. There appears to be a clear pattern of gender differentiation along a number of these dimensions: girls tend to have lower academic self-images, more negative body-images and slightly less sense of control, while they are more likely to be currently involved in domestic labour.

Table 8.8 summarises the effects of attendance at coeducational schools on personal and social-development outcomes. "Total effects" refer to the impact of coeducation controlling for social background and academic ability alone. It allows us to estimate the impact of coeducation on pupils of similar backgrounds and ability. Coeducational and single-sex schools may also differ in terms of pupil, parental and teacher expectations, pupil–teacher interaction, peer relations and school process. These differences are controlled for in assessing the impact of coeducation on pupils' personal and social development (see Tables 8.2 and 8.3). "Direct effects" refer to the impact of coed when all of these factors are taken into account.

Table 8.8: The Effects of Coeducation on Social- and Personal-Development Outcomes, Controlling for Other Relevant Variables

	Academic Self-Image	Control	Body Image	Gender Role Expectations	Domestic Labour
Junior Cert					
Girls: Total Effects	.113	-.035	-.039	.046	.336*
Direct Effects	.036	-.101	-.055	047	.215*
Boys: Total Effects	-.139	-.039	-.205*	.057	-.034
Direct Effects	-.141*	-.129	-.142	.008	-.029
Leaving Cert					
Girls: Total Effects	.158*	-.006	.084	.021	.171*
Direct Effects	.042	-.126*	-.014	.054	.152*
Boys: Total Effects	.072	.030	-.173*	.152*	.145*
Direct Effects	.015	-.079	-.246*	.184*	.114

* Approximates to statistical significance at the <.05 level.
Source: Tables A7.5, A7.6, A7.8 and A7.9.

Coeducation has some effects in relation to a number of the specified outcomes. Firstly, academic self-image tends to be somewhat lower among boys in coed schools than among their counterparts in single-sex school. This finding differs from international studies which indicate that the effects of coeducation on self-image are negative for girls and broadly neutral for boys (see, for example, Bryk et al., 1993). This pattern may occur because boys in coed schools are using girls as a reference group and, given girls' higher performance in exams (see Chapter 6), are likely to depress their evaluations of their own academic abilities.

Secondly, evaluations of personal appearance/attractiveness tend to be lower among boys in coed schools than among their counterparts in single-sex schools. This appears to be a "pure" coed effect — that is, being in a school with girls causes boys to become more self-conscious of, and critical about, their personal appearance.

The pattern for current domestic labour and gender role expectations is difficult to explain. While girls in coed schools tend to have higher domestic workloads, there is some indication that Leaving Cert boys in coed schools have less traditional attitudes (both in terms of practice and ideology) that their counterparts in single-sex schools.

In terms of the restricted range of personal and social-development outcomes considered in the study, coeducation appears to have surprisingly few clear effects. Any effect present tends to apply to boys more than to girls, with some negative effects apparent on boys' body-image and academic self-image (at Junior Cert level), and some positive effects on gender role attitudes (at Leaving Cert level). Thus, the closer interaction with girls in coed schools appears to be associated with more critical self judgments among boys. In contrast, disadvantages to girls, in terms of lower academic self-image, lower sense of control and more negative body-image, tend to occur across all types of school.

9

Pupil Stress Levels

Chapter 8 examined the impact of coeducation and other schooling factors on a range of social-development outcomes. Current stress levels cannot be regarded as a relatively enduring outcome in the same sense, being subject to greater fluctuations over the course of second-level schooling. However, pupils' current stress/distress levels are indicative of their experiences of the educational system during the crucial exam years. Much media attention has been given to the "points race" and its impact on second-level pupils. However, little attention has been given to the processes shaping educational achievement pressures and pupils' and schools' responses to these stresses. This chapter examines the levels of stress among Junior and Leaving Cert pupils, and the effects of personal, familial and schooling factors on these stress levels.

9.1   STRESS LEVELS AMONG PUPILS

The scale used to measure stress amongst pupils in both the Junior and Leaving Cert samples is an adaptation of the General Health Questionnaire (GHQ) 28-item "stress" scale (Goldberg, 1972, 1978). The full scale has been widely used internationally to measure non-psychotic, or minor psychiatric, stressful symptoms or disorders in the general population (see Winefield et al., 1989; 1993). The shorter 12-item measure has been widely used in previous Irish studies, particularly on the effects of unemployment. It has been shown to have high reliability and validity as a measure of current psycho-social stress and to be moderately predictive of clinically significant psychological illness (Whelan et al., 1991; Hannan, Ó Riain, 1993). Because of severe limitations on space in the administered questionnaire, we could include only six items of the 12-question GHQ "stress" measure. While this reduced scale is less useful as a predictor of psychiatric problems, it represents a reliable (alpha = .72) measure of current stress/distress levels[1]

Table 9.1: Percentage of Junior and Leaving Cert Respondents Reporting Stress

GHQ "Stress" Items	Percentage of Respondents who Give Negative ("Stressed") Responses					
	Junior Cert Sample		Leaving Cert Sample		School Leavers 1992*	
	Male	Female	Male	Female	Male	Female
	%	%	%	%	%	%
1."Able to concentrate on what you are doing" (% Less/Much Less than Usual)	19.1	29.4	27.1	40.9	1.9	4.0
2. "Playing a useful part in things" (% Less/Much Less than Usual)	13.0	18.0	12.9	19.9	5.3	3.9
3. "Capable of making decisions about things" (% Less/Much Less than Usual)	6.0	10.5	7.1	14.6	3.3	3.5
4. "Lost much sleep over worry" (% More/Much More than Usual)	19.2	35.4	21.3	40.5	7.7	8.5
5. "Felt constantly under strain" (% More/Much More than Usual)	28.8	47.1	37.1	57.7	11.9	13.5
6. "Losing confidence in yourself" (% More/Much More than Usual)	17.3	29.4	20.5	35.8	6.5	8.1
N	2,870	2,975	2,260	2,510	606	615

* These results are from a follow-up survey of 1986 school-leavers; this group was interviewed at approximately 22–24 years of age. For items 1 and 2, a slightly different response category was used, so results are not fully comparable.

---

[1]   Junior and Leaving Cert pupils were mostly interviewed in February/ March; it is possible that measured stress levels would be higher closer to the exams.

experienced by pupils within schools (see Appendix A8.1). It must be noted that the scale represents a measure of current, rather than chronic, stress. Pupils were asked to compare their feelings of strain, for example, to their "usual' situation — hence, if young people are in a more or less constantly pressurised situation, this will not necessarily be revealed by indicators of current stress.

Three main patterns of stress are apparent among the sample of pupils. Firstly, levels of stress are much higher among Junior and Leaving Cert students than among young adults or older people (see Hannan, Ó Riain, 1993; Whelan et al., 1991). Secondly, the stress levels among girls at both Junior and Leaving Cert level are significantly and consistently higher than among boys. This difference does not hold for young adults (Hannan, Ó Riain, 1993), although older women report higher levels of stress than men (Whelan et al., 1991). These gender differences tend to be greater on the most pressing items, such as difficulty in sleeping and feeling constantly under strain. Thirdly, students at Leaving Cert level are significantly more stressed than those at Junior Cert level. This increase holds roughly equally for both girls and boys, and, in both cases, inability to concentrate, feeling of strain, loss of sleep, and loss of confidence show the greatest increases. Evidently, exam years are extremely stressful for students, particularly for those doing the Leaving Cert. However, these raised stress levels do not appear to persist into young adult life where successful transitions to the labour market and early adulthood substantially reduce stress levels (Hannan, Ó Riain, 1993).

Given the contrast with adults and recent school-leavers, it appears likely that these higher stress levels are caused mainly by achievement pressures at school. In the following analyses, therefore, we focus mainly on the likely stressful events or processes associated with educational achievement pressures. While a more comprehensive analysis of individual stress levels would require more detailed information on pupils' life histories, our measures of education-related stressors are quite extensive and the analyses very revealing.

9.2 FACTORS AFFECTING STRESS LEVELS

Pearlin's (1981; 1989) model appears the most useful in examining the causes and dimensions of stress: its *sources*, *mediators* and *outcomes*. The outcome of interest in the following analyses is the

pupil's score on the modified GHQ stress measure. Likely sources
of stress are examined under the following headings: (i) personal/
familial factors; (ii) interaction among peers, particularly among
pupils within the same school; (iii) the nature of pupil–teacher
interaction; and (iv), schooling process and school composition factors (a detailed specification of variables is presented in Appendix
Table A8.2).

(i) Personal/Familial Sources of Stress

The most likely chronic stressors in a pupil's background appear
to be high levels of economic strain within the family — for
example, through unemployment and/or large families. Measures
of more acute stressful life events, such as bereavement or illness,
are unfortunately not available. In addition to economic factors,
parents' expectations of the pupil are potential sources of stress,
especially where these expectations exceed pupil ability — these
subjective factors are likely to be more important than "objective"
ones, such as socioeconomic status. Furthermore, pupils may
experience role strain through combining high study hours with
part-time employment and/or a high degree of involvement in
domestic labour within the home.

(ii) Peer Interaction

Pupils' experience of bullying/aggression from other pupils is particularly likely to increase stress levels. In addition, the student's
ability to compete successfully in classroom interaction with other
classmates is likely to be important.

(iii) Pupil–Teacher Interaction

The nature and quality of interaction with teachers, the extent of
negative or positive feedback in class, or the degree of support for
pupil participation in class discussion, are likely to impact significantly on student stress levels. These effects may operate at a contextual level as well, with some schools characterised by higher
levels of positive pupil–teacher interaction.

(iv) School Process and Composition

In addition to pupil–teacher interaction within the school, the way
in which the school is organised is likely to have a significant

impact. For example, a pupil's allocation to a highly competitive streamed class may act as a source of stress. Similarly, the disciplinary policy of the school may be an important factor.

In Pearlin's model, the effects of these stressors can be moderated or neutralised by factors which provide resources or ways of coping with stress (see also Banks et al., 1984, 1988; Whelan et al., 1991). At the school level, the quality of pastoral care provision is likely to mediate significantly or help to buffer the effects of stressors. Similarly, the involvement of the school in organising sports and other recreational activities may serve to reduce stress levels. At the individual level, personal resources, such as a strong sense of control over one's own life, may mediate the effects of potential stressors. While some researchers (Ross and Mirowsky, 1989, for example) view "locus of control" as an enduring personality trait mainly determined by early childhood socialisation, control appears to be highly responsive to social context (see Kohn and Schooler, 1982) and is treated here as a mediating factor.

The remainder of this chapter tests this model, and related hypotheses, using multi-level modelling techniques in relation to Junior and Leaving Cert pupils.

9.3 PERSONAL AND FAMILIAL FACTORS

Tables 9.2 and 9.3 present the findings for Junior Cert and Leaving Cert pupils respectively. While levels of stress are higher among Leaving Cert pupils, the factors shaping pupils' stress levels are remarkably similar for both groups. It is apparent that the potential contribution of school-level factors to stress levels is relatively minor: only 4–5 per cent of the variation in overall stress levels is attributable to the school level, while 95–96 per cent of the variation occurs between pupils within schools.

Contrary to our hypotheses (see section 9.2), objective background factors, such as social class, do not impact on stress levels. Other measures of social background, such as parental unemployment and family size, did not appear to have any impact on pupil stress levels and were not included in the final model. The findings in relation to unemployment are surprising given the strong impact of unemployment on the stress levels of both unemployed persons and their spouses (Whelan et al., 1991; Hannan,

Ó Riain, 1993). However, family circumstances may have a longer-term effect, impacting on chronic rather than current stress levels.[2]

Among both Junior and Leaving Cert pupils, girls experience substantially higher levels of stress than boys,[3] a difference of approximately half a standard deviation. This gender effect persists even when other sources of stress are controlled for. Thus, girls' higher stress levels cannot be explained by their experiencing higher levels of other potential stressors but by a differing relationship between stressors and stress levels for girls. In particular, parental expectations appear to have a much stronger effect on girls' experience of stress than on their male counterparts, an effect which is apparent for both Junior and Leaving Cert pupils (see Appendix Tables A8.4–A8.7).

Qualitative studies have highlighted the differences between boys and girls in the process of identity development during adolescence. Teenage girls are confronted by conflicting sets of expectations: they are expected to develop the "masculine" characteristics of autonomy and high educational/career aspirations, while at the same time they are expected to maintain "feminine'" personality traits, such as being gentle, unassertive and caring for others (Anyon, 1983; Hudson, 1984; Lees, 1993). While such studies have not explicitly focused on the impact of these conflicting expectations on stress levels among girls,[4] they appear to provide a possible explanation for the gender differences found among pupils in our sample.

Those with higher verbal/numerical ability (among Junior Cert pupils) and those with higher junior-cycle exam performance (among Leaving Cert pupils) tend to exhibit higher stress levels. It is likely that stress is not related to academic ability/performance per se, but rather to the associated expectations and pressures impinging on higher-ability pupils.

---

[2]   For example, young people from unemployed families may not be experiencing more felt strain "than usual", although the levels of strain they experience may be higher than the rest of the population.

[3]   Stress levels among girls are significantly more variable than among their male counterparts (see Table A8.3).

[4]   However, it has been argued that the development of anorexia nervosa can be seen in the context of these contradictory cultural expectations for adolescent girls (MacSween, 1993).

Table 9.2: Multi-level Models of Stress for Junior Cert Pupils (N = 3,706)

Fixed Effects	Model 1	Model 2	Model 3	Model 4	Model 5	Model 6
Intercept	-.014	-.279	-.178	-.032	-.574	-.376
Background Variables:						
Gender (Girls = 1)		.526*	.435*	.367*	.532*	.435*
Social Class		-.003	-.002	.001	.009	.005
Ability		.002*	.002*	.002	.003*	.003*
School Type:						
Coed School			-.171*	-.176*	-.138*	-.112*
Coed-Gender Interaction			.134	.158*	.061	.081
Parental Expectations:						
Own Expectations				-.356*	-.262*	-.183*
Parental Expectations				.157*	.132*	.134*
Parental Pressure				.026	.035*	.049*
Lack of Parental Support				.090*	.076*	.007
Hours of Study				.038*	.051*	.050*
Involvement in Domestic Labour				.011	-.006	.009
Part-time Job				.027	.015	.034
School Process/Interaction:						
Homework Rules					-.095*	-.091*
Positive Teacher Interaction					-.119*	-.015
Negative Teacher Interaction					.224*	.209*
Average Positive Interaction in School					-.215	-.253*
Average Negative Interaction in School					.068	.110
Bullying					.705*	.499*
Restricted Subject Choice					.103*	.114*
Mediating Variables:						
Pastoral-Care Provision						.007
Recreation						-.032*
Social Life						.004
Social-Skills Development						-.046*
Control						-.227*
Academic Self-Image						.049*
Body-Image						-.107*
Random Effects:						
Variance at School Level	0.047*	0.142*	0.011*	0.009	0.004	0.002
Variance at Pupil Level	0.954*	0.920*	0.919*	0.882*	0.791*	0.719*
% Variance Explained:						
School Level	—	69.5	76.2	79.8	91.8	95.0
Pupil Level	—	3.6	3.5	7.5	17.0	24.6
Proportion of Remaining Variance at:						
School Level	4.7	1.5	1.2	1.1	0.5	0.3
Pupil Level	95.3	98.5	98.8	98.9	99.5	99.7
Deviance	10442.9	10250.6	10241.2	10086.5	9664.9	9307.7
Reduction in Deviance	—	<.001	<.01	<.001	<.001	<.001

* Indicates significance at the <.05 level.

Table 9.3: Multi-level Models of Stress for Leaving Cert Pupils (N = 3,852)

Fixed Effects	Model 1	Model 2	Model 3	Model 4	Model 5	Model 6
Intercept	-.012	-.266	-.223	-.107	-.580	-.652
Background Variables:						
Gender (Girls = 1)		.490*	.483*	.462*	.594*	.486*
Social Class		-.007	-.006	.001	.008	.007
Junior Cert GPA		.021*	.020*	.022	.028*	.026*
Inter Cert GPA		.077	.071	.096	.130*	.149*
School Type:						
Coed School			-.073	-.058	-.003	.013
Coed-Gender Interaction			.003	-.006	-.079	-.051
Parental Expectations:						
Own Expectations				-.323*	-.263*	-.175*
Educational Aspirations				.043*	.047*	.071*
Parental Expectations				.105*	.082*	.095*
Parental Pressure				.040	.047	.055*
Lack of Parental Support				.049	.034	-.003
Hours of Study				.011	.027*	.025
Involvement in Domestic Labour				.003	-.004	-.003
Part-time Job				-.010	-.020	.010
School Process / Interaction:						
Homework Rules					-.047	-.033
Positive Teacher Interaction					-.123*	-.013
Negative Teacher Interaction					.207*	.152*
Average Positive Interaction in School					-.071	.004
Average Negative Interaction in School					.008	-.032
Bullying					.593*	.443*
Restricted Subject Choice					.138*	.130*
Mediating Variables:						
Pastoral-Care Provision						.006
Recreation						-.025*
Social Life						.007
Social-Skills Development						-.027*
Control						-.228*
Academic Self-Image						-.002
Body-Image						-.070*
Random Effects:						
Variance at School Level	0.058*	0.022*	0.021*	0.016*	0.015*	0.016*
Variance at Pupil Level	0.944*	0.914*	0.914*	0.882*	0.820*	0.759*
% Variance Explained:						
School Level	—	62.4	64.3	72.5	73.7	72.6
Pupil Level	—	3.2	3.2	6.6	13.2	19.6
Proportion of Remaining Variance at:						
School Level	5.8	2.3	2.2	1.8	1.8	2.1
Pupil Level	94.2	97.7	97.8	98.2	98.2	97.9
Deviance	10832.6	10651.8	10649.0	10501.4	10218.8	9927.8
Reduction in Deviance	—	<.001	n.s.	<.001	<.001	<.001

* Indicates significance at the <.05 level.

9.4 EXPECTATIONAL PRESSURES

As hypothesised, there appears to be a clear relationship between parental expectations and stress levels among pupils. Controlling for ability and pupils' own educational expectations, stress levels are higher (by one-third to one-half of a standard deviation) among those whose parents expect them to do very well in their forthcoming exam than among those whose parents expect them to do well below average. In addition, lack of parental support, where pupils do not discuss their educational and career plans with their parents, tends to increase stress levels.

Contrary to the effects of parental expectations, own expectations in relation to exam performance are associated with lower stress levels. This pattern is likely to reflect the pupils' confidence in their own abilities, so it is only when parents' expectations are higher than the pupil's that higher expectations become sources of stress.[5] Among Leaving Cert pupils, aspirations to go on to higher education serve to increase stress levels. Similarly, more hours spent at study are associated with higher stress levels, although this pattern holds only for girls (Tables A8.4 and A8.6).

The hypothesis of role strain between school work and part-time employment or domestic labour impacting on stress levels is only tentatively confirmed. Involvement in domestic labour slightly increases stress levels for boys (but not for girls); the effect is small and significant only for the Junior Cert group. This pattern may, however, be more complex than role strain between study and outside-work demands, and may relate to conflicting notions of "masculinity" and involvement in work which is seen as stereotypically "female". Holding a part-time job slightly increases stress for girls, but not for boys, although the effect is not statistically significant. In conjunction with background factors, expectational pressures explain approximately 7 per cent of individual variance in stress levels.

---

[5]   When the discrepancy between own and parents' expectations is tested, it is found that stress levels are higher where parents have higher expectations than pupils.

9.5 SCHOOLING PROCESS AND INTERACTION WITH TEACHERS AND PEERS

The findings from Model 5 (Tables 9.2 and 9.3) indicate that taking account of differences in pupil–pupil and pupil–teacher interaction within the school substantially increases the amount of variance explained in stress levels. The strongest effect appears to be from bullying: pupils who experience bullying on a more frequent basis report significantly higher levels of stress than other pupils (Tables 9.2 and 9.3).

The extent to which pupils report negative interaction with teachers (such as being given out to, or ignored, by teachers) significantly increases stress levels. Conversely, positive teacher interaction (such as praise and positive feedback) decreases pupil stress levels, particularly among boys. The model also tests whether pupil–teacher interaction acts as a contextual effect — that is, whether schools reporting more positive pupil–teacher interaction have an effect on stress levels over and above the individual effect. There is some evidence that high average positive interaction within a school reduces stress levels at the Junior Cert level, at least among girls, although the results are somewhat inconclusive at the Leaving Cert level. Other contextual measures, such as average social class and average unemployment levels within schools, were found to have no impact on stress levels.

Pupils were asked whether there were any subjects they would like to have taken but could not — this item is included in the model as "restricted subject choice". This factor is associated with higher stress levels among both Junior and Leaving Cert pupils (Tables 9.2 and 9.3). A further test was carried out to investigate whether a high level of pupils within a school reporting restricted subject choice had an additional impact on individual pupil stress levels — this aggregate variable was found to have no appreciable effect on stress levels. Thus, it is not that higher stress levels are associated with more rigid subject-choice rules within schools, but that pupils are more likely to experience increased stress when their individual subject preferences/needs are not met by the school.

In general, school organisation tends to have little effect on pupil stress levels. Only homework rules serve to lower stress levels, a process which is significant at the Junior Cert only. This is likely to operate in the same way as positive pupil–teacher interaction with regular feedback to pupils on work performance reducing anxiety and stress. Other aspects of school organisation, such as streaming/banding, do not appear to impact on pupil stress levels. Thus, school-related stressors appear to be mainly operative at the intra-personal or interpersonal level rather than at the formal organisational level.

9.6 MEDIATING VARIABLES

So far we have examined only the direct effects of stressor variables on students' sense of well-being. The research literature on stress, however, also emphasises the role of mediating factors, factors that moderate or change the effect of stressor variables. These effects appear to operate mainly through the material, social and social-psychological resources or capacities which help or hinder individuals in coping with stressful experiences (see Pearlin et al., 1981; Pearlin, 1989; Whelan et al., 1991; Hannan, Ó Riain, 1993).

Contrary to our hypothesis, the provision of a formal pastoral-care programme does not appear to reduce stress levels among individual pupils.[6] Rather, the important factor appears to be the school "ethos" as expressed through teacher treatment of pupils, and the school's impact on the personal and social development of pupils. Thus, the impact of potential stressors is lessened where pupils feel that their schooling has contributed to their personal and social development.

For Junior and Leaving Cert pupils, particularly boys, participation in sports appears to be associated with lower stress levels. A more active social life (for example, going to discos, dating) does not have the same ameliorative effect.

In the research literature, "locus of control" is proposed as the classic social psychological variable mediating the effects of unemployment, for example, on stress levels: where individuals are confident of their ability to control events, stressors, such as unemployment, have significantly lower impact (see Hannan, Ó Riain, 1993: 193–9). Control has a highly significant impact on

---

[6] This measure is based on principals' (and guidance counsellors') reports of pastoral-care provision in the school. Consequently, the measure reflects the degree of formalisation of provision rather than its "quality" or "effectiveness".

pupil stress levels, with a one-point increase in locus of control resulting in almost a quarter of a standard deviation decrease in stress levels. Thus, the stronger the sense of control, the less impact other stressor variables have on individual stress levels. The following table illustrates the mediating impact of locus of control on potential stressors for Junior Cert pupils.

Table 9.4: Correlation between Sources of Stress and Stress, Mediated by Control, for Junior Cert Pupils

| | Level of Control | | |
Stressor Variables	Low	Medium	High
	Correlations with Stress		
Bullying	.28*	.22*	.16*
Negative Teacher Interaction	.11*	.11*	.03

* Indicates significance at the <.05 level.

The lower the level of control, the higher the correlation between the stressor variables and stress levels: where pupils are passive and fatalistic, these stressors have much stronger effects. Conversely, where sense of control is high, the effect of potential stressors is reduced, and, in the case of negative teacher interaction, it has no significant impact on stress among pupils with a relatively high sense of control (Table 9.4).

Having a high body-image (for example, seeing oneself as attractive/good-looking) also has a mediating effect, significantly reducing stress levels. This is likely to operate in the same way as control, with pupils who have a positive body-image having greater personal resources to cope with potentially stressful contexts. The pattern for academic self-image is somewhat less clear. Among Junior Cert pupils, particularly girls, those who see themselves as more academically competent report higher stress levels, a pattern which is most likely related to associated achievement pressures. In contrast, a higher academic self-image reduces stress levels for Leaving Cert girls, while increasing stress levels for boys. It appears likely that it is overall (global) self-image, rather than a component part (such as academic self-image), that serves important mediating functions (Rosenberg et al., 1995).

9.7 THE IMPACT OF COEDUCATION

Controlling for the social and ability background of pupils, being in a coeducational school is found to reduce stress levels somewhat among pupils, significantly so in the case of Junior Cert boys (Table A8.5, Model 3). The effect of coed on stress levels decreases slightly when school process and mediating variables are introduced into the model, indicating that some of the effects on boys are associated with more positive pupil–teacher interaction, less restricted subject choice and higher levels of social-skills development within coed schools. However, controlling for all of these factors, being in a coed school is still associated with a significant reduction in stress levels for Junior Cert boys. Table 9.5 indicates predicted stress levels by school type, using boys in single-sex schools as a reference point.

Among Junior Cert pupils, girls have the highest stress levels (regardless of the coed/single-sex distinction) while boys in coed schools have the lowest levels, significantly lower than among their counterparts in single-sex schools. This pattern varies by type of coed school, with the lowest stress levels found among boys in vocational schools. Stress levels are also slightly lower among girls in vocational schools than among other girls, although the difference is not statistically significant. There is much less variation in stress levels among Leaving Cert pupils, although boys in vocational schools report somewhat lower stress scores than those in other school types.

Table 9.5: Predicted Stress Levels by Gender and School Type

	Junior Cert		Leaving Cert	
School Type	**Boys**	**Girls**	**Boys**	**Girls**
Single-Sex Secondary	0	+.4	0	+.5
Coed, of which:	-.1	+.4	+.01	+.4
Secondary	-.05	+.4	-.02	+.5
Vocational	-.2	+.3	-.05	+.4
Community/Comprehensive	-.1	+.5	+.10	+.5

Source: Calculated from Model 6 in Tables 9.2 and 9.3, and A8.8.

In summary, being in a coeducational school appears to be associated with lower stress levels among Junior Cert boys. This does not appear to be a "pure" coed effect as boys in coed secondary schools closely resemble their counterparts in single-sex schools in their experiences of stress. The effects on Leaving Cert pupils are less clear-cut, with no significant variation by school type. In overall terms, being in a coed school does not have the same ameliorative effect for girls as for boys.

9.8 CONCLUSIONS

The analyses indicate strikingly high levels of current stress among both Junior and Leaving Cert pupils, particularly among girls. Stress is found to be significantly higher among those in their exam years than among young adults. Stress levels among the pupils are primarily influenced by educational achievement pressures and the nature of interaction within the schools. While much of the variation in stress levels occurs between pupils within schools, schools can intervene through teacher–pupil interaction, and potentially through controlling levels of bullying, to reduce pupil stress levels. More formal and structured school interventions, such as pastoral-care programmes, are found to have no appreciable impact on the stress levels of pupils, when they are not underpinned by a positive school climate.

Controlling for other factors, being in a coeducational school seems to be associated with somewhat lower stress levels among Junior Cert boys. This is not related to coeducation per se, but to the type of coed school, being particularly marked in vocational schools. The reasons for this pattern are unclear, but appear likely to relate to aspects of school ethos that are not included in the model. Among Leaving Cert pupils, there are no clear differences in stress levels by school type.

10

Conclusions and Recommendations

This study has been guided by three general questions:

- Does the educational achievement of pupils, particularly girls, in coeducational schools differ from that of pupils in single-sex schools?

- Does coeducation affect the personal and social development of pupils?

- If so, what accounts for these differences in achievement, and in personal and social development?

This chapter presents the main conclusions of our research, and discusses the implications for policy development.

10.1 THE EFFECTS OF COEDUCATION ON EDUCATIONAL ACHIEVEMENT

Existing research suggested two main hypotheses concerning the impact of coeducation on educational achievement:

(1) Girls in coed schools tend to underperform relative to girls in single-sex schools, and to boys in coed schools.

(2) These differences are related to the way in which coed schools "manage" gender differences among their pupils: that is, the majority of coed schools are run in ways which reproduce gender differences in the wider society.

One of the main purposes of the research was to test whether these hypotheses held in the Irish context.

The study found that coeducational and single-sex schools differ in a number of respects (see Chapters 4 and 5):

- Single-sex schools tend to be more selective in their intake than coed schools. This results in a very different social and ability profile of pupils in the two school types.

- Coed schools are more likely to allocate pupils to classes on the basis of their academic ability ("streaming" or "banding").

- Coed and single-sex schools differ in the type of curriculum taught and the way in which subjects and levels are made available to classes and pupils.

However, these differences are related not to coeducation as such, but rather to the historical origins of the secondary, vocational and community/comprehensive sectors; coed secondary schools more closely resemble single-sex secondary schools than they do other coed schools. If we are to assess the relative academic performance of pupils in coed and single-sex schools, we need to control for these other differences in order to compare "like with like".

10.1.1 Coeducation and Junior Certificate Performance

Comparing "like with like", we come to the following conclusions:

Coeducation has a slight negative effect on girls' overall examination performance: girls in single-sex schools are at a slight advantage compared to coed girls, though girls in coed schools still outperform coed boys. Even allowing for the fact that "current ability" may itself be influenced by coeducation, the coed effect is substantively very small. Most of the difference in performance between coed and single-sex schools is, in fact, due to differences in the social background and ability of their pupil intakes.

The impact of coeducation on exam performance is strongest among pupils of below-average academic ability. Among lower-ability pupils, boys in coed schools do somewhat better, and coed girls slightly worse, than their counterparts in single-sex schools. In contrast, being in a coeducational school has little substantive impact on exam performance among middle- and higher-ability pupils.

Differences among types of coed schools are greater than the overall difference between coed and single-sex schools. In particular, being in a vocational school is associated with a "boost" in boys' performance, especially among lower-ability boys. This is likely to relate to the type of curriculum offered, with an emphasis on technical/practical subjects helping to improve overall performance among boys of low academic ability. There is no equivalent curricular boost for girls of lower academic ability.

Performance in Junior Certificate Mathematics shows a clear pattern of coed/ single-sex differences. Girls' performance in coed schools is significantly lower than in single-sex schools, by about half a grade. This difference holds across all types of coed schools — secondary, vocational and community/ comprehensive.

10.1.2 Coeducation and Leaving Certificate Performance

Being in a coeducational school has no significant impact on Leaving Certificate performance, when we control for social background, prior performance and other schooling factors. Schools differ significantly from one another in average performance, but this is primarily because of the type of pupils attending them, and the way in which pupils are allocated to classes, not whether they are coeducational or single-sex.

Mathematics performance, however, continues to differentiate coed from single-sex schools, with attendance at a coed school having a negative effect for both girls and boys. Girls in vocational and community/comprehensive schools, in particular, score more than half a grade lower than girls in single-sex secondary schools, even controlling for Maths grade in the Junior Cert. This pattern is of particular concern, since it indicates a cumulative process of under-performance in Maths among girls in coed schools over the whole period of second-level schooling.

10.1.3 Other Factors Influencing Educational Performance

Gender

Controlling for social background and ability factors, girls significantly outperform boys at the Junior Certificate level. Being in a coed school narrows this gap slightly, but girls in coed schools still outperform their male counterparts. Girls also continue to outperform boys at the Leaving Certificate level, although the differences are less than at the junior-cycle level.

Social Background
Differences among pupils in educational performance are primarily related to individual differences in academic ability and social background. Even controlling for ability and other differences, pupils from lower socioeconomic backgrounds continue to be at a disadvantage within the schooling system. In addition, the concentration of pupils from a particular social background within a school has an effect on exam performance, over and above the individual level effect. Thus, pupils tend to do worse in schools with a high concentration of pupils from working-class or unemployed backgrounds, regardless of their own social background.

School Process
Much of the difference between schools is related to pupil composition. However, even controlling for pupil-composition differences, there is considerable variance between schools and school types in their impact on academic achievement. By implication then, schools vary in their "effectiveness", both overall and with particular groups of pupils. Case-studies of these effective schools could identify elements of "good practice" for use in programmes to improve school effectiveness.

Certain school-level processes appear to have a consistent negative effect on academic performance. Controlling for all other variables, the use of streaming has a negative impact on average academic performance at the Junior Cert level. Streaming has a particularly negative effect on pupils allocated to bottom/remedial classes, with these pupils scoring one-third of a grade per subject less in the Junior Cert, and over one grade per subject less in the Leaving Cert, than those of the same ability in mixed-ability classes. A change to mixed-ability "base" classes, and the "setting" of levels, is, therefore, likely to secure a marked improvement in pupil performance. Further research is needed to identify the optimal combination of "pure" mixed-ability teaching (where pupils of all abilities are taught in the same class) and "setting" (where certain subjects are taught in separate higher and ordinary level classes).

10.2 COEDUCATION AND PERSONAL/SOCIAL DEVELOPMENT

Pupils in coeducational schools have a more positive view of their schools' impact on their social/personal development than pupils in single-sex schools. However, coeducation has surprisingly few effects on more objective measures of pupils' personal and social development. The only consistent effects are for boys: Junior Cert boys in coed schools have somewhat lower academic self-images and lower senses of control, and coed boys at both Junior and Leaving Certificate levels are more critical of their appearance than their counterparts in single-sex schools. Thus, being in a coed school seems to make boys more self-critical; in contrast, girls have less confidence and lower senses of control than boys, no matter what kind of school they attend.

Coeducation has some effect on gender role expectations: in particular, Leaving Cert boys have less traditional views of work and family roles when they attend coed schools. It is not clear that the same positive coed effects apply to girls since coed girls appear to have somewhat higher domestic workloads than girls in single-sex schools.

Perhaps the most notable finding is the pattern of gender differences in the measures of personal and social development used. Even given their higher level of achievement, girls are less confident about their academic abilities, do not feel the same sense of control over their lives, and are more critical of their appearance than boys with similar backgrounds and schooling experiences. In addition, girls are still subject to traditional gender stereotyping, carrying a much heavier domestic workload than boys.

Several aspects of the schooling process are more important than school type as influences on pupils' personal and social development. In particular, the quality of relations with teachers and other pupils strongly influences pupils' feelings of control, academic self-confidence, and evaluations of their appearance. These informal pupil–teacher and pupil–pupil relations seem to be much more important than formally structured interventions such as pastoral-care programmes.

10.3 COEDUCATION AND STRESS

Stress levels are disturbingly high among Junior Certificate, and particularly among Leaving Certificate, pupils. Difficulty in sleeping, feeling constantly under strain, loss of self-confidence and inability to concentrate are the most frequently reported symptoms. Stress is very closely related to other aspects of personal and social development, with highly stressed pupils reporting lower academic self-images, lower senses of control, and more negative body images.

In general, coeducation does not appear to impact on stress levels. However, boys in coed schools (particularly vocational schools) appear to be less stressed than boys in single-sex schools at the Junior Cert level, although the difference is relatively small and does not persist to the Leaving Cert level. Girls report much higher stress levels than boys within both types of school.

Stress levels are primarily influenced by educational achievement pressures and the quality of interpersonal relationships within the school and the family. Stress levels are particularly high where parents and teachers have very high expectations of the pupil, and these expectations are not proportionate to the pupil's own expectations and abilities. Stress levels are lower where the quality of interpersonal relations within the school is high — that is, where pupils receive more positive feedback and less negative sanctioning from teachers, and have good relations with their peers. Thus, while much of the variation in stress occurs between pupils within schools, schools can intervene through teacher–pupil interaction, and particularly through controlling levels of conflict (bullying) among pupils, to reduce pupil stress levels.

10.4 RECOMMENDATIONS

The second-level school system in Ireland is characterised by substantial institutional diversity as well as high levels of individual autonomy relative to other developed countries (OECD, 1992). The State funds the second-level system, sets rules for periods of instruction, and sets standards in curricula and examinations. However, outside these broad parameters, school authorities possess a considerable degree of freedom — for example, in selecting pupils and teachers, and deciding the curricular mix to be provided in the school. Since the 1960s, the State has set specific social objectives for schools, emphasising equality of access and treatment for pupils of all social backgrounds and ability levels (Department of Education, 1966; *Ár nDaltaí Uile*, 1969). However, the State has neither the authority over schools nor the institutional instruments available to it to ensure that these objectives are met. The relative failure of State policy in reducing social-class inequalities in educational achievement is clear from the study findings and from other national research (see also Breen, 1995; Higher Education Authority, 1995).

State policy for gender equality in education has been clearly emphasised in the *Green Paper* (1992,: 67–72) and the *Report of the National Education Convention* (1994). Though less explicit in the *White Paper* (1995), gender equity in terms of treatment and outcomes is clearly emphasised. As is the case with social-class equality, this policy objective is unlikely to lead to effective action "on the ground" unless the underlying reasons for policy failure to reduce inequalities in educational achievement are corrected. The State needs to develop better instruments to promote the achievement of gender (and social-class) equality goals among individual schools and local school systems. The role of the educational system in promoting gender equity is particularly important, given rapidly changing gender roles in the economy and the family. Besides monitoring the school system to "ensure that equality is being promoted" (*White Paper*, 1995: 196), significant sanctioning power needs to be available to the Department and the proposed Regional Education Boards to ensure equality of treatment at both a school and local catchment-area level.

The remainder of this section discusses the main policy issues raised by the study and proposes an integrated set of policy recommendations at a State, local and school level. These recommendations are summarised in Appendix 9.1.

10.4.1 Educational Achievement

Coeducation appears to have a slight negative effect on girls' educational achievement, although the effect is mainly caused by the dampening effect of coeducation on the achievement of lower-ability girls. Coed schools appear to have widened their curricula, and access to "non-academic" subjects, to cater for the needs of lower-ability boys, but not of lower-ability girls. We therefore recommend:

- The issuing of guidelines by the Department of Education to coed schools to ensure equality of access to, and treatment within, subjects and levels for girls and boys of all ability levels

- The provision of specific in-service courses for the principals and management of coed schools, in order to enhance gender fairness in school organisation and curricular arrangements

- The development of new "gender fair" vocational/technical and applied subjects to encourage achievement among girls of below-average academic ability

- Improved provision of, and access to, vocational/technical subjects for lower-ability boys in single-sex schools.

Educational underachievement in Mathematics is apparent among girls in coed schools. It is, therefore, recommended that:

- Further research be conducted on girls' achievement in other "male" subjects, particularly the sciences, in order to assess whether this pattern is common to related subjects

- Positive action should be taken at the State and school level to encourage girls' take-up of, and performance in, these subject areas. Appropriate measures would include the extension of schemes, such as the Department of Education's Intervention Projects in Physics and Chemistry, along with a reconsideration of school-imposed restrictions on pupil eligibility to take particular subjects and levels.

- Positive action should be underpinned by positive teacher attitudes. All teacher training and in-career development programmes should incorporate a strong emphasis on gender equality issues as is emphasised in the *White Paper* (1995: 130). In addition, teachers in coed schools should be given specific in-service training in how to handle classes with both girls and boys effectively, to ensure gender equity.

Schools differ in their "effectiveness" concerning the educational achievement of their pupils. The main issue is not whether a school is coed or single-sex, but how the school handles gender, class and academic-ability differences among pupils, with schools varying widely in the nature and effectiveness of their schooling processes. The following interventions are, therefore, recommended:

- Further research to identify "models of good practice" for school effectiveness, drawing on detailed case-studies of schools which are effective across a range of outcomes (such as overall academic achievement, achievement in particular subject areas, personal and social development)

- A more proactive role by the State (perhaps, through extending the remit of the National Council for Curriculum and Assessment) in developing and diffusing models of good practice in schooling process and pedagogical practice as a basis for school-improvement programmes

- Such intervention should be based on a "whole school" approach, with equal attention to the formal school organisation and the informal climate of the school (for example, through teacher expectations and support for achievement, positive teacher–pupil interaction, and so on). This approach should be developed in consultation with school management, principals and teachers, and perhaps implemented by the proposed Regional Education Boards (see *White Paper*, 1995: 187).

Certain elements of the schooling process have clear effects on educational achievement. In particular, streaming tends to result in underperformance among those in the bottom classes.

- The State needs to provide schools with information on more effective ways in which ability and aptitude differences among pupils can be handled. This approach should be supported by the provision of in-service programmes on mixed-ability teaching.

- A move towards mixed-ability "base" classes, with provision of separate higher and ordinary level classes ("setting") in particular subjects, would appear to be an effective way of improving educational performance.

The findings indicate very wide variances in the social background and ability levels of pupils in different schools, with equally wide variances in their outcomes. While many "disadvantaged" pupils are not in "disadvantaged" schools (see Kellaghan et al., 1995), the social-class mix of a school has an additional "structural effect", with pupils having higher grades in more selective schools. Conversely, exam grades tend to be lower where schools suffer from "cream-off", and contain high proportions of working-class pupils or pupils from unemployed backgrounds. We therefore recommend that:

- The State take a more proactive role in discouraging schools from selecting pupils on ability or background criteria — perhaps, by making the receipt of some school-level optional resources conditional on schools meeting their local social responsibilities

- In addition to providing extra resources to "disadvantaged" schools (through the current Schemes of Assistance to Schools in Designated Areas of Disadvantage), the Department of Education needs to provide help to such schools to improve their effectiveness at both a school and classroom level. This is particularly true for schools suffering from "cream-off".

In more general terms, the study raises issues about the nature of the current examination system, and its use as a selection mechanism for further education and training. In recent years, the system has increasingly focused on one dimension of pupil achievement — overall academic grades or "points" — with a consequent neglect of alternative certification arrangements and channels of mobility into post-school education, training and employment. The significance of appropriate subject specialisations at second level, for instance, has been increasingly ignored. As expressed clearly in a consultative paper of the NCCA (1994), the Leaving Certificate examination "has come to be regarded less as a test of achievement and more as a means of discriminating between students for the purposes of selection" into higher education (op. cit.: 15). The overall effect has been to make it much more difficult for pupils of lower academic ability either to maximise their educational achievement or to gain access to further education/ training. We, therefore:

- Call for an active debate about the nature and effectiveness of current channels of mobility into further education and training, and their consequences for different types of second-level pupils; and for an opening-up of alternative selection criteria, such as subject area requirements for specific vocational and technical courses

- Welcome recent innovations (such as the Vocational and Applied Leaving Certificate) designed to cater to those with different aptitudes and abilities. We caution, however, that their success depends on their recognition in terms of access to further education/training and the labour market

- Given the disadvantages of, and stress associated with, our current exam system, there is an urgent need to reach agreement on ongoing methods of assessment for all examinations, similar to those agreed for the Applied Leaving Certificate (see NCCA, 1994; Department of Education, circular S73/95, 1995).

10.4.2 Personal and Social Development

As well as being differentially effective in terms of academic performance, schools vary in the personal and social development of their pupils. The findings indicate the importance of good teacher–pupil and peer relations in the development of adolescent girls and boys. We therefore recommend that:

- Further research be carried out to identify the elements of "good practice" in schools' approaches to pupil development, and related issues such as bullying and disciplinary problems

- As suggested in the *White Paper* (1995: 161–3), personal/social development should be central to any assessment of a school's effectiveness

- Schools should be helped to develop effective policies to reduce bullying behaviour among pupils.

The findings indicate that formally structured programmes (such as pastoral-care programmes) are of limited use unless accompanied by a school climate that is beneficial to pupil development. Consequently, we recommend that:

- Formal programmes dealing with pupil development should be integrated into a "whole school" approach to educational development, underpinned by supportive teacher attitudes, expectations and practice

- These programmes should be supported by "whole school" training for both school management and teachers.

The lower self-confidence among girls in all school types gives cause for concern. Girls appear to absorb negative messages about their selves and their appearances from a wide range of sources (such as the media, popular culture, peer groups etc.). However, schools do have the potential to challenge these stereotypes. We therefore recommend that:

- Government policy should be more proactive in encouraging gender equity within schools, not only in relation to subject performance and take-up, but also in relation to the social development of pupils.

- Schools, both coed and single-sex, should develop their own policies to promote gender equity: a broad view of gender equity should be adopted with policies applying not only to girls in single-sex and coed schools, but also to boys in single-sex schools.

- Teacher training and subsequent staff-development programmes for principals and teachers should incorporate a specific focus on gender equity.

- Programmes, such as assertiveness training, should be developed to enhance self-image and locus of control among girls, with separate provision of such courses for girls within coed schools.

10.4.3 Stress

Stress levels are disturbingly high among Junior and Leaving Certificate pupils. As with other aspects of personal and social development, the stress levels of pupils are strongly influenced by the climate of the school. Stress levels could be reduced by:

- The advancement of a "whole school" approach to pupil development

- School-level interventions on bullying and inter-peer conflict

- The development of practical programmes designed to enhance coping and problem-solving skills among pupils

- Support given to schools to balance their academic objectives with the provision of sports and other recreational and cultural activities which help to reduce stress levels among pupils.

A good deal of pupil stress is caused by high expectational pressures in relation to exam performance and "points". This is especially marked where parents and teachers expect more of pupils than pupils themselves feel they can deliver. It is important that schools are responsive to the different abilities and preferences of pupils, catering for less "academic" pupils (who may have high capabilities in other areas of the curriculum) as well as those with high academic ability and educational aspirations. We therefore welcome innovations, such as the Vocational and Applied Leaving Certificate, the introduction of Foundation level subjects at Junior and Leaving Cert level, and the Junior Cert Schools Programme. We strongly recommend, however, that these developments be buttressed by changes in the institutional rules regarding access to further education, training and apprentice-ships.

While it may fall outside the scope of the study, it is difficult to discuss stress levels among pupils without mentioning the "points race" and the attendant media publicity. The findings of the study do not allow us to disentangle the effects of the particular points system from more general expectational pressures. However, it is clear that parent and teacher expectational pressures are signifi-cant factors in pupils' experiences of stress. Perhaps it is an appropriate time for a debate on the social and personal costs of a system geared towards high grades, and for a re-evaluation of the most appropriate way to meet pupils' needs and aspirations. A number of European countries have adopted alternative approaches to allocating higher-education places (such as the specification of minimum entrance criteria, with random selection thereafter) which may potentially reduce stress levels among exam candidates. Similarly, alternative methods of pupil evaluation (such as continuous assessment over the senior cycle) may help to reduce the high stress of the exam years.

While expectational pressures increase stress levels among pupils, they may actually reduce the ability of young people to perform to their full potential. Further research is needed on the impact of stress on academic performance, on the way stress levels interact with other dimensions of personal/social develop-ment, and the ways in which effective school programmes help both to reduce stress levels and to improve pupil development.

10.5 CONCLUSION

To conclude, this study set out to answer some basic questions about the effects of coeducation on girls' educational achievement and personal and social development. Coeducation was found to have a slight negative effect on performance among Junior Cert girls, though this is mainly limited to those of lower academic ability. It has no appreciable impact on their overall Leaving Cert performance or on their personal/social development. In contrast, coeducation has clear negative effects on girls' performance in Mathematics.

However, the study also indicates the fundamental importance of broader schooling influences on educational achievement and personal/social development. Schools, both coed and single-sex,

vary significantly from each other in their effectiveness in relation to overall educational performance, the performance of
different groups (girls and boys, different ability groups), and in
pupils' personal/ social development. The multi-dimensional
nature of school objectives and processes needs to be taken into
account in the development of any school improvement programmes, regardless of school type. Coed schools, however, face
more complex organisational and instructional tasks because they
cater for the needs of both girls and boys, and consequently
require specific support to carry out these tasks. In the context of
increased amalgamations of smaller single-sex schools into coed
schools, the new school managements and staff require substantial assistance in constructing a new and effective school organisation around more complex school objectives and more diverse
school clientèle.

Appendix

APPENDIX 1.1: THE IRISH EDUCATIONAL SYSTEM

There are three types of second-level school in Ireland: secondary, vocational, and community/comprehensive. Secondary schools have traditionally been more academic in orientation, in contrast to a greater practical and technical focus in vocational schools. Community and comprehensive schools were established in an attempt to bridge the gap between the secondary and vocational sectors, by providing a broad curriculum catering for pupils of different backgrounds and ability levels. Secondary schools may be single-sex or coeducational, while the vast majority of vocational and community/comprehensive schools are coeducational. All school types are publicly aided. Voluntary secondary schools are privately owned and controlled, although subject to public regulation and inspection. Vocational schools are administered by local education authorities, Vocational Education Committees.

Pupils enter second-level education at around 12 years of age. The junior cycle consists of three years, leading to the Junior Certificate examination, usually taken at the age of 15 or 16. There is a national curriculum within which pupils have a choice of subjects. Pupils usually take eight or nine subjects in the Junior Certificate examination, with little subject specialisation. The examination is nationally standardised and assessed. Until 1992, there were two State exams at junior-cycle level: the Group Certificate, which was vocational in orientation, and the Intermediate Certificate, which was more academic in orientation.

The senior cycle consists of a two-year programme. In some schools, this is preceded by a Transition Year, with an emphasis on education in its broadest sense and on pupil development. Pupils sit the Leaving Certificate at around 17 or 18 years of age, usually taking six or seven subjects. Leaving Certificate examination assessment is nationally standardised, and examination es are extremely important in securing access to employment d to further education (Breen, Hannan and O'Leary, 1995). In recent years, a range of programmes (such as the Leaving Certificate Vocational Programme, and the Leaving Certificate Applied Programme) have been developed to cater for pupils with more vocational orientations.

Appendix 2

APPENDIX 2.1: LEAVING CERTIFICATE SCHEDULE — 1993/94

Survey of Young People's Experiences and Views on Education

The purpose of this questionnaire is to get your views about your education and about your future career. We are interviewing students in over 120 schools in Ireland in the study. The answers will be combined to form a general picture of their views. The information provided will be of great value in assessing the suitability of current educational programmes and in developing ways to help young people with their educational and job-seeking problems.

The answers which you give <u>will be treated with the strictest confidence.</u> No one at the school will see the completed questionnaires. The research workers are the only people who will ever see your questionnaire. We are interested in Group Averages only and not in any single individual's answers.

S____

Most of the questions can be answered by ticking the appropriate box like this:

Y____

Are you at school? Yes ☐ No ☐

C____

or in some questions where there is a choice of answer, by circling the appropriate number ... 1 ... 2 ... 3

P____

SKIPPING QUESTIONS

Some questions with a YES/NO or AGREE/DISAGREE answer, have a box around one of the answers. Where that is the case and your answer is in the <u>BOX</u> please go on to answer all the other questions in the <u>BOX</u>. If not, skip or go on to the next question. For example:

Do you smoke?   Yes ☐   No ☐ → Next Question

IF YES: About how many cigarettes per day? _____?

Before turning to the first page of the questionnaire please complete the following basic details:

Class Year: _____

Class Name/No.:_____

Pupil Number (if you know it)   ☐☐☐☐☐☐   Numb

What is your name (block capitals): _____

Date: _____   N

(This is needed for sampling purposes only and will <u>never</u> be published. Once back in the office you will be assigned a code number and this "face sheet" will be kept separately from the rest of the questionnaire.)

S___
Y___
C___

Leaving Cert. Schedule — 1993/94

Q1. What is your date of birth? ☐☐ day ☐☐ month ☐☐ year   P___

Q2. What is your sex?   Male ☐₁   Female ☐₂

Q3. Are you   a day pupil   ☐₁

                                     a boarder   ☐₂

Q4. Was the Primary School you attended directly linked or attached to this school?

                    Yes ☐₁   No ☐₂

Q5. Was the final year (sixth class) in your Primary School single-sex or mixed (girls and boys)?

girls only ☐₁   boys only ☐₂   girls and boys ☐₃

Q6. At the time you left primary school what second-level school did your parents want you to go to?

	This School	Another School

(a) My parents wanted me to go to: ☐₁ →Q.7   ☐₂ →Q.6(b)

(b) If your parents wanted you to go to another school was it?

Single-sex secondary school   ☐₁

Mixed-sex secondary school   ☐₂

Vocational (Tech) school   ☐₃

Q7. How far, approximately, is your present school from your home?

                    ☐☐ mile(s)

Q8. Are there any other second-level schools nearer your home, or easier to get to, that you could have gone to? Yes ☐₁ No ☐₂

Q9. We want now to ask how many sisters and brothers you have. If you are a twin count the other twin as older.

How many: older sisters have you?   _____
             older brothers have you?   _____
             younger sisters have you?   _____
             younger brothers have you?   _____

A1.1
A1.2
A1.3
A2

A3

A4

A5

A6.1

A6.2

A7

A8

A9.1
A9.2
A9.3
A9.4

Q10. (a) How many of your sisters and brothers are in or have been
to second level schools? _____   A10.1

(b) How many of these are in or went to your school?

sisters _____   A10.2
brothers_____   A10.3

Q11. For each subject you took for the Junior (or Inter) Cert., please:

(i)   Tick the box ❑ for each subject you took in the Junior Cert.
(or Inter Cert.) exam
(ii) Circle the number indicating the level (Foundation, Ordinary
(Pass), Higher (Honours)) at which you took the subject
(iii) Fill in the grade you received in the subject in the exam.

(i) What subjects taken? Subject		(ii) What level taken? Foundation level	Ordinary level	Higher level	(iii) What grade received?	
Irish	☐	1	2	3	_____	A11.1-3
English	☐	1	2	3	_____	A11.4-6
Maths	☐	1	2	3	_____	A11.7-9
History	☐		2	3	_____	A11.10-12
Geography	☐		2	3	_____	A11.13-15
French	☐		2	3	_____	A11.16-18
Science	☐		2	3	_____	A11.19-21
Business Studies	☐		2	3	_____	A11.22-24
Commerce	☐		2	3	_____	A11.25-26
Art	☐		2	3	_____	A11.27-28
Music	☐		2	3	_____	A11.29-30
Home Economics	☐		2	3	_____	A11.31-32
Mechanical Drawing	☐		2	3	_____	A11.33-34
Woodwork	☐		2	3	_____	A11.35-36
Metalwork	☐		2	3	_____	A11.37-38
Technology	☐		2	3	_____	A11.39-40
Latin or Greek	☐		2	3	_____	A11.41-42
Classical Studies	☐		2	3	_____	A11.52-54
German	☐		2	3	_____	A11.55-57
Spanish	☐		2	3	_____	A11.58-60
Italian	☐		2	3	_____	A11.61-63
Other (specify) _____	☐		2	3	_____	A11.64-66

Q12. Here is a list of reasons you could give for choosing subjects for the <u>Leaving Cert</u>. How important was each of the following reasons in your case? (Circle one number on each line that provides the answer most true in your case.)

<u>I picked my subjects because:</u>	Very important <u>reason</u>	Somewhat important <u>reason</u>	Not an important <u>reason</u>	
They were the most interesting	1	2	3	A12.1
I would need them to get into further education or training	1	2	3	A12.2
I had got good marks in them in the Junior (or Inter) Cert. exam	1	2	3	A12.3
I really liked the subjects	1	2	3	A12.4
It is easier to get a good job if you take and do well in these subjects	1	2	3	A12.5

Q13. For each subject you are taking for the Leaving Cert., please:
   (i) Tick the box for each subject you are <u>now</u> taking at school for the <u>Leaving Cert.</u>
   (ii) Circle the appropriate number indicating whether you are taking the Ordinary (pass) or Higher (honours) level — if you haven't fully decided on the Ordinary or Higher level, circle the level you will be most likely to take.

(i) What subjects are you taking?	(ii) What level are you taking?		
		Ordinary	Higher
Irish	☐	1	2	A13.1-2
English	☐	1	2	A13.3-4
Maths	☐	1	2	A13.5-6
History	☐	1	2	A13.7-8
Geography	☐	1	2	A13.9-10
French	☐	1	2	A13.11-12
Physics	☐	1	2	A13.13-14
Chemistry	☐	1	2	A13.15-16
Biology	☐	1	2	A13.17-18
Physics and Chemistry	☐	1	2	A13.19-20
Applied Maths	☐	1	2	A13.21-22
Mechanics	☐	1	2	A13.23-24
Economics	☐	1	2	A13.25-26
Business Organisation	☐	1	2	A13.27-28
Accounting	☐	1	2	A13.29-30
Economic History	☐	1	2	A13.31-32
Art	☐	1	2	A13.33-34
Music	☐	1	2	A13.35-36
Home Econ. (Soc. & Sci.)	☐	1	2	A13.37-38
Home Econ. (General)	☐	1	2	A13.39-40
Technical Drawing	☐	1	2	A13.41-42
Engineering	☐	1	2	A13.43-44
Construction Studies	☐	1	2	A13.45-46
Latin or Greek	☐	1	2	A13.47-48
Classical Studies	☐	1	2	A13.49-50
Spanish	☐	1	2	A13.51-52
German	☐	1	2	A13.53-54
Italian	☐	1	2	A13.55-56
Agric. Science	☐	1	2	A13.57-58
Agric. Economics	☐	1	2	A13.59-60
Other (specify) _____	☐	1	2	A13.61-62

Q14. (a) Taking <u>only</u> those subjects you are taking at **higher
(honours) level**, how many grades, A to D, do you expect
to get in the Leaving Certificate examination?

How many As or Bs?	_____	A14.1
How many Cs?	_____	A14.2
How many Ds?	_____	A14.3

Q14 (b) Did you do a transition year after the Junior (or Inter)

Cert?   Yes ❑₁ No ❑₂   A14.5

Q14 (b) Did you do the Leaving cert. exam before? Yes ❑₁ No ❑₂   A14.6

Q15 (a) Thinking back to when you came back to school after the
Junior (or Inter) Cert. Were there any subjects which you
would have really liked to have taken but didn't or
couldn't?   A15.1

Yes ❑₁   No ❑₂ →Go to Q.16
                                                          A15.2

Q15 (b) If YES, please write the names of (up to two) such subjects
which you would have like to but didn't take, in order of
your preference for them.   A15.3

1. _____   2. _____

Q15 (c) Taking the first subject you wrote down for Q15(b), how
important, if at all, was each of the following reasons for
not taking the subject? (Please circle one number on each
line.)

	Very important reason	Somewhat important reason	Not an important reason	
I had to choose between it and another subject which I preferred to take at the time	1	2	3	A15.4
It was only available to those who had taken it or who had got a certain result in it or a related subject, in the JC exam	1	2	3	A15.5
A teacher or Guidance Counsellor advised me to take another subject instead	1	2	3	A15.6
It wasn't taught in my school	1	2	3	A15.7

Q16 (a) Have you changed from the Higher (honours) level to
Ordinary (pass) level in any subject since you started the
Leaving Cert. Course?

                    Yes ☐₁   No ☐₂ →Go to Q.17   A16.1

Q16 (b) If YES: In which subjects? 1. _____ 2. _____

                                                                A16.2

Q16 (c) Taking the first subject mentioned how important were the
following reasons for changing level in this subject?

                                                                A16.3

	Very important reason	Somewhat important reason	Not an important reason	
I found the level too difficult	1	2	3	A16.4
I didn't think the teaching was very good	1	2	3	A16.5
The subject/level was taking up too much time	1	2	3	A16.6
The teacher or Guidance Counsellor advised me to change level	1	2	3	A16.7

Q17 Had you a choice or were you allocated to a higher (honours),
or to an ordinary (pass) level class in <u>Maths</u> in the Leaving
Certificate?

(i) Yes, I had a choice   ☐₁ A17.1

(ii) No, I was allocated to the level — I really had no choice ☐₂

Q18 (a) Were there any subjects which you took at the beginning of
the Leaving Cert. course but have since dropped in favour
of another subject(s)?

                    Yes ☐₁   No ☐₂ →Go to Q.18(c)   A18.1

                                                            ___A18.2
Q18 (b) If YES: I have switched from   1._____ to _____ since ___A18.3
                                    starting the Leaving Cert. course ___A18.4

                    and from   2._____ to _____   ___A18.5

Q18 (c) In making your decision about subjects, and levels to take in your Leaving Cert. Course how important was the help and advice of the following people in these decisions? (Please answer about each person circling one number on each line.)

	Very important	Somewhat important	Not important	
1. The (Career) Guidance Counsellor	1	2	3	A18.6
2. Subject Teachers	1	2	3	A18.7
3. Your Mother	1	2	3	A18.8
4. Your Father	1	2	3	A18.9

Q19. Over the last two weeks that you have spent in class, *how often* have you had the following experiences (circle one number on each line).

	Very Often	Often	A Few Times	Never	
Have you been told that your work is good?	1	2	3	4	A13.1
Have you been asked questions in class?	1	2	3	4	A19.2
Have you been given out to because your work is untidy or not done on time?	1	2	3	4	A19.3
Have you been praised for answering a difficult question correctly?	1	2	3	4	A19.4
Have you wanted to ask or answer questions in class but were ignored?	1	2	3	4	A19.5
Have you been given out to for misbehaving in class?	1	2	3	4	A19.6
Have you been praised because your written work is well done?	1	2	3	4	A19.7
Have you wanted to ask or answer a question in class but didn't because you were worried what other people in the class would think of you?	1	2	3	4	A19.8

Q20. How strongly would you agree or disagree with each of the following statements? (Circle one number on each line for the answer that is most true in your case.)

	Strongly Agree	Agree	Disagree	Strongly Disagree	
I wouldn't ask a teacher to explain something if I didn't understand it	1	2	3	4	A20.1
I am very satisfied with most of the subjects I have taken	1	2	3	4	A20.2
Teachers pay more attention in class to what some pupils say than to others	1	2	3	4	A20.3
If I could choose again I would choose some different subjects from the ones I am taking	1	2	3	4	A20.4
I find most teachers are hard to talk to	1	2	3	4	A20.5
I can do just about anything I set my mind to	1	2	3	4	A20.6
I'm usually well ahead of others in my year in school	1	2	3	4	A20.7
I am as good at school work as most other people of my age	1	2	3	4	A20.8
I have been given a lot of help by my teachers in choosing my subjects/levels	1	2	3	4	A20.9
I'm hardly ever able to do what my teachers expect of me	1	2	3	4	A20.10
What happens to me in the future really depends on me	1	2	3	4	A20.11
I'm usually well ahead of others in my class	1	2	3	4	A20.12
There is really no way I can solve some of the problems I have	1	2	3	4	A20.13
For the most part, school life is a happy one for me	1	2	3	4	A20.14

Q21. How well do your parents and your teachers expect you to perform in the Leaving Certificate? How well do you expect to do? (Please answer about each person, circling one number on each line.)

	Very Well	Well	Just Below Average	Well Below Average	
1. Your father?	1	2	3	4	A21.1
2. Your mother?	1	2	3	4	A21.2
3. Your teachers?	1	2	3	4	A21.3
4. And yourself?	1	2	3	4	A21.4

Q22 Thinking of everyone in your year at school, how would you place yourself in your year?

Top/Well Above Average	Just Above Average	Average	Just Below Average	Well Below Average	
1	2	3	4	5	A22

Q23. What, in your opinion is the highest Certificate or Qualification which (i) your father, (ii) your mother, (iii) your teachers, and (iv) you yourself expect you to get as a result of your education? (For each person tick one box on each line.)

	Junior Cert.	Leaving Cert.	Third Level Cert/ Diploma	University degree	
1. Highest Cert. your father expects you to get	☐1	☐2	☐3	☐4	A23.1
2. Highest Cert. your mother expects you to get	☐1	☐2	☐3	☐4	A23.2
3. Highest Cert. your teachers expect you to get	☐1	☐2	☐3	☐4	A23.3
4. Highest Cert. you expect to get	☐1	☐2	☐3	☐4	A23.4

Q24 (a) Do you intend to go on for further education after your
Leaving Cert?

Definitely Yes ☐₁ Probably Yes ☐₂   No ☐₃ →Go to Q.25 | A24.1

Q24 (b) *If YES, what exact course do you intend to pursue?*
(e.g.: Secretarial Course, A Nursing Diploma, Engineering
Degree, Business Diploma etc.) _____

_____ | A24.2

Q24 (c) If YES: Where do you intend to pursue this course?

At a University	☐₁
Teacher Training College	☐₂
At an RTC	☐₃
At a College of Technology	☐₄
At a Training Hospital	☐₅
At an Agricultural College	☐₆
Other (Explain)_____	☐₇

A24.3

Q25. Looking to the future, when you finally finish your education,
we would like to know about the kind of work you have been
considering.

(i) If you had your choice, what job would you really like to
get? _____

_____ | A25.1

(ii) If you couldn't get that job what kind of job would you be
just satisfied with? _____

_____ | A25.2

Q26. In making up your mind about what you would like to do after
the Leaving Certificate — for third-level education and/or about
jobs — how important are the following people in helping you to
make up your mind?

	Very important	Important	Not important	
1. Your Mother	1	2	3	A26.1
2. Your Father	1	2	3	A26.2
3. Some other family member or relation	1	2	3	A26.3
4. A teacher(s) in school	1	2	3	A26.4
5. Guidance Counsellor	1	2	3	A2635

Q27. How strongly do you agree or disagree with each of the following statements? (Circle one number on each line.)

	Strongly Agree	Agree	Disagree	Strongly Disagree	
I prefer subjects in which I have to work out problems such as in Maths or Science	1	2	3	4	A27.1
I have more confidence in dealing with a subject like English than with any Science subject	1	2	3	4	A27.2
I usually have to give up on difficult problems in Mathematics	1	2	3	4	A27.3
I feel that I will never really be able to understand Maths	1	2	3	4	A27.4
I really like subjects where I can work with my hands, like woodwork or home economics	1	2	3	4	A27.5

Q28. For each of the following 5 subjects state, by circling the appropriate number, whether you think the subject is:
(i)   *Useful* or not,
(ii) *Interesting* or not, and
(iii) *Difficult* or not.

	(i) This subject is Useful		(ii) This subject is Interesting		(iii) This subject is Difficult		
	Yes	No	Yes	No	Yes	No	
Maths	1	2	1	2	1	2	A28.1-3
Technical Drawing	1	2	1	2	1	2	A28.4-6
French	1	2	1	2	1	2	A28.7-9
Physics	1	2	1	2	1	2	A28.10-12
Biology	1	2	1	2	1	2	A28.13-15

Q.29 Over the past <u>two weeks that you have been in school</u>, about how many hours after school in the evening or night have you usually spent on a typical week night (Monday to Friday) on each of the three activities below.

1. How many hours each evening doing homework given?

    _____ hrs per evening   A29.1

2. How many hours each evening doing study other than homework?

    _____ hrs per evening   A29.2

3. How many hours each evening watching TV or other pastimes?

    _____ hrs per evening   A29.3

Q30 For most of your subjects, how is your homework checked? (Tick one box only.)

It is collected and given back with <u>a lot</u> of comments
and/or corrections $\square_1$

It is collected and given back with <u>a little</u> comment
and/or corrections $\square_2$ A30

Pupils check their own homework in class in
discussion with the teacher $\square_3$

It is not usually checked $\square_4$

Q31 (a)   Have you had grinds or private tuition during the <u>last 3 months</u> for any subject you are studying at school?

            Yes $\square_1$ No $\square_2$ A31.1

Q31 (b) If YES: Approximately how many hours or classes of private tuition have you received in this period? _____   A31.2

Q32 (a) Do you ever receive help with homework/study from your parents or brother/sister?

Yes, often $\square_1$ Yes, sometimes $\square_2$ Never $\square_3$ →Go to Q.33   A32.1

Q32 (b) If YES, what was the <u>main</u> subject in which you received help? _____

                                                      A32.2

Q33. In the last two weeks how often have you done any of the following jobs at home? (If you are a boarder think about the work you do at home during the holidays.) Circle one number on each line.

		Never	once or twice	3 to 5 times	6 times or more	
1.	Made your bed	1	2	3	4	A33.1
2.	Swept the floor or used the vacuum cleaner	1	2	3	4	A33.2
3.	Set the table for meals	1	2	3	4	A33.3
4.	Did the dishes or cleaned up after meals	1	2	3	4	A33.4
5.	Prepared the dinner or tea	1	2	3	4	A33.5
6.	Did any ironing	1	2	3	4	A33.6
7.	Put out the rubbish or cleaned up the yard	1	2	3	4	A33.7

Q34. Answer section (a) below <u>if you are in a single-sex school</u>. If you are in a <u>mixed-sex school then go to and answer section (b)</u>.

(a) For Pupils in Single-Sex Schools Only (others go to Q.34(b))

In the last two weeks that you have spent <u>in school</u> how often, if at all, have the following things happened?

	Never	1 or 2 times	3+ times	
Have you been jeered at or mocked by other pupils?	1	2	3	A34.1
Have you experienced being bullied or physically pushed around by other pupils?	1	2	3	A34.2
Have you been upset by things said behind your back by other pupils?	1	2	3	A34.3
Have you been pestered or bullied on the way to or from school?	1	2	3	A34.4

Go to Q. 35.

(b)   For Pupils in Mixed-Sex Schools Only

In the last two weeks that you have spent <u>in school</u> how often, if at all, have the following things happened? (Answer for behaviour by <u>both</u> boys and girls.)

	Never	1 or 2 times	3+ times	
Have you been jeered at or mocked by other pupils?				
(i) by boys	1	2	3	A34.5
(ii) by girls	1	2	3	A34.6
Have you experienced being bullied or physically pushed around by other pupils?				
(i) by boys	1	2	3	A34.7
(ii) by girls	1	2	3	A34.8
Have you been upset by things said behind your back by other pupils?				
(i) by boys	1	2	3	A34.9
(ii) by girls	1	2	3	A34.10
Have you been pestered or bullied on the way to or from school?				
(i) by boys	1	2	3	A34.11
(ii) by girls	1	2	3	A34.12

Q35. How many times in the <u>past two weeks</u> that you have spent in school (not during holidays) have you?

	Never	Once or twice	3 or more times	
Taken part in <u>any</u> sports <u>organised by your school</u> outside class time	1	2	3	A35.1
Taken part in a music group or society or debate/play that was organised <u>by your school</u> outside class time	1	2	3	A35.2
Taken part in <u>any</u> sports that were <u>not</u> organised by the school	1	2	3	A35.3
Been to a disco, a concert or the cinema	1	2	3	A35.4
Taken alcohol with friends	1	2	3	A35.5
Been out on a date	1	2	3	A35.6

Q36. Do you have a regular girlfriend/boyfriend?   Yes ☐₁ No ☐₂ | A36

Q37. How strongly would you agree or disagree with each of the following statements?

	Strongly Agree	Agree	Disagree	Strongly Disagree	
I have little control over the things that happen to me	1	2	3	4	A37.1
Many pupils in my class care too much about how they look and dress	1	2	3	4	A37.2
There is a lot I can do to change my life if I really want to	1	2	3	4	A37.3
I don't like competing at schoolwork with others in my class	1	2	3	4	A37.4
I often feel helpless in trying to deal with the problems I have	1	2	3	4	A37.5
I would personally prefer to be in a single-sex school rather than a mixed-sex school	1	2	3	4	A37.6

Q38. In general, to what extent do you feel that your second-level education has benefited you in the following ways?

	Yes a lot	Yes some	No help	
In increasing your self-confidence	1	2	3	A38.1
In helping you develop into a well-balanced person	1	2	3	A38.2
In building good relations with friends of the opposite sex	1	2	3	A38.3
In being able to talk and communicate well with others	1	2	3	A38.4
In helping you to make new friends	1	2	3	A38.5

Q39. Supposing that you were much older and were working and
married and you had children. There are a number of possible
arrangements that you and your spouse could make about working and minding the children. Read all five possible arrangements below. Then indicated by ticking one box in each <u>row</u>

(i) what would you be most likely to do? and
(ii) what do you think your mother would expect?

	1	2	3	4	5
	You would give up your job to mind your children on a full-time basis	You would work part-time and mind the children. Your spouse would work full-time	You would both work full-time and would pay some-one else to mind the children	You would work full-time. Your spouse would work part-time and mind the children	You would work full-time. Your spouse would mind the children full-time

	1	2	3	4	5	
(i) What would you be most likely to do?	☐₁	☐₂	☐₃	☐₄	☐₅	A39.1
(ii) What do you think your mother would expect?	☐₁	☐₂	☐₃	☐₄	☐₅	A39.2

Q40. Now we'd like to ask you about <u>how you feel about your school</u>.
For each pair of adjectives tick one space from the seven
spaces to show where you would place your school in relation
to the two adjectives. An example is given in the first line.

<u>My school is ...</u>

e.g. Big	☐☐☐☐☐☐☐	Small	
1. Strict	☐☐☐☐☐☐☐	Easy going	A40.1
2. Organised	☐☐☐☐☐☐☐	Disorganised	A40.2
3. Friendly	☐☐☐☐☐☐☐	Unfriendly	A40.3

Q41. <u>How do you feel about yourself</u> in relation to the following pairs of adjectives? For each pair of adjectives tick one space from the seven spaces to show where you would place yourself in relation to the two adjectives. For example, if you feel you are very tall tick the box nearest to tall or if not tick where you feel you are on the scale from tall to small.

<u>I am</u>

1. Tall	[ ]	Small	A41.1
2. Carefree	[ ]	Worried	A41.2
3. Plain	[ ]	Good-looking	A41.3
4. Thin	[ ]	Fat	A41.4
5. Awkward	[ ]	Graceful	A41.5
6. Attractive	[ ]	Unattractive	A41.6

Q42. Here are some statements regarding the way you have been feeling over the last few weeks. For each statement circle the number next to the answer which best suits or describes the way you have been feeling recently.

1. Been able to concentrate on whatever you're doing?

Better than usual.........1   Same as usual.........2   Less than usual.........3   Much less than usual.........4   A12.1

2. Felt that you were playing a useful part in things?

More than usual.........1   Same as usual.........2   Less than usual.........3   Much less than usual.........4   A42.2

3. Felt capable of making decisions about things?

More than usual.........1   Same as usual.........2   Less than usual.........3   Much less than usual.........4   A42.3

4. Lost much sleep over worry?

Not at all.........1   No more than usual...2   Rather more than usual......3   Much more than usual.........4   A42.4

5. Felt constantly under strain?

Not at all.........1   No more than usual...2   Rather more than usual......3   Much more than usual.........4   A42.5

6. Been losing confidence in yourself?

Not at all.........1   No more than usual...2   Rather more than usual......3   Much more than usual.........4   A42.6

We would like to ask you some questions about your
family. We need answers to these questions for classifi-
cation purposes only. As we have said all of your answers
are completely confidential and will never be published
in any circumstances.

Q43. What are the *highest* levels of education (a) your father and (b)
your mother completed? (If you are unsure, make your best
guess.)

	Father (a)	Mother (b)	
Primary School	$\square_1$	$\square_1$	
Group or Intermediate Cert.	$\square_2$	$\square_2$	
Leaving Cert.	$\square_3$	$\square_3$	
Third-Level Diploma or Cert. (e.g. Nursing, RTC)	$\square_4$	$\square_4$	
University Degree	$\square_5$	$\square_5$	A43.1
Parent not present	$\square_6$	$\square_6$	A43.2

Q44. What is the employment situation of (a) your father and (b)
your mother?

	Father (a)	Mother (b)	
At work (full-time)	$\square_1$	$\square_1$	A44.1
At work (part-time)	$\square_2$	$\square_2$	A44.2
Unemployed	$\square_3$	$\square_3$	
Retired	$\square_4$	$\square_4$	
Full-time in home duties	$\square_5$	$\square_5$	
Parent not present	$\square_6$	$\square_6$	

Q45 (a) What is the name or title of your father's job? (If he is no
longer at work, what did he do when he had a job?)

_____   A45.1

Q45 (b) What exactly does/did he do at work? _____

_____

Q46 (a) What is the name or title of your mother's job? (If she is no
longer at work, what did she do when she had a job?)

_____ | A46.1

Q46 (b) What exactly does/did she do at work? _____

_____

Q47.   If your parents are farmers, how many acres of land do | A47
        they farm? _____ (approx.)

Q48 (a) In the evenings after school or at weekends etc. Do you | A48.1
        work in a paid part-time job?

                    Yes ☐₁   No ☐₂ | A48.2

Q48 (b) If YES: On average how many hours a week do you work?

                    ☐☐ hours per week

Thank you very much for your co-operation. We would like to stress,
once again, that the information which you have given us is completely confidential and will be used for research purposes only.
Your answers will only be seen by the researcher and will not be
revealed to anyone else. All of your answers will be coded, and be
added together to get an overall or average view of what Leaving
Cert. students think, as well as what courses and subjects they are
taking, and what they intend to do.

Finally, if there is time, and there is anything else you would like to
tell us about your education, please use the remaining space to tell
us what you think.

APPENDIX 2.2: INSTRUCTIONS FOR THE SAMPLING OF CLASSES WITHIN SCHOOLS

(a) Mixed-Ability Classes

Where all classes in the relevant year are mixed-ability, arrange the classes in order of their number or name. Then take every second class starting from both the top and the bottom of the list of classes. Where there is an odd number of classes, add the additional class "upwards"; where there is an even number of classes, add the additional class "downwards". Where this leaves a "gap" of two classes or more, use the latter rule to close the gap. The following figure summarises the rules used according to the number of classes within the relevant year group.

Figure A2.1: Class Sampling Scheme and Number of Classes in Years

Ranked ID of Class	Number of Classes in Years in School													
	1	2	3	4	5	6	7	8	9	10	11	12	13	14
1	X	X	X	X	X	X	X	X	X	X	X	X	X	X
2		X												
3			X		X	X		X	X	X	X	X	X	X
4				X			X							
5					X							X	X	X
6						X		X	X	X	X			
7							X							
8								X		X		X	X	X
9									X		X			
10										X		X		X
11											X		X	
12												X		X
13													X	
14														X

Note: X Indicates sampled class.

(b) Mostly Mixed-Ability Classes, but with Bottom or Top Class of Lower/Higher Ability

Arrange classes as above, ranked by number/name for mixed-ability classes, and with bottom or top class(es) in bottom and top position. If only 1/2 classes in bottom or top "band", then use the sampling table for mixed-ability classes, making sure to sample at least one of the top of bottom band. Where these rules result in oversampling of classes, reduce the relevant number among the mixed-ability classes.

(c) Broad Banding, with Relatively Equal Number of Classes in Each Band

Generally treat each band as if it were a separate school, and sample as per mixed-ability table. If this results in oversampling, distribute the allowed number of sampled classes, with the higher proportion in those bands with a greater number of classes.

(d) Broad Banding with Unequal Number of Classes in Each Band

Arrange classes, ranking bands by their ability, and classes within bands by their number/name. As far as possible, use the same rule for sampling within bands as for mixed-ability classes. If this leads to oversampling, put the greater number of sampled classes in the band with the larger number of classes.

(e) Fully Streamed Classes

Rank classes from top to bottom in terms of ability. Then select as for mixed-ability classes, selecting top and bottom classes and taking every second one from the top and bottom.

APPENDIX 2.3: STATISTICAL MODELLING TECHNIQUES

In *multiple regression* procedures, the dependent variable is seen as a linear function of more than one independent variable. A multiple regression model of educational performance can be presented as follows:

$$Y_i = \beta_0 + \beta_1 X_1 + \beta_2 X_2 + \varepsilon_i$$

where Y_i is the grade point average (GPA) of pupil i;

β_0 is the intercept, the average value of GPA when each independent variable equals zero;

β_1 represents the average change in GPA with a unit change in variable X_1, which is ability score on entry to second-level schooling;

β_2 represents the difference in mean GPA between girls and boys (where X_2 is a dummy variable with 1 = girls);

ε_i is the differential in grade point average (GPA) for pupil i.

Multiple regression techniques make a number of assumptions:

• The expected mean value of the error term (ε_i) is 0.

• The variance of the error term is constant for all values of X (homoscedasticity).

• The error terms are uncorrelated (no autocorrelation); the independent variable is uncorrelated with the error term.

• The error term is normally distributed.

Social systems have a hierarchical organisation: for example, people (level 1) live within households (level 2) within local-authority areas (level 3), and pupils (level 1) learn within schools (level 2). The existence of hierarchically organised data means that we need to take this hierarchy into account when analysing data (Goldstein, 1995). Regression techniques assume that there is no autocorrelation within the data — that is, that pupils represent independent observations, rather than being clustered within schools. However, members of groups (such as schools) are not "independent" in this way. Groups rarely form at random and, once formed, the members of a group interact with each other to create even greater homogeneity (Jones, 1992). Treating pupils within a school as independent observations results in mis-estimated precision, incorrect standard errors, confidence limits and tests (Jones, 1991). Consequently, using regression techniques for research on schools increases the risks of finding differences and relationships where none exist.

In contrast to regression procedures, *multi-level modelling* techniques take the clustering of individuals within groups into account, and automatically adjust standard errors for auto-correlation in the sample. Multi-level modelling also has sub-stantive benefits for educational research. Firstly, this approach better reflects the complexity of the social world since it recog-nises the context within which human behaviour occurs. Secondly, it allows us to separate contextual effects from composition effects, and thus to assess school-level differences controlling for differences in pupil intake.

Multi-level models fall into two categories: random intercepts models and fully random models. The random intercepts model allows for a different average grade score between schools. It can be specified as follows:

$$Y_{ij} = \beta_0 + \beta_1 x_{1ij} + (\mu_j + \varepsilon_{ij})$$

where Y_{ij} is the grade point average (GPA) of pupil i in school j;
        x_1 is the independent variable, ability-test score on entry, centred on its mean value;
        β_0 is the fixed intercept term, representing the average GPA for an individual of average prior ability;
        β_1 is the fixed slope term between prior ability and GPA — that is, the change in GPA associated with a unit change in prior ability;
        μ_j is the differential (or unexplained variance) in GPA for school j;
        ε_{ij} is the differential in grade point average (GPA) for pupil i in school j.

The random intercepts model can be extended to a fully random model — that is, to allow the relationship between prior ability and grade point average to vary between schools.

APPENDIX 2.4: AN ASSESSMENT OF ACADEMIC ABILITY MEASURES FOR JUNIOR CERT. PUPILS

First-year AH2 test scores were available for 998 pupils within 21 schools in the sample. These scores were graded (A to E) and numeric scores in third year were converted into grades to ensure comparability between the two years.[1] Eleven of the schools are coed (three secondary, four community/comprehensive, four vocational) and ten single-sex (seven girls', three boys'). These schools are somewhat different from the total sample of schools, especially in relation to the high prevalence of streaming/banding. Performance in the first-year AH2 test was found to be highly correlated with both third-year test scores ($r = .72$)[2] and Junior Cert. exam performance ($r = .65$). As might be expected, ability in third year was more highly correlated than first-year scores with Junior Cert. exam performance ($r = .79$).

Two sets of analyses were carried out for this subsample of schools in order to assess whether using third-year ability scores produced substantially different results from analyses relying on first-year (entry) ability scores. The first set of models estimates the impact of background and schooling factors, controlling for the effects of ability-test scores on entry to second-level schooling (see Table A2.1). This analysis was repeated using third-year ability scores instead of entry scores (see Table A2.2).

The two sets of analyses are broadly similar. However, some differences are apparent: firstly, the impact of social class and parental unemployment appears somewhat stronger; secondly, the impact of being older than the average is stronger when first-year scores are used. The impact of coeducation on Junior Cert. exam performance is not significant for either model. In the final model (Model 6), the coeducation term is slightly larger when third-year scores are used, although the coed-gender interaction term does not vary substantially between the two sets of analyses.

---

[1] Information on full numeric scores is available for 485 pupils in nine schools. However, the number of schools is too small to be analysed using multi-level modelling.

[2] This correlation is very high given that AH2 tests are slightly different from DATS tests, and that scores have been recoded into grades — one would expect that DATS first- and third-year scores would be more highly correlated.

Table A2.1: Use of First-Year AH2 Scores in Model of GPA for Junior Cert Pupils (N = 998; 21 Schools)

Fixed Effects	Model 1	Model 2	Model 3	Model 4	Model 5	Model 6
Intercept	6.620*	6.950*	4.497*	4.623*	4.688*	5.726*
Family Background Variables:						
Gender (Girls = 1)		.684*	.529*	.612	.531	.662
Social Class		-.245*	-.149*	-.148*	-.145*	-.081*
Father Unemployed		-.748*	-.486*	-.484*	-.479*	-.364*
Mother Unemployed		-.292	-.169*	-.169	-.166	-.126
Mother's Education		.129*	.070	.068	.065	.032
Mother in Professional Job		.144	-.042	-.042	-.037	.091
No. of Siblings		-.057*	-.038	-.038	-.037	-.018
Birth Order		-.346*	-.132	-.132	-.137	-.133
Farm Daughter		.441	.226	.222	.211	.434
West of Ireland		.658	-.082	-.146	-.184	.230
Under 14½ Years		.128	-.206	-.207	-.214	-.203
14½–15 Years		.095	.014	.016	.013	-.014
15½–16 Years		-.504*	-.255*	-.256*	-.251*	-.138
16 Years and Over		-1.511*	-.880*	-.877*	-.875*	-.457*
Ability (First Year)			1.00*	0.99*	0.99*	.059*
School Type:						
Coed School				-.261	-.075	.093
Coed-Gender Interaction				-.105	-.023	-.295
Selectivity:						
Parental Choice					.034	.040
School Cream-off					-.280	-.282
School Process / Organisation:						
Streaming						.323
Class Position:						
Top Class						.273
Middle Class						-.888
Bottom/Remedial Class						-1.787*
Average Social Class						-.265
Homework Rules						.424
Random Effects:						
Variance at School Level	0.705*	0.248*	0.351*	0.324*	0.280*	0.210*
Variance at Pupil Level	2.938*	2.398*	1.556*	1.555*	1.554*	1.251*
% Variance Explained:						
School Level	—	64.9	50.2	54.0	60.3	70.2
Pupil Level	—	18.4	47.0	47.1	47.1	57.4
Proportion of Remaining Variance at:						
School Level	19.4	9.4	18.4	17.3	15.3	14.4
Pupil Level	80.6	90.6	81.6	82.7	84.7	85.6
Deviance	3960.0	3742.8	3324.2	3322.7	3319.2	3101.2
Reduction in Deviance	—	<.001	<.001	n.s.	n.s.	<.001

* Indicates significance at the <.05 level.

Table A2.2: Use of Third-Year DATS Scores in Model of GPA for Junior Cert Pupils (N = 998; 21 Schools)

Fixed Effects	Model 1	Model 2	Model 3	Model 4	Model 5	Model 6
Intercept	6.620*	6.950*	4.075*	3.993*	3.871*	4.749*
Family Background Variables:						
Gender (Girls = 1)		.684*	.264*	.488	.437	.580
Social Class		-.245*	-.078*	-.078*	-.075*	-.046
Father Unemployed		-.748*	-.270*	-.268*	-.264*	-.230*
Mother Unemployed		-.292	-.151	-.150	-.147	-.117
Mother's Education		.129*	.029	.028	.025	.009
Mother in Professional Job		.144	.043	.042	.049	.118
No. of Siblings		-.057*	-.015	-.015	-.014	-.006
Birth Order		-.346*	-.075	-.074	-.080	-.087
Farm Daughter		.441	.329	.326	.304	.413*
West of Ireland		.658	.175	.191	.180	.386
Under 14½ Years		.128	.020	.020	.012	-.056
14½–15 Years		.095	-.057	-.055	-.056	-.064
15½–16 Years		-.504*	-.083	-.083	-.077	-.036
16 Years and Over		-1.511*	-.493*	-.492*	-.492*	-.255
Ability (Third Year)			1.05*	1.05*	1.05*	0.79*
School Type:						
Coed School				.080	.190	.259
Coed-Gender Interaction				-.142	-.090	-.297
Selectivity:						
Parental Choice					.057	.056*
School Cream-off					-.157	-.164
School Process / Organisation:						
Streaming						.270
Class Position:						
Top Class						.089
Middle Class						-.580*
Bottom/Remedial Class						-1.395*
Average Social Class						-.234
Homework Rules						.387
Random Effects:						
Variance at School Level	0.705*	0.248*	0.130*	0.128*	0.114*	0.123*
Variance at Pupil Level	2.938*	2.938*	1.173*	1.173*	1.169*	1.020*
% Variance Explained:						
School Level	—	64.9	81.5	81.8	83.8	82.5
Pupil Level	—	18.4	60.1	60.1	60.2	65.3
Proportion of Remaining Variance at:						
School Level	19.4	9.4	10.0	9.9	8.9	10.8
Pupil Level	80.6	90.6	90.0	90.1	91.1	89.2
Deviance	3960.0	3742.8	3029.5	3029.2	3023.7	2891.8
Reduction in Deviance	—	<.001	<.001	n.s.	n.s.	<.001

* Indicates significance at the <.05 level.

In order to investigate the potential impact of school type on ability-test performance, a multi-level model was developed using third-year ability scores as the dependent variable, and entry scores as one of the explanatory variables (see Table A2.3). Controlling for ability at entry, social class and father's unemployment have a direct effect on ability scores in third year. A similar pattern is evident for those who are older than the average. Being in the bottom or remedial class of a streamed/banded school has a negative impact on third-year ability scores, even when first-year scores are controlled for. The coefficients for coeducation indicate that there is some falling off in ability scores within coed schools, although this effect is not statistically significant.

Table A2.3: Prediction of Third-Year Ability Scores among Junior Cert Pupils (N = 998; 21 Schools)

Fixed Effects	Model 1	Model 2	Model 3	Model 4	Model 5	Model 6
Intercept	2.453*	2.737*	0.852*	1.087*	1.229*	1.981*
Family Background Variables:						
Gender (Girls = 1)		.304*	.185*	.112	.085	.067
Social Class		-.159*	-.084*	-.083*	-.082*	-.047*
Father Unemployed		-.455*	-.260*	-.261*	-.255*	-.192*
Mother Unemployed		-.135	-.039	-.040	-.039	-.018
Mother's Education		.095*	.052*	.050	.050	.031
Mother in Professional Job		.097	-.046	-.045	-.047	.011
No. of Siblings		-.040*	-.025	-.024	-.024	-.015
Birth Order		-.258*	-.091	-.092	-.093	-.088
Farm Daughter		.108	-.053	-.049	-.045	.097
West of Ireland		.458*	-.104	-.191	.216	-.078
Under 14½ Years		.103	-.156	-.159*	-.161	-.151*
14½–15 Years		.144	.084	.083	.080	.068
15½–16 Years		-.400*	-.211*	-.212*	-.210*	-.143*
16 Years and Over		-.967*	-.487*	-.482*	-.479*	-.269*
Ability (First Year)			.766*	.766*	.764*	.550*
School Type:						
Coed School				-.363	-.288	-.204
Coed-Gender Interaction				.062	.089	.031
Selectivity:						
Parental Choice					-.014	-.014
School Cream-off					-.118	-.134
School Process / Organisation:						
Streaming						.075
Class Position:						
Top Class						.287
Middle Class						-.497
Bottom/Remedial Class						-.751*
Average Social Class						-.146
Homework Rules						.103
Random Effects:						
Variance at School Level	0.278*	0.102*	0.110*	0.085*	0.078*	0.052*
Variance at Pupil Level	1.336*	1.108*	0.618*	0.618*	0.617*	0.530*
% Variance Explained:						
School Level	—	63.5	60.7	69.5	71.9	81.3
Pupil Level	—	17.1	53.8	53.8	53.8	60.4
Proportion of Remaining Variance at:						
School Level	17.2	8.4	15.1	12.1	11.2	8.9
Pupil Level	82.8	91.6	84.9	87.9	88.8	91.1
Deviance	3170.5	2969.7	2397.9	2393.2	2391.2	2233.9
Reduction in Deviance	—	<.001	<.001	n.s.	n.s.	<.001

* Indicates significance at the <.05 level.

Appendix 3

Table A3.1: Female Enrolment in Coed Schools

	Coed Secondary	Vocational	Comm./ Comp.	Total
No. of Female Students (000)	33.8	41.1	22.0	96.8
Females as Proportion of all Students (%)	46.5	43.6	46.3	45.2
Survey Results				
Females as Proportion (%)	54.2	39.8	48.2	45.8
Standard deviation (schools surveyed)	10.8	10.2	4.1	11.1

Excludes single-sex non-secondary schools.
Sources: Department of Education, Statistical Report 1993/94.
National Survey on Coeducation.

Table A3.2: Change in Aggregate First-Year Enrolments and Full-Time Teacher Numbers, 1989/90–1993/94

	Coed Secondary	Vocational	Comm./ Comp.	Total
*First Year Enrolments**				
Total Enrolled, 1989/90 (000)	42.6	15.8	8.2	66.6
Total Enrolled, 1993/94 (000)	44.3	16.6	10.0	70.9
% Increase (1989–93)	3.9	5.1	21.9	6.4
*Teacher Numbers***				
Total no. 1989/90 (000)	11.6	4.8	2.3	18.7
Total no. 1993/94 (000)	12.5	5.1	2.7	20.4
% Increase since 1989/90	7.6	6.2	18.4	8.6

* Refers to all pupils enrolled in first year, not just new entrants.
** Figures exclude Dept's estimates for full-time equivalents (FTEQ) in respect of part-time teachers. These are not available in respect of secondary teachers in 1989/90. Inclusion of FTEQ data would substantially increase the percentage growth in teacher numbers.
Source: Department of Education, Statistical Reports: 1989/90, 1993/94.

Table A3.3: Restrictions on Entry by Type of School

	Single-Sex	COED			All Types
		Secondary	Vocational	Comm./Comp	
Schools Limiting Entry (%)	34	20	3	29	22
(No.)	(15)	(4)	(1)	(5)	(25)
Total No. of Schools	44	20	33	17	114
Of Those Limiting Entry, Criteria Cited:	*Number of Schools*				
Sibling at School	14	4	1	5	24
Attended Feeder School	9	1	1	4	15
Attended Local Primary School	7	—	1	4	12
Attended Attached School	8	2	—	1	11
Ability/Entrance Exam	4	1	—	1	6

Source: National Survey on Coeducation.

Table A3.4: Preference of Disappointed Parents by School Type Child Attends

School Type Attended	Type of School Parents Would Have Preferred		
	Single-Sex	Coed Secondary/ Community/Comp.	Vocational
Single Sex %	51	40	10
Coed Secondary %	43	30	26
Community/ Comprehensive %	43	50	6
Vocational %	53	34	13
All Schools %	49	38	13
No. Pupils	276	213	74

Source: National Survey on Coeducation.

Table A3.5: Parental Socioeconomic Status and Choice of School (1994 Junior Cert Pupils)

Social Class	Percentage of Pupils Not Attending Nearest Available School	Percentage of Parents who Do Not Obtain Their Choice of School
Upper Middle Class	59	10
Middle Class	46	8
Lower Middle Class	50	10
Upper Working Class/ Skilled Manual	46	10
Working Class/Semi-skilled Manual	52	12
Lower Working Class/ Unskilled Manual	48	13
All Social Classes	49	10
No. of Pupils	2,909	577

Source: National Survey on Coeducation.

Table A3.6: Social Class Composition at Leaving Cert Level by School Type

	Single-Sex	Coed			Total
		Sec'y	Vocational	Comm./Comp.	
	%	%	%	%	%
Upper Middle Class	19	19	7	13	16
Middle Class	28	31	21	26	27
Lower Middle Class	21	21	21	18	21
Upper Working Class/ Skilled Manual	21	17	34	28	23
Working Class/ Semi-skilled and Unskilled Manual	11	13	17	14	13
Total %	100	100	100	100	100
No.	2,245	893	902	628	4,669

Social-class classifications are based on the 1986 Census of Population "social-class" categorisation.

Totals may not sum to 100 per cent because of rounding. Table excludes 144 cases (3 per cent) where parental occupation was not recorded by pupils. It is suspected, based on examination of other variables, that many of these cases would fall into the lower social classes.

Source: National Survey on Coeducation.

Table A3.7: Distribution of Schools by Proportion of Pupil Intake Coming from Backgrounds of Poverty, as Perceived by School Principals

Intake in Poverty	Secondary			Vocational	Comm./ Comp.	All Types
	Girls Only	Boys Only	Coed			
	%	%	%	%	%	%
< 10%	46	56	65	41	56	51
10%–20%	35	33	25	12	6	22
20%–30%	8	6	5	24	17	13
> 30%	12	6	5	24	22	15
Total %	100	100	100	100	100	100
No.	26	18	20	34	18	116

Note: Table shows the distribution of principals in each type of school according to their perception of the degree of poverty among their pupils' families. For example, the first figure in column 2 indicates that 46 per cent of principals in girls' secondary schools felt that less than 10 per cent of their pupils came from backgrounds of poverty.

Source: National Survey on Coeducation.

Table A3.8: Distribution of Schools by Proportion of Pupil Intake Coming from Backgrounds of Unemployment, as Perceived by School Principals

Intake with Parent(s) Unemployed	Secondary			Vocational	Comm./ Comp.	All Types
	Girls Only	Boys Only	Coed			
	%	%	%	%	%	%
< 10%	15	39	45	6	17	22
10%–20%	15	33	15	26	33	24
20%–30%	42	17	15	18	22	23
> 30%	27	11	25	50	28	31
Total %	100	100	100	100	100	100
No.	26	18	20	34	18	116
Estimated % Rate of Un-employment	13	12	11	24	19	16

The unemployment rate is based on Junior Cert pupil responses and is calculated as the number of pupils with at least one unemployed parent as a proportion of the total number of pupils.

Source: National Survey on Coeducation.

Table A3.9: Distribution of Schools by Proportion of Pupil Intake Coming from Backgrounds of Alcoholism, as Perceived by School Principals

Intake with Problems	Secondary Girls Only	Secondary Boys Only	Secondary Coed	Vocational	Comm./ Comp.	All Types
	%	%	%	%	%	%
< 10%	72	94	68	74	88	78
10%–20%	4	6	32	21	6	14
20%–30%	20	—	—	3	—	5
> 30%	4	—	—	3	6	3
Total %	100	100	100	100	100	100
No.	25	17	19	34	17	112

Note: This table aims to illustrate the point made in footnote 13, and does not purport to provide an accurate or reliable indicator of the prevalence of alcoholism which (as stated earlier) is extremely difficult to estimate.

Source: National Survey on Coeducation

Table A3.10: Average Verbal Reasoning Score by Type of School

	Single-Sex Secondary Boys Only	Single-Sex Secondary Girls Only	Coed Secondary	Coed Vocational	Coed Comm./ Comp
Mean Score					
All Pupils*	28.9	28.1	27.5	21.4	23.4
Boys*	28.9	—	28.4	21.4	23.7
Girls*	—	28.1	26.6	21.5	23.0
Less able pupils** as a proportion of total enrolment	12.3	14.4	13.7	28.6	25.5

*   Significant, p<.01.

**   Defined as the proportion of pupils within each school type falling more than one standard deviation below the aggregate mean VR score

Source: National Survey on Coeducation.

Table A3.11: Average Numerical Ability Score by Type of School

	Single-Sex Secondary		Coed		
	Boys Only	Girls Only	Secondary	Vocational	Comm./ Comp
Mean Score					
All Pupils*	23.5	20.6	21.5	16.7	19.9
Boys*	23.5	—	21.9	15.9	21.1
Girls*	—	20.6	21.0	17.9	18.6
Less able pupils** as a proportion of total enrolment	11.6	17.3	15.3	34.4	29.9

*   Significant, $p < .01$

** Defined as the proportion of pupils within each school type falling more than one standard deviation below the aggregate mean NA score

Source: National Survey on Coeducation.

Appendix 4

Table A4.1: Allocation of Pupils to Classes in Year of Entry by School Type

	Girls' Secondary	Boys' Secondary	Coed Secondary	Vocational	Comm./ Comp.	Total
	%	%	%	%	%	%
Mixed Ability	64	53	94	40	33	56
Banding	24	29	—	3	39	18
Streaming	12	18	6	57	28	27
Total %	100	100	100	100	100	100
No.	25	17	18	30	18	108

Table excludes schools with one class only/no base classes.
Source: National Survey on Coeducation.

Table A4.2: Allocation to Classes of Leaving Cert Pupils by School Type

	Girls' Secondary	Boys' Secondary	Coed Secondary	Vocational	Comm./ Comp.	Total
	%	%	%	%	%	%
Mixed Ability	75	64	88	50	40	64
Banding	13	—	6	—	33	10
Streaming	13	36	6	50	27	25
Total %	100	100	100	100	100	100
No.	24	14	16	18	15	87

Table excludes schools with one class only/no base classes. Systems involving gender segregation are included under appropriate headings (for example, within-gender streamed schools under Streaming).
Source: National Survey on Coeducation.

Table A4.3: Gender Bias in Provision of Separate Higher/Ordinary Level Classes in Coed Schools

	Coed Secondary	Vocational	Comm./ Comp.	All Coed Schools
Junior Cert				
% Schools with Female Bias	5	3	6	4
% Schools with Male Bias	0	6	11	6
Leaving Cert				
% Schools with Female Bias	16	3	13	10
% Schools with Male Bias	0	0	0	0
Total No. Coed Schools				
Junior Cert	19	29	15	63
Leaving Cert	20	34	18	72

Source: National Survey on Coeducation.

Table A4.4: Proportion of Schools within Each School Type Limiting Access to Higher Level Courses in Selected Subjects at Leaving Cert Level to Certain Classes

Subject at higher level	Girls' Sec'y	Boys' Sec'y	Coed Sec'y	Vocational	Comm./ Comp.	All Schools	No. of Schools
	%	%	%	%	%	%	
Maths	13	29	20	57	67	34	82
Physics	6	7	7	36	54	21	73
Biology	0	8	0	25	47	14	83
English	13	21	7	40	67	28	82
Irish	8	21	7	37	60	25	84
French	0	7	0	27	60	17	83

Table includes only schools in which there is more than one base class at Leaving Cert. level and in which relevant subjects are taught at higher level.
Source: National Survey on Coeducation.

Table A4.5: Take-up of Selected Subjects for Inter Cert 1980, by Gender

Subject	% Pupils Taking Subject		Ratio	Log of Ratio
	M	F	M - F	
Languages				
French	56	71	.80	- .22
German	3	10	.33	-1.11
Spanish	4	5	.80	- .31
Arts and Humanities				
Art	27	47	.57	- .56
Music A & B	6	22	.28	-1.27
Practical / Technical				
Home Economics	0	70	.01	-4.61
Woodwork	37	0	428.01	6.06
Metalwork	21	0	2,846.89	7.95
Mechanical Drawing	45	0	160.07	5.08
Other				
Higher Maths	31	24	1.27	.24
Science A & E	90	57	1.58	.46
Commerce	49	66	.73	- .31

Source: Hannan, Breen et al. (1983), p. 116, slightly amended to ensure
consistency with 1993 data as follows:
Science (1993) = Science A & E (1980); Music (1993) = Music A & B
(1980).

Table A4.6: Take-up of Selected Subjects for Leaving Cert 1980, by Gender

Subject	% Pupils Taking Subject		Ratio	Log of Ratio
	M	F	M - F	
Languages				
French	53	69	.76	- .27
German	2	6	.40	- .92
Spanish	3	4	.64	- .45
Arts and Humanities				
History	38	34	1.11	.10
Geography	53	43	1.21	.19
Art	12	21	.58	- .54
Music (A & B)	1	4	.19	-1.64
Practical / Technical				
Home Econ. (Gen)	0	22	.01	-4.61
Building Construction	10	0	982.97	6.89
Engineering	9	0	1,824.21	7.51
Technical Drawing	18	0	219.74	5.39
Sciences				
Higher Maths	15	4	3.78	1.33
Applied Maths	4	0	29.30	3.38
Physics	28	3	8.26	2.11
Chemistry	28	10	2.84	1.04
Biology	40	62	.65	- .43
Home Econ. (S&S)	4	37	.12	-2.12
Business				
Accounting	24	23	1.03	.03
Business Org.	26	30	.87	- .14
Economics	30	15	1.98	.68

Source: Hannan, Breen et al. (1983), p. 116. Figures for Music slightly amended.

Appendix 5

Table A5.1 : Disaggregation of the Effects of Coeducation on Junior Cert Performance by School Type (as in Model 6, Tables 6.2, 6.4 and 6.5)

Type of School	Total	Girls	Boys
Coed Secondary	-.033	-.205	-.038
Coed Secondary–Gender Interaction	-.186		
Vocational	.312*	-.070	.402*
Vocational–Gender Interaction	-.350*		
Community/Comprehensive	.183	.004	.219
Community–Gender Interaction	-.219		

* Indicates significance at the <.05 level.

Table A5.2: Multi-level Models of Grade Point Average for Junior Cert Secondary School Pupils (N = 2,849)

Fixed Effects	Model 1	Model 2	Model 3	Model 4	Model 5	Model 6
Intercept	6.762*	6.998*	6.895*	6.910*	6.761*	6.518*
Family Background Variables:						
Gender (Girls=1)		.433*	.428*	.456*	.497*	.710*
Social Class		-.224*	-.221*	-.222*	-.155*	-.086*
Father Unemployed		-.485*	-.481*	-.482*	-.429*	-.193*
Mother Unemployed		-.339*	-.336*	-.335*	-.214	-.081
Mother's Education		.110*	.106*	.107*	.046	.009
Mother in Professional Job		.159	.167*	.166*	.091	.002
No. of Siblings		-.047*	-.047*	-.047*	-.020	-.018
Birth Order		-.206*	-.210*	-.212*	-.164	-.016
Farm Daughter		.236	.234	.237	.203	.195*
West of Ireland		.299*	.294*	.312*	.370*	.241*
Under 14½ Years		.080	.078	.078	.024	.006
14½–15 Years		.128	.129	.128	.096	.045
15½–16 Years		-.343*	-.325*	-.326*	-.154*	-.018
16 Years and Over		-1.574*	-1.552*	-1.555*	-1.163*	-.596*
Selectivity:						
Parental Choice			.062*	.062*	.046*	.027
School Cream-off			-.144*	-.131	-.077	.022
School Type:						
Coed School				-.125	-.167	-.068
Coed-Gender Interaction				-.053	-.173	-.177
School Process / Organisation:						
Streaming					-.001	-.043
Class position:						
Top Class					.634*	.232*
Middle Class					-.457*	-.152
Bottom/Remedial Class					-1.713*	-.527*
Average Social Class					-.383*	-.189*
Homework Rules					.223	.113
VRNA						.162*
VRNA Squared						-.001*
Random Effects:						
Variance at School Level	0.369*	0.154*	0.141*	0.135*	0.156*	0.073*
Variance at Pupil Level	2.495*	2.142*	2.136*	2.136*	1.593*	0.914*
% Variance Explained:						
School Level	—	58.3	61.9	63.5	57.7	80.2
Pupil Level	—	14.1	14.4	14.4	36.2	63.4
Proportion of Remaining Variance at:						
School Level	12.9	6.7	6.2	5.9	8.9	7.4
Pupil Level	87.1	93.3	93.8	94.1	91.1	92.6
Deviance	10816.5	10345.4	10332.7	10331.0	9516.2	7922.8
Reduction in Deviance	—	<.001	<.01	n.s.	<.001	<.001

* Indicates significance at the <.05 level.

Table A5.3: Variance by Gender in Junior Cert Exam Performance (as in Model 6, Tables 6.2, 6.7 and 6.8)

Gender	Total	English	Maths
Girls	0.871*	1.766*	2.224*
Boys	1.024	2.243	2.607

* Indicates significance at the <.05 level.

Source: Model 6 (in Tables 6.2, 6.7 and 6.8) is elaborated to allow gender to be random at level 1; the coefficients allow for a comparison of the extent to which girls' and boys' GPAs vary from that predicted by the average line for their school.

Table A5.4: OLS Regression Model of Junior Cert Exam Performance for Girls and Boys

Explanatory Variables	Girls	Boys
Intercept	2.356*	2.242*
Family Background Variables:		
Social Class	-.092*	-.041*
Father Unemployed	-.368*	-.020
Mother Unemployed	.026	-.210*
Mother's Education	.005	.023
Mother in Professional Job	-.045	.043
No. of Siblings	-.030*	-.014
Birth Order	-.026	-.103
Farm Daughter	.229*	.128
West of Ireland	.066	.311*
Under 14½ Years	-.012	-.026
14½–15 Years	.037	-.009
15½–16 Years	-.010	-.137
16 and Over	-.508*	-.324*
Selectivity:		
Parental Choice	.033*	.036*
School Cream-off	.007	-.035
School Type:		
Coed School	-.095*	.169*
School Process / Organisation:		
Streaming	-.105*	-.084*
Class Position:		
Top Class	.362*	.494*
Middle Class	-.083	.078
Bottom/Remedial Class	-.284*	-.345*
Average Social Class	-.171*	-.244*
Homework Rules	.164*	.156*
Ability (VRNA)	.174*	.140*
Ability Squared	-.001*	-.001*
R^2	.669	.653

* Indicates significance at the <.05 level.

Table A5.5: Multi-level Models of Grade Point Average for Low-Ability Junior Cert Pupils (N = 1,443)

Fixed Effects	Model 1	Model 2	Model 3	Model 4	Model 5	Model 6
Intercept	4.880*	5.090*	5.054*	4.577*	4.754*	4.534*
Family Background Variables:						
Gender (Girls = 1)		.472*	.461*	1.226*	.962*	1.048*
Social Class		-.094*	-.091*	-.097*	-.073*	-.052*
Father Unemployed		-.344*	-.344*	-.346*	-.376*	-.297*
Mother Unemployed		-.104	-.095	-.094	-.064	-.028
Mother's Education		.024	.024	.021	.026	-.009
Mother in Professional Job		.266	.266	.258	.131	.095
No. of Siblings		-.048*	-.047*	-.045*	-.039*	-.030*
Birth Order		-.176	-.186	-.189	-.171	-.110
Farm Daughter		.462*	.464*	.445*	.416*	.367*
West of Ireland		.261	.236	.169	.148	.123
Under 14½ Years		.321*	.317*	.305*	.238*	.187
14½–15 Years		.167	.163	.154	.094	.045
15½–16 Years		-.213*	-.204*	-.213*	-.126	-.048
16 Years and Over		-.632*	-.625*	-.630*	-.575*	-.391*
Selectivity:						
Parental Choice			.045	.047	.054*	.027
School Cream-off			-.094	-.101	.009	.038
School Type:						
Coed School				.596*	.451*	.571*
Coed-Gender Interaction				-.891*	-.761*	-.765*
School Process / Organisation:						
Streaming					-.370*	-.305*
Class Position:						
Top Class					1.285*	.930*
Middle Class					.993*	.684*
Bottom/Remedial Class					-.071	.169
Average Social Class					-.421*	-.348*
Homework Rules					.376*	.236*
VRNA						.052
VRNA Squared						.001
Random Effects:						
Variance at School Level	0.526*	0.325*	0.318*	0.271*	0.215*	0.152*
Variance at Pupil Level	1.871*	1.724*	1.720*	1.715*	1.518*	1.149*
% Variance Explained:						
School Level	—	38.2	39.4	48.4	59.1	71.1
Pupil Level	—	7.9	8.1	8.3	18.9	38.6
Proportion of Remaining Variance at:						
School Level	21.9	15.8	15.6	13.7	12.4	10.0
Pupil Level	78.1	84.2	84.4	86.3	87.6	90.0
Deviance	5155.2	5007.3	5002.6	4987.9	4804.2	12937.8
Reduction in Deviance	—	<.001	n.s.	<.001	<.001	<.001

* Indicates significance at the <.05 level.

Table A5.6: Multi-level Models of Grade Point Average for Middle-Ability Junior Cert Pupils (N = 1,539)

Fixed Effects	Model 1	Model 2	Model 3	Model 4	Model 5	Model 6
Intercept	6.618*	6.627*	6.470*	6.442*	6.224*	6.214*
Family Background Variables:						
Gender (Girls = 1)		.770*	.751*	.808*	.824*	.878*
Social Class		-.137*	-.135*	-.135*	-.104*	-.095*
Father Unemployed		-.109	-.108	-.108	-.064	-.058
Mother Unemployed		-.236	-.227	-.226	-.194	-.121
Mother's Education		.030	.027	.027	.014	.018
Mother in Professional Job		.043	.050	.051	.061	-.004
No. of Siblings		-.031	-.030	-.030	-.025	-.024
Birth Order		-.068	-.070	-.071	-.067	-.081
Farm Daughter		.363*	.364*	.364*	.352*	.251*
West of Ireland		.204	.189	.186	.266*	.260*
Under 14½ Years		-.099	-.109	-.110	-.116	-.145
14½–15 Years		.107	.102	.102	.111	.067
15½–16 Years		-.173	-.161	-.162	-.110	-.135
16 Years and Over		-.892*	-.867*	-.868*	-.726*	-.612*
Selectivity:						
Parental Choice			.073*	.073*	.056*	.044*
School Cream-off			-.099	-.097	.003	.028
School Type:						
Coed School				.032	.041	.076
Coed-Gender Interaction				-.074	-.178	-.213
School Process / Organisation:						
Streaming					-.049	-.041
Class Position:						
Top Class					.491*	.422*
Middle Class					-.084	-.039
Bottom/Remedial Class					-.658*	-.522*
Average Social Class					-.452*	-.391*
Homework Rules					.168	.130
VRNA						.261*
VRNA Squared						-.002
Random Effects:						
Variance at School Level	0.340*	0.159*	0.150*	0.149*	0.153*	0.146*
Variance at Pupil Level	1.383*	1.219*	1.211*	1.211*	1.095*	0.976*
% Variance Explained:						
School Level	—	53.2	56.0	56.1	54.8	57.1
Pupil Level	—	11.9	12.4	12.4	20.8	29.4
Proportion of Remaining Variance at:						
School Level	19.7	11.5	11.0	11.0	12.3	13.0
Pupil Level	80.3	88.5	89.0	89.0	87.7	87.0
Deviance	5018.6	4779.6	4765.8	4765.6	4619.5	4446.6
Reduction in Deviance	—	<.001	<.01	n.s.	<.001	<.001

* Indicates significance at the <.05 level.

Table A5.7: Multi-level Models of Grade Point Average for High-Ability Junior Cert Pupils (N = 1,605)

Fixed Effects	Model 1	Model 2	Model 3	Model 4	Model 5	Model 6
Intercept	7.819*	7.720*	7.690*	7.745*	7.590*	7.533*
Family Background Variables:						
Gender (Girls = 1)		.461*	.453*	.366*	.379*	.411*
Social Class		-.085*	-.082*	-.082*	-.070*	-.056*
Father Unemployed		-.021	-.005	-.006	-.020	.006
Mother Unemployed		-.220*	-.229*	-.230*	-.221*	-.181
Mother's Education		.028	.024	.024	.014	.011
Mother in Professional Job		.018	.024	.024	.009	-.017
No. of Siblings		-.016	-.016	-.016	-.008	-.007
Birth Order		-.031	-.034	-.036	-.054	-.030
Farm Daughter		.076	.077	.075	.059	.021
West of Ireland		.150	.130	.136	.228*	.199*
Under 14½ Years		.058	.060	.058	.058	.072
14½–15 Years		.034	.037	.035	.032	.019
15½–16 Years		-.029	-.016	-.014	-.047	-.030
16 Years and Over		-.131	-.112	-.107	-.081	-.044
Selectivity:						
Parental Choice			.034*	.034*	.025	.026
School Cream-off			-.084	-.080	-.044	-.031
School Type:						
Coed School				-.084	-.064	-.045
Coed-Gender Interaction				.116	.051	.032
School Process / Organisation:						
Streaming					.001	.023
Class Position:						
Top Class					.189	.102
Middle Class					-.858*	-.781*
Bottom/Remedial Class					-.455*	-.381*
Average Social Class					-.120	-.109
Homework Rules					.115	.108
VRNA						.143*
VRNA Squared						-.001*
Random Effects:						
Variance at School Level	0.148*	0.101*	0.098*	0.097*	0.092*	0.096*
Variance at Pupil Level	0.683*	0.643*	0.640*	0.640*	0.600*	0.566*
% Variance Explained:						
School Level	—	31.6	33.6	34.4	37.6	35.0
Pupil Level	—	5.9	6.3	6.3	12.3	17.1
Proportion of Remaining Variance at:						
School Level	17.8	13.6	13.3	13.2	13.3	14.5
Pupil Level	82.2	86.4	86.7	86.8	86.7	85.5
Deviance	4078.0	3959.3	3951.3	3950.4	3845.2	3760.9
Reduction in Deviance	—	<.001	<.05	n.s.	<.001	<.001

* Indicates significance at the <.05 level.

Table A5.8: Disaggregation of the Effects of Coeducation by School Type and Ability Group (as in Model 6, Tables A5.5–A5.8)

Type of School	Low Ability	Middle Ability	High Ability
Coed Secondary	.290	-.170	-.198
Coed Secondary-Gender Interaction	-.566*	-.027	.016
Vocational	.739*	.346*	. 040
Vocational-Gender Interaction	-.756*	-.448*	.051
Community/Comprehensive	.591*	-.063	.186
Community-Gender Interaction	-.913*	.025	.084

* Indicates significance at the <.05 level.

Table A5.9: Random Slopes Model for Junior Cert Pupils

Fixed Effects	Random Slopes Model
Intercept	6.289*
Family Background Variables:	
Gender	.643*
Social Class	-.069*
Father Unemployed	-.096
Mother Unemployed	-.103
Mother's Education	.008
Mother in Professional Job	.022
No. of Siblings	-.019*
Birth Order	-.051
Farm Daughter	.162*
West of Ireland	.212*
Under 14½ Years	.024
14½–15 Years	.043
15½–16 Years	-.065*
16 and Over	-.396*
Selectivity:	
Parental Choice	.031*
School Cream-off	.008
School Type:	
Coed School	.080
Coed-Gender Interaction	-.202
School Process / Organisation:	
Streaming	-.093
Class Position:	
Top Class	.426*
Middle Class	-.083
Bottom/Remedial Class	-.380*
Average Social Class	-.255*
Homework rules	.124
Ability	.149*
Ability Squared	-.001*
Random Effects	
School Level:	
Intercept Variance	.1025*
Variance in Ability Slope	-.0011*
Covariance	.0001*
Pupil Level:	
Intercept Variance	.9058*
Variance in Ability Slope	-.0079*
Covariance	.0000

* Indicates significance at the <.05 level.

Note: At the school level, the "variance in ability slope" term indicates that schools differ significantly in the relationship between current ability measures and JC exam performance. At the pupil level, the "variance in ability slope" term indicates that, within schools, higher-ability pupils are less variable in their exam performance than lower-ability pupils.

Table A5.10: Multi-level Model of English and Maths Performance for Junior Cert Boys and Girls

	English Grade		Maths Grade	
	Girls	Boys	Girls	Boys
Intercept	7.132*	6.646*	6.005*	5.706*
Family Background Variables:				
Social Class	-.078*	-.024	-.119*	-.082*
Father Unemployed	-.190	.032	-.256*	.021
Mother Unemployed	-.177	-.106	-.108	-.469*
Mother's Education	.001	-.001	.099*	.003
Mother in Professional Job	-.058	.279*	-.063	.150
No. of Siblings	-.054*	-.017	-.052*	-.017
Birth Order	.035	.017	.015	-.169
Farm Child	.179	-.145	.255*	.113
West of Ireland	.415*	.031	-.077	.144
Under 14½ Years	-.005	-.267*	.060	.045
14½–15 Years	.107	-.035	.099	.014
15½-16 Years	-.079	-.225*	-.155	-.333*
16 Years and Over	-.724*	-.716*	-.622*	-.460*
Selectivity:				
Parental Choice	.029	-.002	.036	.039
School Cream-off	.014	.007	.138	.051
School Type:				
Coed School	-.078	-.132	-.558*	-.088
School Process / Organisation:				
Streaming	-.026	-.066	-.254*	-.147
Class Position:				
Top Class	.454*	.734*	.606*	.794*
Middle Class	-.223	-.341	.535*	.365
Bottom/Remedial Class	-.767*	-.736*	-.196	-.586*
Average Social Class	-.224	-.485*	-.310*	-.346*
Homework Rules	.016	-.405*	.135	.003
Ability				
Verbal Reasoning Ability (VRA)	.191*	166*	—	—
VRA Squared	-.002*	-.001*	—	—
Numerical Ability	—	—	.274*	.222*
Numerical Ability Squared	—	—	-.002*	-.000
Random Effects:				
Variance at School Level	0.159*	0.270*	0.175*	0.160*
Variance at Pupil Level	1.750*	2.201*	2.204*	2.586*
Variance Explained:				
School Level	73.7	75.1	88.2	90.6
Pupil Level	45.0	46.4	62.2	63.1

* Indicates significance at the <.05 level.

Table A5.11: Disaggregation of English Performance among Coed Schools by School Type (as in Model 6, Tables 6.7 and A5.10)

Type of School	Total	Girls	Boys
Coed Secondary	-.128	-.123	-.119
Coed Secondary-Gender Interaction	-.026		
Vocational	-.321	-.026	-.190
Vocational-Gender Interaction	.242		
Community/Comprehensive	-.171	-.052	-.041
Community-Gender Interaction	.065		

* Indicates significance at the <.05 level.

Table A5.12: Disaggregation of Maths Performance among Coed Schools by School Type (as in Model 6, Tables 6.8 and A5.10)

Type of School	Total	Girls	Boys
Coed Secondary	-.229	-.562*	-.214
Coed Secondary-Gender Interaction	-.335		
Vocational	.028	-.456*	.103
Vocational-Gender Interaction	-.421*		
Community/Comprehensive	-.238	-.698*	-.167
Community-Gender Interaction	-.507*		

* Indicates significance at the <.05 level.

Appendix 6

Table A6.1: Allocation of Points to Leaving Certificate Subject Grades

Grade	Higher Level	Ordinary Level
A1	20	12
A2	18	10
B1	17	9
B2	16	8
B3	15	7
C1	14	6
C2	13	5
C3	12	4
D1	11	3
D2	10	2
D3	9	1
Other	0	0

Note: The scores are based on a modified version of the CAO/CAS "points" system. No bonus points are awarded for higher level Mathematics.

Table A6.2: Allocation of Scores to Junior and Inter Certificate Subjects

Grade	Higher	Ordinary	Foundation	Common
A	10	7	4	8
B	9	6	3	7
C	8	5	2	6
D	7	4	1	5

Note: Adapted from the scoring system used in Breen (1986).

Table A6.3: Disaggregation of the Effect of Coeducation on Leaving Cert Grade Point Average by School Type (as in Model 6, Tables 7.2, 7.4 and 7.5)

	Total	Girls	Boys
Coed Secondary	.216	.407	.119
Coed Secondary-Gender Interaction	.130		
Vocational	.159	-.125	.262
Vocational-Gender Interaction	-.347		
Community/Comprehensive	.124	-.402	.277
Community-Gender Interaction	-.482		

Table A6.4: Multi-level Models of Grade Point Average for Leaving Cert Secondary School Pupils (N = 2,706)

Fixed Effects	Model 1	Model 2	Model 3	Model 4	Model 5	Model 6
Intercept	8.709*	8.488*	8.137*	8.124*	8.271*	8.173*
Family Background Variables:						
Gender (Girls = 1)		1.436*	.569*	.394	.380	.406
Social Class		-.471*	-.120*	-.119*	-.118*	-.103*
Father Unemployed		-.711*	-.050	-.048	-.045	-.070
Mother Unemployed		-.949*	-.340	-.401	-.395	-.368
Mother's Education		.310*	.153*	.153*	.151*	.147*
Mother in Professional Job		.736*	.423*	.420*	.420*	.405*
No. of Siblings		-.025	.048	.047	.048	.046
Birth Order		-.485*	.068	.068	.070	.109
Farm Daughter		.056	-.077	-.096	-.094	-.093
West of Ireland		.328	-.483	-.567	-.626*	-.500
16 Years and Under		.162	-.074	-.073	-.071	-.085
18 Years and Over		-.737*	.021	.019	.014	.039
Educational Background:						
Junior/Inter Cert GPA			1.881*	1.883*	1.879*	1.819*
Inter Cert			2.052*	2.056*	2.054*	1.846*
Repeating Leaving Cert			2.022*	2.014*	2.019*	2.019*
School Type:						
Coed School				.330	.365	.276
Coed-Gender Interaction				.234	.249	.189
Selectivity:						
School Cream-off					-.185	-.106
School Process / Organisation:						
Streaming						.233
Class Position:						
Top Class						-.076
Middle Class						-.821
Bottom/Remedial Class						-1.507*
Average Social Class						-.486*
Random Effects:						
Variance at School Level	2.945*	1.599*	1.119*	1.077*	1.053*	0.911*
Variance at Pupil Level	15.670*	14.470*	6.358*	6.356*	6.356*	6.255*
% Variance Explained:						
School Level	—	45.7	62.0	63.4	64.2	69.1
Pupil Level	—	7.7	59.4	59.4	59.4	60.1
Proportion of Remaining Variance at:						
School Level	15.8	10.0	15.0	14.5	14.2	12.7
Pupil Level	84.2	90.0	85.0	85.5	85.8	87.3
Deviance	15262.4	15016.8	12816.9	12814.3	12812.8	12762.8
Reduction in Deviance	—	<.001	<.001	n.s.	n.s.	<.001

* Indicates significance at the <.05 level.

Table A6.5: Variance by Gender in Leaving Cert Grade Point Average

	Total	English	Maths
Girls	5.66*	11.62*	9.93*
Boys	6.58	12.36	12.76

* Indicates significance at the <.05 level.

Source: Model 6 (in Tables 7.2, 7.7 and 7.8) is elaborated to allow gender to be random at level 1; the coefficients indicate that, within schools, girls' exam performance is significantly less variable than that of boys.

Table A6.6: Multi-level Models of Grade Point Average for Low-Ability Leaving Cert Pupils (N = 1,333)

Fixed Effects	Model 1	Model 2	Model 3	Model 4	Model 5	Model 6
Intercept	4.480*	4.623*	4.361*	4.353*	4.679*	4.650*
Family Background Variables:						
Gender (Girls = 1)		.039	-.066	-.061	-.097	-.126
Social Class		-.129*	-.078	-.078	-.067	-.042
Father Unemployed		-.408	-.302	-.302	-.296	-.219
Mother Unemployed		-.841*	-.729*	-.729*	-.715*	-.723*
Mother's Education		.145*	.149*	.149*	.137*	.107
Mother in Professional Job		.222	.226	.226	.215	.148
No. of Siblings		-.020	-.001	-.001	.002	.008
Birth Order		.236	.160	.160	.186	.188
Farm Daughter		.283	.093	.093	.095	.064
West of Ireland		-.056	-.303	-.303	-.430	-.568
16 Years and Under		-.416*	-.313	-.313	-.341*	-.324
18 Years and Over		.391*	.003	.003	.011	.057
Educational Background:						
Junior/Inter Cert GPA			.447*	.447*	.435*	.417*
Inter Cert			.686*	.687*	.732*	.502
Repeating Leaving Cert			2.749*	2.749*	2.763*	2.769*
School Type:						
Coed School				.012	.210	.383
Coed-Gender Interaction				-.005	.015	-.014
Selectivity:						
School Cream-off					-.407*	-.283*
School Process / Organisation:						
Streaming						.076
Class Position:						
Top Class						-.057
Middle Class						-1.128*
Bottom/Remedial Class						-1.078*
Average Social Class						-.691*
Random Effects:						
Variance at School Level	1.276*	0.874*	0.923*	0.923*	0.740*	0.548*
Variance at Pupil Level	6.072*	5.930*	5.185*	5.185*	5.181*	5.116*
% Variance Explained:						
School Level	—	31.5	27.7	27.7	42.0	57.1
Pupil Level	—	2.3	14.6	14.6	14.7	15.7
Proportion of Remaining Variance at:						
School Level	17.4	12.8	15.1	15.1	12.5	9.7
Pupil Level	82.6	87.2	84.9	84.9	87.5	90.3
Deviance	6318.5	6262.1	6095.9	6095.9	6079.9	6045.6
Reduction in Deviance	—	<.001	<.001	n.s.	<.001	<.001

* Indicates significance at the <.05 level.

Table A6.7: Multi-level Models of Grade Point Average for Middle-Ability Leaving Cert Pupils (N = 1,504)

Fixed Effects	Model 1	Model 2	Model 3	Model 4	Model 5	Model 6
Intercept	7.586*	7.458*	6.950*	6.897*	6.995*	6.960*
Family Background Variables:						
Gender (Girls = 1)		.286	.090	.271	.265	.297
Social Class		-.171*	-.121*	-.120*	-.118*	-.087
Father Unemployed		-.165	.070	.074	.078	.101
Mother Unemployed		-.068	.266	.266	.259	.295
Mother's Education		.048	.038	.037	.035	.006
Mother in Professional Job		.313	.137	.139	.136	.160
No. of Siblings		.027	.048	.048	.050	.053
Birth Order		.258	.447*	.444*	.445*	.442*
Farm Daughter		.203	.509*	.516*	.510*	.492*
West of Ireland		-.316	-.320	-.327	-.373	-.396
16 Years and Under		-.038	.059	.060	.064	.080
18 Years and Over		.772*	.099	.099	.093	.084
Educational Background:						
Junior/Inter Cert GPA			2.242*	2.240*	2.237*	2.182*
Inter Cert			3.189*	3.168*	3.169*	2.885*
Repeating Leaving Cert			1.221*	1.234*	1.249*	1.397*
School Type:						
Coed School				.038	.113	.252
Coed-Gender Interaction				-.228	-.231	-.304
Selectivity:						
School Cream-off					-.138	.007
School Process / Organisation:						
Streaming						-.046
Class Position:						
Top Class						-.123
Middle Class						-.326
Bottom/Remedial Class						-.655
Average Social Class						-.761*
Random Effects:						
Variance at School Level	2.008*	1.549*	0.868*	0.863*	0.854*	0.681*
Variance at Pupil Level	6.554*	6.458*	4.824*	4.824*	4.820*	4.798*
% Variance Explained:						
School Level	—	22.9	56.8	57.0	57.5	66.1
Pupil Level	—	1.5	26.4	26.4	26.5	26.8
Proportion of Remaining Variance at:						
School Level	23.5	19.3	15.2	15.2	15.1	12.4
Pupil Level	76.5	80.7	84.8	84.8	84.9	87.6
Deviance	7266.6	7224.3	6763.7	6763.2	6761.4	6738.6
Reduction in Deviance	—	<.001	<.001	n.s.	n.s.	<.001

* Indicates significance at the <.05 level.

Table A6.8: Multi-level Models of Grade Point Average for High-Ability Leaving Cert Pupils (N = 1,597)

Fixed Effects	Model 1	Model 2	Model 3	Model 4	Model 5	Model 6
Intercept	12.150*	12.020*	11.630*	11.460*	11.520*	11.630*
Family Background Variables:						
Gender (Girls = 1)		.683*	.381*	.642*	.653*	.651*
Social Class		-.198*	.017	.017	.019	.026
Father Unemployed		-.465	-.100	-.095	-.100	-.079
Mother Unemployed		-.204	-.013	-.019	-.006	-.013
Mother's Education		.271*	.158*	.157*	.154*	.151*
Mother in Professional Job		.252	-.098	-.098	-.097	-.111
No. of Siblings		-.083*	-.031	-.031	-.030	-.031
Birth Order		-.184	.052	.051	.051	.055
Farm Daughter		-.245	.140	.154	.163	.150
West of Ireland		-.172	-.004	-.005	-.027	-.053
16 Years and Under		.025	.110	.116	.121	.137
18 Years and Over		.115	.011	.015	.001	-.030
Educational Background:						
Junior/Inter Cert GPA			3.747*	3.754*	3.753*	3.739*
Inter Cert			5.519*	5.519*	5.514*	5.349*
Repeating Leaving Cert			1.291*	1.303*	1.321*	1.334*
School Type:						
Coed School				.225	.283	.301
Coed-Gender Interaction				-.340	-.354	-.361
Selectivity:						
School Cream-off					-.118	-.101
School Process / Organisation:						
Streaming						-.044
Class Position:						
Top Class						-.124
Middle Class						-.523
Bottom/Remedial Class						-.395
Average Social Class						-.213
Random Effects:						
Variance at School Level	1.450*	1.041*	0.392*	0.385*	0.373*	0.372*
Variance at Pupil Level	6.795*	6.469*	3.089*	3.089*	3.089*	3.075*
% Variance Explained:						
School Level	—	28.2	73.0	73.5	74.3	74.4
Pupil Level	—	4.8	54.5	54.5	54.5	54.7
Proportion of Remaining Variance at:						
School Level	17.6	13.9	11.3	11.1	10.8	10.8
Pupil Level	82.4	86.1	88.7	88.9	89.2	89.2
Deviance	7258.5	7166.5	6043.9	6042.5	6040.6	6034.1
Reduction in Deviance	—	<.001	<.001	n.s.	n.s.	n.s.

* Indicates significance at the <.05 level.

Table A6.9: Disaggregation of the Effects of Coeducation on Leaving Cert Grade Point Average by Ability and School Type (as in Model 6, Tables A6.6–A6.8)

School Type	Low Ability	Middle Ability	High Ability
Coed Secondary	.346	.344	.211
Coed Secondary-Gender Interaction	.409	-.177	-.420
Vocational	.372	.283	.447
Vocational-Gender Interaction	-.083	-.060	-.373
Community/Comprehensive	.371	.101	.310
Community-Gender Interaction	-.315	-.666	-.277

Table A6.10: Disaggregation of the Effects of Coeducation on Leaving Cert English Performance by School Type (as in Model 6, Tables 7.7 and A6.11)

School Type	Total	Girls	Boys
Coed Secondary	-.361	.172	-.398
Coed Secondary-Gender Interaction	.589		
Vocational	-.626	-.613	-.525
Vocational-Gender Interaction	-.067		
Community/Comprehensive	.167	.013	.272
Community-Gender Interaction	-.168		

Table A6.11: Disaggregation of the Effects of Coeducation on Leaving Cert Maths Performance by School Type (as in Model 6, Tables 7.8 and A6.12)

School Type	Total	Girls	Boys
Coed Secondary	-.358	-.205	-.418
Coed Secondary-Gender Interaction	.124		
Vocational	-.702	-.609	-.420
Vocational-Gender Interaction	.274		
Community/Comprehensive	-.713	-.740*	-.563
Community-Gender Interaction	-.064		

* Indicates significance at the <.05 level.

Table A6.12: Multi-level Model of English and Maths Performance for Leaving Cert Boys and Girls

	English Grade		Maths Grade	
	Girls	Boys	Girls	Boys
Intercept	9.954*	8.035*	7.734*	7.471*
Family Background Variables:				
Social Class	-.300*	-.185*	-.186*	-.049
Father Unemployed	-.492*	.560	.058	.431
Mother Unemployed	.078	-.565	.262	-.197
Mother's Education	.182*	.073	.214*	.034
Mother in Professional Job	.526*	.472	.156	.331
No. of Siblings	-.060	.041	.009	.084
Birth Order	.059	-.116	-.065	.235
Farm Child	.057	-.556*	.004	-.180
West of Ireland	-.213	-.655	-.279	-.009
16 Years and Under	.311	.193	.471*	.340
18 Years and Over	-.433	-.503*	-.424*	-.206
Educational Background:				
Junior/ Inter Cert GPA	1.569*	1.276*	1.180*	1.126*
Inter Cert	-.072	.091	-.791*	-1.514*
Repeating Leaving Cert	1.067*	1.257*	.408	1.323*
School Type:				
Coed School	-.091	-.244	-.479	-.462
Selectivity:				
School Cream-off	-.091	-.206	.100	-.226
School Process / Organisation:				
Streaming	.117	-.033	.242	.375*
Class Position:				
Top Class	.061	1.180*	-.548	-.284
Middle Class	-.913	-.863	-.422	-1.612*
Bottom/Remedial Class	-2.176*	-1.757*	-.816	-1.538*
Average Social Class	-.680*	-1.478*	-.603*	-1.170*
Random Effects:				
Variance at School Level	1.188*	1.173*	0.680*	0.764*
Variance at Pupil Level	11.450*	12.050*	9.881*	12.640*
Variance Explained:				
School Level	73.2	79.3	80.1	81.0
Pupil Level	44.7	43.1	42.1	37.9

* Indicates significance at the <.05 level.

Appendix 7

Table A7.1: Pupils' Perceptions of the Personal- and Social-Development Aspects of Their Second-Level Education

% Reporting Benefit ("a Lot") in Relation to:	Junior Cert				Leaving Cert			
	Girls		Boys		Girls		Boys	
	Single-Sex	Coed	Single-Sex	Coed	Single-Sex	Coed	Single-Sex	Coed
Self-confidence	36.3	40.7	32.7	35.1	37.9	49.1	31.0	41.6
Well-balanced person	29.5	38.1	31.8	31.2	34.1	44.2	28.8	36.6
Good Relations with Opposite Sex	23.9	62.0	28.5	55.8	18.9	66.8	18.8	64.6
Talk/Communicate with Others	48.6	66.0	45.3	56.5	46.0	67.1	35.5	60.5
Make New Friends	73.3	76.8	63.7	68.9	72.4	77.6	59.8	72.5
Mean on Personal/ Social Development Scale	11.3	12.5	11.2	12.1	11.2	12.8	10.7	12.5

Table A7.2: Derivation of Social-Developmental Outcome Measures

Variables	Description
Academic Self-Image	Likert scale based on the following items:
	(1) I can do just about anything I set my mind to
	(2) I'm usually well ahead of others in my year in school
	(3) I am as good at school work as most other people my age
	(4) I'm hardly ever able to do what my teachers expect of me (reversed)
	(5) I'm usually well ahead of others in my class.
	Reliability: alpha of .67 (JC) and .68 (LC)
	Original scores range from 1 to 4; standardised to have a mean of zero and a standard deviation of one
Locus of Control	Likert scale based on the following items:
	(1) I have little control over the things that happen to me (reversed)
	(2) There is a lot I can do to change my life if I really want to
	(3) I often feel helpless in trying to deal with the problems I have (reversed)
	(4) What happens in the future really depends on me
	(5) I can do just about anything I set my mind to
	(6) There is really no way I can solve some of the problems I have.
	Reliability: alpha of .50 (JC) and .53 (LC).
	Original scores range from 1 to 4; standardised to have a mean of zero and a standard deviation of one
Body-Image	Likert scale based on the pupils' selection from adjective pairs:
	(1) Plain — Good-looking
	(2) Fat — Thin
	(3) Awkward — Graceful
	(4) Unattractive — Attractive.
	Reliability: alpha of .64 (JC, LC).
	Original scores range from 1 to 7; standardised to have a mean of zero and a standard deviation of one.

Table A7.2 (continued)

Variables	Description
Gender Role Expectations	One item scale with the following categories:
	(1) You would give up your job to mind your children on a full-time basis
	(2) You would work part-time and mind the children. Your spouse would work full-time
	(3) You would both work full-time and would pay someone else to mind the children
	(4) You would work full-time. Your spouse would work part-time and mind the children
	(5) You would work full-time. Your spouse would mind the children full-time.
	Categories are reversed for boys.
	Original scores range from 1 (traditional) to 5 (non-traditional); standardised to have a mean of zero and a standard deviation of one
Involvement in Domestic Labour	Likert scale based on involvement in the following tasks:
	(1) Made your bed
	(2) Swept the floor or used the vacuum cleaner
	(3) Set the table for meals
	(4) Did the dishes or cleaned up after meals
	(5) Did any ironing
	(6) Put out the rubbish or cleaned up the yard.
	Reliability: alpha of .74 (JC) and .73 (LC)
	Original scores range from 1 to 4; standardised to have a mean of zero and a standard deviation of one.

Table A7.3: Derivation of Explanatory Variables in Models of Developmental Outcomes

Variables	Description
Family / Educational Background	
Gender	Dummy variable where 1 = Girl.
Social Class	Census Social Class scale ranging from 0 (higher professional) to 5 (unskilled manual worker) based on the occupational status of parents.
Mother's Education	Highest level of mother's education ranging from 0 (primary education) to 4 (university degree).
Mother's Employment	Dummy variable where 1 = mother in full-time or part-time employment.
No. of Siblings	Number of siblings; only child is coded as 0.
Ability (Junior Cert Analysis)	VRNA, combined verbal reasoning and numerical-ability scores; centred on its mean value.
Junior/Inter Cert GPA (Leaving Cert Analysis)	Grade point average in Junior/Inter Cert. scored as in Table A6.2; centred on its mean value.
Inter Cert (Leaving Cert Analysis)	Dummy variable where 1 = sat Inter rather than Junior Cert.
School Type	
Coeducation	Dummy variable where 1 = attendance at a co-educational or co-institutional school.
Educational Expectations	
Own Expectations	Expected performance in forthcoming exam — ranges from 0 (well below average) to 3 (very well).
Educational Aspirations (Leaving Cert analysis)	Highest expected qualification — ranges from 0 (Junior Cert) to 3 (University Degree).
Parental Expectations	Parents' expectations re performance in forthcoming exam — ranges from 0 (well below average) to 3 (very well).
Teachers' Expectations	Teachers' expectations re performance in forthcoming exam — ranges from 0 (well below average) to 3 (very well).
Parental Pressure	Degree of parental pressure based on parental expectations, high study hours and grinds/outside tuition — ranges from 0 (low) to 3 (high).
Lack of Parental Support	Parental help/advice considered "not important" in decision about subjects, education/career aspirations, and help with homework/study — ranges from 0 (high parental support) to 2 (lack of parental support).

Table A7.3 (continued)

Variables	Description
Mother's Gender Role Expectations	Mother's perceived gender role expectations — ranges from 0 (traditional) to 4 (non-traditional).
Hours of Study	Usual hours of study (incl. homework) on a weekday evening.
Part-time Job	Dummy variable where 1 = holds a part-time job.
School Interaction	
Bullying	Likert scale based on frequency of following items:
	(1) Been jeered at or mocked by other pupils
	(2) Experienced being bullied or physically pushed around by other pupils
	(3) Been upset by things said about you behind your back by other pupils
	(4) Been pestered or bullied on the way to or from school.
	Reliability: alpha is .64 (JC) and .61 (LC).
	Values range from 0 (low) to 2 (high).
Positive Teacher Interaction	Likert scale based on frequency of following items:
	(1) Have you been told that your work is good?
	(2) Have you been asked questions in class?
	(3) Have you been praised for answering a difficult question correctly?
	(4) Have you been praised because your written work is well done?
	Reliability: alpha is .68 (JC) and .67 (LC).
	Ranges from 0 (low) to 3 (high).
Negative Teacher Interaction	Likert scale based on frequency of following items:
	(1) Have you been given out to because your work is untidy or not done on time?
	(2) Have you wanted to ask or answer questions in class but were ignored?
	(3) Have you been given out to for misbehaving in class?
	(4) Teachers pay more attention in class to what some pupils say than to others.
	(5) I find most teachers hard to talk to.
	Reliability: alpha is .59 (JC) and .61 (LC).
	Values range from 0 (low) to 3 (high).

Table A7.3 (continued)

Variables	Description
School Process / Context	
Homework Rules (Junior Cert Analysis)	Extent to which the school has and enforces rules on the setting, doing and checking of homework; values range from 0 (few rules) to 2 (a no. of rules which are enforced).
Class Position: Top Class Middle Class Bottom Class	Set of dummy variables where 1 defines membership of top, middle and bottom/remedial classes in streamed/ banded schools respectively; 0 represents being in mixed-ability class.
Average Social Class	Average social class of pupils within the school; centred on its mean value.
Mediating Variables	
Pastoral-Care Provision	Nature and organisation of pastoral-care provision in the school (as reported by principals and guidance counsellors) — values range from 0 (no formal programme) to 6 (highly developed/organised programme).
Recreation	Frequency of involvement in: (1) Sports organised by the school outside class time (2) School music group/society/debate/play outside class time (3) Sports that were not organised by the school. Values range from 0 (low) to 6 (high).
Social Life	Based on: (1) Frequency of going to a disco, a concert or the cinema (2) Frequency of going out on a date (3) Having a regular girlfriend/ boyfriend. Values range from 0 (low) to 5 (high).
Social-Skills Development	Perception of benefits of second-level education re: (1) Increasing your self confidence (2) Helping you develop into a well-balanced person (3) Building good relations with friends of the opposite sex (4) Being able to talk and communicate well with others (5) Helping you to make new friends. Values range from 0 (negative) to 10 (positive).

Table A7.4: Variance of Social Psychological Outcomes by Gender for Junior and Leaving Cert Pupils, Controlling for All Other Relevant Factors (as in Tables 8.2 and 8.3)

	Academic Self-Image	Control	Body-Image	Gender Role Expectations	Involvement in Domestic Labour
Junior Cert:					
Girls	0.578*	0.784	0.913*	0.629*	.837
Boys	0.658	0.811	0.725	0.914	.819
Leaving Cert:					
Girls	0.558*	0.762*	0.882*	0.616*	.846
Boys	0.711	0.841	0.754	1.037	.841

* Indicates significance at the <.05 level.

Table A7.5: Social Psychological Outcomes among Junior Cert Girls (N = 1,979)

Fixed Effects	Academic Self-Image	Control	Body Image	Gender Role Expectations	Involvement in Domestic Labour
Intercept	-1.656	-.897	-1.224	-1.553	-.658
Family Background					
Social Class	-.053*	-.009	-.038*	-.018	-.008
Mother's Education	-.006	-.047*	.006	.019	-.011
Mother's Employment	-.050	.026	.012	.065	.104*
No. of Siblings	-.014	-.004	.007	.021	.041*
Ability	.016*	.008*	-.005*	.006*	-.001
School Type					
Coed School	.036	-.101	-.055	.047	.215*
Educational Expectations					
Own Expectations	.394*	.304*	.229*	.049	.063
Parents' Expectations	.058	.042	.031	.077	.004
Parental Pressure	.046*	.055*	-.019	.007	-.009
Lack of Parental Support	-.078	-.105*	-.024	.242*	-.196*
Teachers' Expectations	.143*	-.079	.000	-.035	-.006
Mother's Gender Role Expectations	.044*	.041	.046	.453*	-.012
Hours of Study	-.027	-.035	-.004	.063*	.025
Part-time Employment	.006	-.017	.004	.025	.002
Domestic Labour	-.021	-.010	-.041	-.084*	—
School Interaction					
Bullying	-.081	-.421*	-.350*	-.081	.327*
Positive Teacher Interaction	.517*	.186*	.200*	.051	.111*
Negative Teacher Interaction	-.171*	-.224*	-.080	.114*	-.141*
School Process/Context					
Homework Rules	.021	.070	.106	.123*	.012
Class Position:					
Top Class	-.112*	-.030	-.023	-.061	-.036
Middle Class	.018	.009	-.101	-.090	-.012
Bottom Class	.066	-.067	-.030	-.085	.053
Average Social Class	.122*	.020	-.128*	.038	.062
Mediating Variables					
Pastoral-Care Provision	.011	.019	.009	-.013	-.033*
Recreation	.038*	.055*	.012	.030*	.055*
Social Life	-.021	.032*	.114*	-.012	.025
Social-Skills Development	.013	.065*	.046*	.009	.038*
Random Effects					
Variance at School Level	0.013*	0.009	0.008*	0.006	0.021*
Variance at Pupil Level	0.588*	0.795*	0.868*	0.783*	0.874*
% Variance Explained:					
School Level	33.0	58.1	36.0	81.7	73.3
Pupil Level	40.0	18.9	12.1	19.3	5.8

* Indicates significance at the <.05 level.

Table A7.6: Social Psychological Outcomes among Junior Cert Boys (N = 1,727)

Fixed Effects	Academic Self-Image	Control	Body Image	Gender Role Expectations	Involvement in Domestic Labour
Intercept	-1.467	-.780	-.536	-.688	-1.051*
Family Background					
Social Class	-.024	-.000	-.063*	-.035	-.030
Mother's Education	.063*	.029	-.037	.003	.052*
Mother's Employment	.004	.018	-.024	.098*	.135*
No. of Siblings	-.024*	-.017	.017	.012	.012
Ability	.014*	.006*	-.005*	.001	-.002
School Type					
Coed School	-.141*	-.129	-.142	.008	-.029
Educational Expectations					
Own Expectations	.416*	.274*	.203*	-.062	.005
Parents' Expectations	-.033	-.027	-.010	.059	.019
Parental Pressure	.055*	.015	.088*	-.028	-.012
Lack of Parental Support	-.043	-.142*	-.091	.091	-.173*
Teachers' Expectations	.084*	-.023	-.003	-.041	-.019
Mother's Gender Role Expectations	-.003	-.016	-.018	.467*	.039
Hours of Study	.018	-.004	-.020	.027	.114*
Part-time Employment	.029	.010	.045	-.010	.065
Domestic Labour	-.028	.012	-.020	.065*	—
School Interaction					
Bullying	.030	-.393*	-.441*	-.011	.298*
Positive Teacher Interaction	.538*	.255*	.110*	-.028	.171*
Negative Teacher Interaction	-.085*	-.156*	.093*	.008	-.035
School Process / Context					
Homework Rules	-.250*	-.040	.004	.069	-.026
Class Position:					
Top Class	-.126	-.014	-.005	-.026	.110
Middle Class	.079	.154	.078	-.009	-.055
Bottom Class	.117	-.105	-.009	-.034	.032
Average Social Class	.181*	.103	-.084	.036	-.056
Mediating Variables					
Pastoral-Care Provision	.003	.011	-.038	-.009	.010
Recreation	.000	.005	.022	.003	.037*
Social Life	-.005	.013	.101*	.013	.040*
Social-Skills Development	.016	.072*	.029*	-.002	.026*
Random Effects					
Variance at School Level	0.027*	0.019*	0.025*	0.002	0.002
Variance at Pupil Level	0.637*	0.791*	0.838*	0.721*	0.887*
% Variance Explained:					
School Level	53.4	33.5	35.3	59.9	85.3
Pupil Level	32.5	18.4	12.9	27.6	9.9

* Indicates significance at the <.05 level.

Table A7.7: Disaggregation of the Effect of Coeducation on Social Psychological Outcomes among Junior Cert Pupils (as in Table 8.2)

	Academic Self-Image	Control	Body-Image	Gender Role Expectations	Involvement in Domestic Labour
Coed Secondary	-.212*	-.123	-.198*	-.003	-.036
Coed Sec'y-Gender Interaction	.194*	-.054	.123	.036	.289*
Vocational	-.148*	-.133	-.141*	.052	-.106
Voc.-Gender Interaction	.225*	.025	.096	-.058	.382*
Comm./Comp.	-.028	-.032	-.237*	.061	-.077
Comm.-Gender Interaction	.084	.007	.250	.038	.291*

* Indicates significance at the <.05 level.

Table A7.8: Social Psychological Outcomes among Leaving Cert Girls (N = 2,105)

Fixed Effects	Academic Self-Image	Control	Body Image	Gender Role Expectations	Involvement in Domestic Labour
Intercept	-2.573	-1.315	-1.377	-1.208	-.086
Family Background					
Social Class	-.027	-.008	-.008	.004	-.014
Mother's Education	.035*	-.013	.020	-.005	-.027
Mother's Employment	-.000	.033	.020	.012	.069
No. of Siblings	-.017	-.029*	-.005	.004	.018
Junior Cert GPA	.110*	.024	-.046*	.051*	-.036*
Inter Cert	.170*	.093	-.073	-.018	-.012
School Type					
Coed School	.042	-.126*	-.014	.054	.152*
Educational Expectations					
Own Expectations	.389*	.341*	.267*	-.031	-.016
Educational Aspirations	.090*	.072*	.018	.088*	-.007
Parents' Expectations	.170*	.047	.020	.029	-.012
Parental Pressure	.014	.054	-.032	.016	-.051
Lack of Parental Support	.070	-.043	-.012	.144*	-.127*
Teachers' Expectations	.151*	-.044	-.033	.005	-.088*
Mother's Gender Role Expectations	.030	.057*	-.013	.523*	-.048
Hours of Study	-.010	-.037	.023	.012	.032
Part-time Employment	-.019	.071	-.007	.032	-.022
Domestic Labour	-.039*	-.027	-.054*	-.036	—
School Interaction					
Bullying	-.045	-.404*	-.287*	-.017	.059
Positive Teacher Interaction	.467*	.278*	.194*	-.003	.097*
Negative Teacher Interaction	-.170*	-.292*	-.076	.086	-.040
School Process / Context					
Homework Rules	.102*	.042	.053	-.015	-.039
Class Position:					
Top Class	-.078	.051	-.049	-.036	-.154
Middle Class	.066	.055	.086	-.080	-.380*
Bottom Class	-.102	.062	-.206*	-.084	-.078
Average Social Class	.029	.067	-.065	.041	-.023
Mediating Variables					
Pastoral-Care Provision	.009	-.001	-.008	-.003	-.010
Recreation	.015	.029	-.019	.028	.086*
Social Life	.012	.044*	.152*	.008	.047*
Social-Skills Development	.023*	.062*	.055*	-.005	.008
Random Effects					
Variance at School Level	0.008	0.013*	0.004	0.011	0.035*
Variance at Pupil Level	0.589*	0.762*	0.844*	0.784*	0.898*
% Variance Explained:					
School Level	83.3	59.3	79.1	48.4	36.6
Pupil Level	38.1	21.0	14.0	20.0	4.9

* Indicates significance at the <.05 level.

Table A7.9: Social Psychological Outcomes among Leaving Cert Boys (N = 1,747)

Fixed Effects	Academic Self-Image	Control	Body Image	Gender Role Expectations	Involvement in Domestic Labour
Intercept	-2.004	-1.474	-1.050	-.973	-.498
Family Background					
Social Class	-.018	.008	-.011	.018	-.017
Mother's Education	.016	-.005	.048*	-.033	.033
Mother's Employment	-.026	-.015	.048	-.009	.131*
No. of Siblings	-.039*	-.000	.014	-.002	-.005
Junior Cert GPA	.097*	-.007	.015	-.003	-.022
Inter Cert	.154	.060	.010	.001	.042
School Type					
Coed School	.015	-.079	-.246*	.184*	.114
Educational Expectations					
Own Expectations	.375*	.258*	.069	.028	.000
Educational Aspirations	.113*	.132*	.036	.061*	.014
Parents' Expectations	.104*	.057	.076	.053	.043
Parental Pressure	.015	.037	-.038	.018	-.094*
Lack of Parental Support	.024	-.055	-.100*	.125*	-.206*
Teachers' Expectations	.168*	-.012	-.031	-.079	-.065
Mother's Gender Role Expectations	-.030	-.003	-.032	.395*	.017
Hours of Study	-.004	.008	.002	.028	.067*
Part-time Employment	.006	-.006	.029	-.044	.006
Domestic Labour	-.019	-.008	-.058*	.041	—
School Interaction					
Bullying	-.082	-.416*	-.385*	-.010	.194*
Positive Teacher Interaction	.396*	.185*	.153*	.030	.189*
Negative Teacher Interaction	-.041	-.130*	.190*	.061	-.026
School Process / Context					
Homework Rules	.033	.049	-.022	.004	.014
Class Position:					
Top Class	.019	.098	-.087	-.014	.078
Middle Class	-.025	.082	-.202	.209	-.000
Bottom Class	.070	.110	-.110	-.004	-.025
Average Social Class	.108*	-.025	-.020	-.029	.002
Mediating Variables					
Pastoral-Care Provision	.006	-.004	-.002	.009	-.026
Recreation	-.001	.022	.001	.002	.055*
Social Life	.015	.022	.159*	-.022	.056*
Social-Skills Development	-.007	.054*	.049*	-.015	.009
Random Effects					
Variance at School Level	0.005	0.011	0.014	0.016	0.020*
Variance at Pupil Level	0.668*	0.834*	0.831*	0.805*	0.902*
% Variance Explained:					
School Level	46.0	0.0	54.1	51.3	29.1
Pupil Level	32.5	15.6	14.2	16.7	7.1

* Indicates significance at the <.05 level.

Table A7.10: Disaggregation of the Effect of Coeducation on Social Psychological Outcomes among Leaving Cert Pupils (as in Table 8.3)

	Academic Self-Image	Control	Body-Image	Gender Role Expectations	Involvement in Domestic Labour
Coed Secondary	-.049	-.123	-.358*	.212*	.177*
Coed Sec'y-Gender Interaction	.091	.058	.341*	-.091	.011
Vocational	.028	-.165*†	-.129	.303*	.054
Voc.-Gender Interaction	.127	.026	.235*	-.274*	.107
Comm./Comp.	-.022	-.031	-.323*	.070	.109
Comm.-Gender Interaction	.047	-.127	.311	-.084	-.089

* Significant at the <.05 level.
† Not significant before the introduction of mediating variables

Table A7.11: Disaggregation of the Coed Effect among Junior Cert Pupils by School Type and Gender (as in Tables A7.5 and A7.6)

	Academic Self-Image	Control	Body-Image	Gender Role Expectations	Involvement in Domestic Labour
Girls:					
Coed Secondary	-.031	-.183*†	-.094	.051	.238*
Vocational	.111	-.061	-.040	.039	.197*
Community/ Comprehensive	.053	.002	.007	.051	.194‡
Boys:					
Coed Secondary	-.211*	-.115	-.163	-.007	-.017
Vocational	-.126	-.173*†	-.100	.010	-.028
Community/ Comprehensive	.028	-.061	-.190	.040	-.061

* Significant at the <.05 level.
† Below significance before controlling for mediating variables.
‡ Significant before controlling for mediating variables.

Table A7.12: Disaggregation of the Coed Effect among Leaving Cert Pupils by School Type and Gender (as in Tables A7.8 and A7.9)

	Academic Self-Image	Control	Body-Image	Gender Role Expectations	Involvement in Domestic Labour
Girls:					
Coed Secondary	-.014	-.064	-.032	.120	.191*
Vocational	.170*	-.162*†	.043‡	.037	.186*
Community/ Comprehensive	.008	-.180*†	-.040	-.021	.061
Boys:					
Coed Secondary	.006	-.114	-.373*	.196*	.201*
Vocational	.037	-.108	-.060	.274*	.037
Community/ Comprehensive	.002	.024	-.269*	.043	.059

*   Significant at the <.05 level.
†   Below significance before controlling for mediating variables.
‡   Significant before controlling for mediating variables.

Appendix 8

Table A8.1: Derivation of Dependent Variable

Variables	Description
Stress	Likert scale based on the following items:
	(1) Been able to concentrate on whatever you're doing
	(2) Felt that you' were playing a moderately useful part in things
	(3) Felt capable of making decisions about things
	(4) Lost much sleep over worry
	(5) Felt constantly under strain
	(6) Been losing confidence in yourself.
	Reliability: alpha of .72 (JC) and .73 (LC).
	Original scores range from 6 to 24; the variable has been standardised to have a mean of zero and a standard deviation of one.

Table A8.2: Derivation of Explanatory Variables in Models of Stress

Variables	Description
Family / Educational Background	
Gender	Dummy variable where 1 = Girl.
Social Class	Census Social-Class scale ranging from 0 (higher professional) to 5 (unskilled manual worker) based on the occupational status of parents.
Ability (Junior Cert Analysis)	VRNA, combined verbal reasoning and numerical ability scores; centred on its mean value.
Junior/Inter Cert GPA (Leaving Cert Analysis)	Grade point average in Junior/Inter Cert scored as in Table A6.2; centred on its mean value.
Inter Cert (Leaving Cert Analysis)	Dummy variable where 1 = sat Inter rather than Junior Cert.
School Type	
Coeducation	Dummy variable where 1 = attendance at a co-educational or co-institutional school.
Parental Expectations	
Own Expectations	Expected performance in forthcoming exam — ranges from 0 (well below average) to 3 (very well).
Educational Aspirations (Leaving Cert Analysis)	Highest expected qualification; ranges from 0 (Junior Cert) to 3 (University Degree).
Parental Expectations	Parents' expectations re performance in forthcoming exam; ranges from 0 (well below average) to 3 (very well).
Parental Pressure	Degree of parental pressure based on parental expectations, high study hours and grinds/outside tuition — ranges from 0 (low) to 3 (high).
Lack of Parental Support	Parental help/advice considered "not important" in decision about subjects, education/career aspirations, and help with homework/study — ranges from 0 (high parental support) to 2 (lack of parental support).
Hours of Study	Usual hours of study (incl. homework) on a week-day evening.
Involvement in Domestic Labour	Degree of involvement in domestic labour tasks (see Chapter 8).
Part-time Job	Dummy variable where 1 = holds a part-time job.
School Process / Interaction	
Homework Rules	Extent to which the school has and enforces rules on the setting, doing and checking of homework — values range from 0 (few rules) to 2 (a no. of rules which are enforced).

Table A8.2 (continued)

Variables	Description
Positive Teacher Interaction	Likert scale based on frequency of following items:
	(1) Have you been told that your work is good?
	(2) Have you been asked questions in class?
	(3) Have you been praised for answering a difficult question correctly?
	(4) Have you been praised because your written work is well done?
	Reliability: alpha is .68 (JC) and .67 (LC).
	Ranges from 0 (low) to 3 (high).
Average Positive Teacher Interaction	School-level average of positive teacher interaction scale; centred on its mean value.
Negative Teacher Interaction	Likert scale based on frequency of following items:
	(1) Have you been given out to because your work is untidy or not done on time?
	(2) Have you wanted to ask or answer questions in class but were ignored?
	(3) Have you been given out to for misbehaving in class?
	(4) Teachers pay more attention in class to what some pupils say than to others.
	(5) I find most teachers hard to talk to.
	Reliability: alpha is .59 (JC) and .61 (LC).
	Values range from 0 (low) to 3 (high).
Average Negative Teacher Interaction	School-level average of negative teacher interaction; centred on its mean value.
Bullying	Likert scale based on frequency of following items:
	(1) Been jeered at or mocked by other pupils
	(2) Experienced being bullied or physically pushed around by other pupils
	(3) Been upset by things said about you behind your back by other pupils
	(4) Been pestered or bullied on the way to or from school.
	Reliability: alpha is .64 (JC) and .61 (LC).
	Values range from 0 (low) to 2 (high).
Restricted Subject Choice	Dummy variable where 1 = Would like to have taken a subject but couldn't.

Table A8.2 (continued)

Variables	Description
Mediating Variables	
Pastoral-Care Provision	Nature and organisation of pastoral-care provision in the school — values range from 0 (no formal programme) to 6 (highly developed/organised programme).
Recreation	Frequency of involvement in:
	(1) Sports organised by the school outside class time
	(2) School music group/society/debate/play outside class time
	(3) Sports that were not organised by the school.
	Value range from 0 (low) to 6 (high).
Social Life	Based on:
	(1) Frequency of going to a disco, a concert or the cinema
	(2) Frequency of going out on a date
	(3) Having a regular girlfriend/boyfriend.
	Values range from 0 (low) to 5 (high).
Social-Skills Development	Perception of benefits of second-level education re:
	(1) Increasing your self-confidence
	(2) Helping you develop into a well-balanced person
	(3) Building good relations with friends of the opposite sex
	(4) Being able to talk and communicate well with others
	(5) Helping you to make new friends.
	Values range from 0 (negative) to 10 (positive).
Control	Locus of control (see Chapter 8).
Academic Self-Image	See Chapter 8.
Body-Image	See Chapter 8.

Table A8.3: Variance of Stress by Gender among Junior Cert and Leaving Cert Pupils, Controlling for All Other Relevant Factors (as in Tables 9.2 and 9.3)

	Junior Cert Pupils	Leaving Cert Pupils
Girls	0.811*	0.796*
Boys	0.616	0.714

* Significant at the <.05 level.

Table A8.4: Multi-level Models of Stress for Junior Cert Girls (N = 1,979)

Fixed Effects	Model 1	Model 2	Model 3	Model 4	Model 5	Model 6
Intercept	-.007	-.028	-.008	-.153	-.531	-.447
Background Variables:						
Social Class		.011	.011	.010	.018	.013
Ability		.002	.002	.001	.003*	.003
School Type:						
Coed School			-.039	-.008	-.084	-.035
Parental Expectations:						
Own Expectations				-.365*	-.273*	-.192*
Parental Expectations				.205*	.159*	.168*
Parental Pressure				.023	.037	.049*
Lack of Parental Support				.098	.079	.030
Hours of Study				.066*	.072*	.067*
Involvement in Domestic Labour				-.013	-.031	-.017
Part-time Job				.106	.077	.099
School Process/Interaction:						
Homework Rules					-.105*	-.100*
Positive Teacher Interaction					-.071	.031
Negative Teacher Interaction					.210*	.186*
Average Positive Interaction in School					-.355*	-.401*
Average Negative Interaction in School					.041	.059
Bullying					.843*	.621*
Restricted Subject Choice					.115*	.118*
Mediating Variables:						
Pastoral-Care Provision						.015
Recreation						-.022
Social Life						.009
Social-Skills Development						-.047*
Control						-.253*
Academic Self-Image						.067*
Body-Image						-.122*
Random Effects:						
Variance at School Level	0.019*	0.020*	0.020*	0.014	0.007	0.006
Variance at Pupil Level	0.982*	0.980*	0.980*	0.936*	0.828*	0.744*
% Variance Explained:						
School Level	—	0.0	0.0	24.6	64.6	66.6
Pupil Level	—	0.2	0.3	4.7	15.7	24.3
Proportion of Remaining Variance at:						
School Level	1.9	2.0	2.0	1.5	0.8	0.8
Pupil Level	98.1	98.0	98.0	98.5	99.2	99.2
Deviance	5610.4	5607.6	5607.1	5510.2	5257.9	5045.1
Reduction in Deviance	—	n.s.	n.s.	<.001	<.001	<.001

* Significant at the <.05 level.

Table A8.5: Multi-level Models of Stress for Junior Cert Boys (N = 1,811)

Fixed Effects	Model 1	Model 2	Model 3	Model 4	Model 5	Model 6
Intercept	-.018	.032	.139	.609	.020	.269
Background Variables:						
Social Class		-.023	-.020	-.015	-.006	-.006
Ability		.003	.002	.002	.003	.003
School Type:						
Coed School			-.186*	-.188*	-.148*	-.114*
Parental Expectations:						
Own Expectations				-.372*	-.265*	-.180*
Parental Expectations				.109*	.105*	.097*
Parental Pressure				.033	.038	.057*
Lack of Parental Support				.074	.069	-.022
Hours of Study				-.009	.012	.013
Involvement in Domestic Labour				.051*	.035	.052*
Part-time Job				-.062	-.070	-.054
School Process / Interaction:						
Homework Rules					-.046	-.069
Positive Teacher Interaction					-.188*	-.075
Negative Teacher Interaction					.247*	.236*
Average Positive Interaction in School					.004	-.065
Average Negative Interaction in School					.269	.297
Bullying					.621*	.409*
Restricted Subject Choice					.099*	.120*
Mediating Variables:						
Pastoral-Care Provision						.003
Recreation						-.057*
Social Life						.004
Social-Skills Development						-.049*
Control						-.214*
Academic Self-Image						.033
Body-Image						-.086*
Random Effects:						
Variance at School Level	0.021*	0.016	0.008	0.003	0.0	0.0
Variance at Pupil Level	0.978*	0.978*	0.977*	0.941*	0.848*	0.775*
% Variance Explained:						
School Level	—	27.5	62.3	87.4	100.0	100.0
Pupil Level	—	0.0	0.0	3.7	13.3	20.7
Proportion of Remaining Variance at:						
School Level	2.2	1.6	0.8	0.3	0.0	0.0
Pupil Level	97.8	98.4	99.2	99.7	100.0	100.0
Deviance	4891.2	4884.3	4874.0	4801.0	4616.0	4461.7
Reduction in Deviance	—	<.05	<.01	<.001	<.001	<.001

* Significant at the <.05 level.

Table A8.6: Multi-level Models of Stress for Leaving Cert Girls (N = 2,105)

Fixed Effects	Model 1	Model 2	Model 3	Model 4	Model 5	Model 6
Intercept	-.011	-.007	.037	.001	-.448	-.756
Background Variables:						
Social Class		-.003	-.003	-.004	.005	-.001
Junior Cert GPA		.012	.011	.013	.023	.027
Inter Cert		.038	.028	.062	.086	.113
School Type:						
Coed School			-.074	-.072	-.094	-.042
Parental Expectations:						
Own Expectations				-.364*	-.306*	-.169*
Educational Aspirations				.007	.014	.037
Parental Expectations				.171*	.135*	.158*
Parental Pressure				.027	.040	.046
Lack of Parental Support				.082	.062	.038
Hours of Study				.050*	.065*	.060*
Involvement in Domestic Labour				-.010	-.017	-.023
Part-time Job				.041	.026	.062
School Process / Interaction:						
Homework Rules					-.043	-.033
Positive Teacher Interaction					-.083	.072
Negative Teacher Interaction					.279*	.172*
Average Positive Interaction in School					-.031	.114
Average Negative Interaction in School					-.023	-.059
Bullying					.656*	.505*
Restricted Subject Choice					.133*	.121*
Mediating Variables:						
Pastoral-Care Provision						.016
Recreation						-.018
Social Life						.025
Social-Skills Development						-.033*
Control						-.221*
Academic Self-Image						-.057*
Body-Image						-.091*
Random Effects:						
Variance at School Level	0.028*	0.027*	0.026*	0.018*	0.011*	0.012*
Variance at Pupil Level	0.973*	0.973*	0.973*	0.930*	0.862*	0.792*
% Variance Explained:						
School Level	—	3.7	8.5	36.1	59.4	57.6
Pupil Level	—	0.0	0.0	4.5	11.5	18.6
Proportion of Remaining Variance at:						
School Level	2.8	2.7	2.6	1.9	1.3	1.5
Pupil Level	97.2	97.3	97.4	98.1	98.7	98.5
Deviance	5960.5	5959.5	5957.9	5852.6	5683.5	5509.8
Reduction in Deviance	—	n.s.	n.s.	<.001	<.001	<.001

* Significant at the <.05 level.

Table A8.7: Multi-level Models of Stress for Leaving Cert Boys (N = 1,747)

Fixed Effects	Model 1	Model 2	Model 3	Model 4	Model 5	Model 6
Intercept	-.007	.000	.041	.311	-.058	-.027
Background Variables:						
Social Class		-.010	-.008	.009	.015	.015
Junior Cert GPA		.035*	.033*	.036*	.042*	.030
Inter Cert		.163	.166	.188*	.234*	.252*
School Type:						
Coed School			-.069	-.048	.026	.049
Parental Expectations:						
Own Expectations				-.311*	-.250*	-.208*
Educational Aspirations				.086*	.086*	.113*
Parental Expectations				.042	.032	.040
Parental Pressure				.054	.055	.066
Lack of Parental Support				.013	.002	-.046
Hours of Study				-.029	-.009	-.006
Involvement in Domestic Labour				.015	.009	.018
Part-time Job				-.078	-.077	-.055
School Process/Interaction:						
Homework Rules					-.076	-.060
Positive Teacher Interaction					-.168*	-.095*
Negative Teacher Interaction					.150*	.130*
Average Positive Interaction in School					-.095	-.065
Average Negative Interaction in School					.103	.059
Bullying					.560*	.401*
Restricted Subject Choice					.154*	.156*
Mediating Variables:						
Pastoral-Care Provision						.001
Recreation						-.034*
Social Life						-.013
Social-Skills Development						-.023*
Control						-.254*
Academic Self-Image						.056*
Body-Image						-.044
Random Effects:						
Variance at School Level	0.015	0.007	0.005	0.000	0.003	0.006
Variance at Pupil Level	0.986*	0.986*	0.987*	0.957*	0.891*	0.823*
% Variance Explained:						
School Level	—	49.9	64.0	100.0	80.4	59.9
Pupil Level	—	0.0	0.0	3.0	9.6	16.6
Proportion of Remaining Variance at:						
School Level	1.5	0.7	0.5	0.0	0.3	0.7
Pupil Level	98.5	99.3	99.5	100.0	99.7	99.3
Deviance	4954.6	4945.3	4943.7	4880.9	4762.2	4627.9
Reduction in Deviance	—	<.05	n.s.	<.001	<.001	<.001

* Significant at the <.05 level.

Table A8.8: Disaggregation of the Effect of Coeducation on Stress (as in Model 6, Tables 9.2 and 9.3)

	Junior Cert	Leaving Cert
Coed Secondary	-.051	-.018
Coed Secondary-Gender Interaction	.016	.018
Vocational	-.153*	-.050
Vocational-Gender Interaction	.065	-.028
Community/ Comprehensive	-.126†	.143
Community-Gender Interaction	.211*	-.162

*   Significant at the <.05 level.
†   Significant before the introduction of mediating variables.

Appendix 9

APPENDIX 9.1: SUMMARY OF RECOMMENDATIONS

(1) The State should take a more proactive role in promoting gender and class equality objectives among schools and local school systems, as well as in developing effective policy instruments to ensure their implementation.

(2) Schools should develop their own gender-equity policies, focusing on the personal and social development of pupils, as well as on take-up and performance in non-traditional subjects. A broad view of gender equity should be adopted, with policies applying not only to girls in single-sex and coed schools, but also to boys in single-sex schools.

(3) There is a particular need to widen and improve curricular provision for pupils of lower academic ability, particularly girls in coed schools. This could be achieved, for example, through the development and provision of girl-friendly vocational/technical subjects, and other subjects based on non-academic aptitudes and abilities.

(4) The underachievement in Mathematics of girls in coed schools needs to be addressed. Appropriate measures would include teacher support/encouragement for girls pursuing higher level courses, along with a re-evaluation of pedagogical practice in male-dominant subjects. Further research is needed on coed girls' performance in other traditionally "male" subjects.

(5) Gender-equity policies should be underpinned by a strong emphasis on gender issues in teacher training, and in-service training. Particular attention should be paid to the development of "gender fair" teaching practices within coed classes.

(6) "Models of good practice" should be developed to enhance school effectiveness in relation to overall academic achieve-

ment, the achievement of different groups (girls and boys, different ability groups), and personal/social development and stress. Further research is needed to identify the central elements of good practice in these areas. The State should take a proactive role in the diffusion of these models, encouraging the development of "whole school" intervention programmes.

(7) The use of "streaming" and "banding" of pupils within schools should be re-evaluated, with an emphasis on moving towards mixed-ability classes and the wider use of separate higher and ordinary level classes in particular subjects.

(8) The Schemes of Assistance to Schools in Designated Disadvantaged Areas should be developed to take account not only of the need for additional resources but also of school climate and school effectiveness.

(9) The State should develop ways of discouraging schools from being selective on ability and social grounds in their intake, thus facilitating equal educational opportunities for all school children within a community.

(10) The current exam system has been found to have negative consequences in terms of underperformance among less "academic" pupils, and in terms of extremely high stress levels among pupils in their exam years. We, therefore, recommend a re-evaluation of the current system: through investigating the expansion of provision of "non-academic" courses, alternative modes of pupil evaluation (such as continuous assessment), and alternative routes into further education, training and apprenticeships for those with vocational, practical and aesthetic, rather than "academic", skills.

(11) School-level interventions on bullying should be developed and supported.

(12) Given the high levels of stress among pupils, special attention should be given to promoting a positive school climate, promoting positive pupil/teacher relations, and enhancing the self-images, coping and problem-solving capacities of pupils. Support should be given to schools to balance their academic objectives with the provision of sports and other recreational/ cultural activities (such as plays, debates, etc.) which help to reduce stress among pupils.

Bibliography

Ainsworth, M.E. and Batten, E. (1974): The *Effects of Environmental Factors on Secondary Educational Attainment in Manchester: A Plowden Follow-Up*, London: Macmillan.

Allmendinger, J. (1989): "Educational Systems and Labour Market Outcomes", *European Sociological Review*, 5: 231–50.

Anyon, J. (1983): "Intersection of Gender and Class: Accommodation and Resistance by Working Class and Affluent Females to Contradictory Sex-Role Ideologies", in Walker, S. and Barton, L. (Eds.), *Gender, Class and Education*, London: Falmer Press.

Arnot, M. (1983): "A Cloud over Coeducation: An Analysis of the Forms of Transmission of Class and Gender Relations", in Walker, S. and Barton, L. (Eds.), *Gender, Class and Education*, London: Falmer Press.

Baeninger, M. and Newcombe, N. (1989): "The Role of Experience in Spacial Test Performance: A Meta-Analysis", *Sex Roles*, 20: 327–44.

Bandura, A. (1990): "Perceived Self-Efficacy in the Exercise of Personal Agency", *Journal of Applied Sport Psychology*, 2: 128–63.

Banks, M.H. and Ullah, P. (1988): *Youth Unemployment in the 1980s*, London: Croom Helm.

Banks, M.H., Ullah, P. and Warr, P. (1984): "Unemployment and Less Qualified Urban Young People", *Employment Gazette*, 2: 343–6.

Bayder, N. and Brooks-Gunn, J. (1991): "Effects of Maternal Employment and Child-Care Arrangements on Preschoolers' Cognitive and Behavioural Outcomes", *Developmental Psychology*, 27 (6): 932–45.

Berk, S.F. (1985): *The Gender Factory*, New York: Plenum.

Berk, L.E. (Ed.) (1989): *Child Development*, Boston: Allyn and Bacon.

Bernstein, B. (1977): "Social Class, Language and Socialization", in Karabel, J. and Halsey, A.H. (Eds.), *Power and Ideology in Education*, New York: Oxford University Press.

Bidwell, C.E. and Friedkin, N.E. (1986): "The Sociology of Education", in Smelser, N.J. (Ed.), op. cit.: 449–509.

Blake, J. (1989): *Family Size and Achievement*, Berkeley, CA: University of California.

Blau, F.D. and Grossberg, A.J. (1992): "Maternal Labor Supply and Children's Cognitive Development", *Review of Economics and Statistics*, 64: 474–81.

Blin-Stoyle, R. (1983): "Girls and Physics", *Physics Education*, 18: 225–8.

Block, J.J. (1983): "Differential Premises Arising from Differential Socialization of the Sexes", reprinted in Berk, L.E. (Ed.), op. cit.

Bone, A. (1983): *Girls and Girl-Only Schools*, Manchester: Equal Opportunities Commission.

Bourdieu, P. and Passeron, J.C. (1977): *Reproduction in Education, Society and Culture*, Thousand Oaks, CA: Sage.

Breen, R. (1986): *Subject Availability and Student Performance in the Senior Cycle of Irish Post-Primary Schools*, Dublin: ESRI General Research Series, Paper No.129.

Breen, R. (1995): "The Persistence of Class Origin Inequalities among School Leavers in the Republic of Ireland, 1984–1993", ESF Network on Transitions in Youth, Working Paper.

Breen, R., Hannan, D.F. and O'Leary, R. (1995): "Returns to Education: Taking Account of Employers' Perceptions and Use of Educational Credentials", *European Sociological Review*, 11(1): 59–73.

Breen, R. and Whelan, C.T. (1992): "Explaining the Irish Patterns of Social Fluidity: The Role of the Political", in Goldthorpe, J.H. and Whelan, C.T. (Eds.), *The Development of Industrial Society in Ireland*, Oxford: Oxford University Press.

Brookover, W.B, Beady, C., Flood, P., Schweitzer, J. and Wisenbaker, J. (1979): *School Social Systems and Student Achievement: Schools Can Make a Difference*, New York: Praager.

Brophy, J. and Good, T. (1974): *Teacher–Student Relationships: Causes and Consequences*, New York: Holt, Rinehart and Winston.

Bryan, K. and Digby, A. (1986): "Performance in Maths and

Science at 16 Plus: A case for Coeducational Schooling?", *Westminster Studies in Education*, 9(86): 9–19.

Bryk, A., Lee, V. and Holland, P. (1993): *Catholic Schools and the Common Good*, Cambridge, MA: Harvard University Press.

Bryk, A. and Raudenbush, S. (1988): "Toward a More Appropriate Conceptualization of Research on School Effects: A Three-Level Hierarchial Linear Model", *American Journal of Education*, 97: 65–108.

Burstein, L. (1980): "The Analysis of Multilevel Data in Educational Research and Evaluation", *Review of Research in Education*, 8: 158–233.

Burton, L. (Ed.) (1994): *Who Counts? Assessing Maths in Europe*, London: Trentham Books Ltd.

Cairns, E. (1990): "The Relationship Between Adolescent Perceived Self-Competence and Attendance at Single-Sex Secondary School", *British Journal of Educational Psychology*, 60: 207–11.

Canada, K. and Pringle, R. (1995): "The Role of Gender in College Classroom Interactions: A Social Context Approach", *Sociology of Education*, 68: 161–86.

Canny, A., Hughes, G. and Sexton, J.J. (1995): *Occupational Employment Forecasts 1998*, Dublin: FÁS/ESRI.

Carpenter, P. (1985): "Single-Sex Schooling and Girls' Academic Achievements", *The Australian and New Zealand Journal of Sociology*, 21(3): 456–72.

Cherry, R., Eaton, E., Gold, D., Andres, D. and Glorieux, D. (1979): "The Development of Francophone Nursery School Children with Employed and Non-Employed Mothers", reprinted in Berk, L.E. (Ed.) op. cit.

Clancy, P. (1995): *Access to College: Patterns of Continuity and Change*, Dublin: Higher Education Authority.

Cocklin, B. (1982): "The Coeducational versus Single-Sex Schools Debate", *Delta*, 31: 19–31.

Coleman, J.S. (1961): *The Adolescent Society*, New York: Free Press of Glencoe.

Coleman, J.S., Campbell, E., Hobson, C., McPartland, J., Mood, A., Weinfeld, F. and York, R. (1966): *Equality of Educational Opportunity Report*, Washington, DC: US Government Printing Office.

Coleman, J.S., Hoffer, T. and Kilgore, S. (1982): *High School Achievement: Public, Catholic and Private Schools Compared*, New York: Basic Books.

Coleman, J.S. and Hoffer, T. (1987): *Public and Private High Schools: The Impact of Communities*, New York: Basic Books.

Cooper, H. (1989): *Homework*, New York: Longman.

Covington, M.V. (1992): *Making the Grade: A Self-Worth Perspective on Motivation and School Reform*, Cambridge: Cambridge University Press.

Crossman, M. (1987): "Teachers' Interactions with Girls and Boys in Science Lessons", in Kelly, A. (Ed.), op. cit..

Dale, R. (1969): *Mixed or Single-Sex School? Vol. 1, A Research Study in Pupil–Teacher Relationships*, London: Routledge and Kegan Paul.

Dale, R. (1971): *Mixed or Single Sex School? Vol. 2, Some Social Aspects*, London: Routledge and Kegan Paul.

Dale, R. (1974): *Mixed or Single Sex School? Vol. 3, Attainment, Attitudes and Overview*, London: Routledge and Kegan Paul.

Daly, P.G. (1992): "School Effectiveness in Northern Ireland", Ph.D. Thesis, Queens University, Belfast.

Daly, P. (1994): "The Effects of Single-Sex and Coeducational Secondary Schooling on Girls' Achievement", Paper to the International Congress for School Effectiveness and Improvement, Melbourne.

Daly, P. (1995): "Science Course Participation and Science Achievement in Single Sex and Co-educational Schools", Paper to the International Congress for School Effectiveness and Improvement, Leeuwarden.

D'Amico, R.J., Haurin, R.J. and Mott F.L. (1983): "The Effect of Mother's Employment on Adolescent and Early Adult Outcomes of Young Men and Women", in Hayes, C.D. and Kammerman, S.B. (Eds.), *Children of Working Parents: Experiences and Outcomes*, Washington, DC: National Academy.

Davies, M. and Kandel, D. (1981): "Parental and Peer Influences on Adolescents' Educational Plans: Some Further Evidence", *American Journal of Sociology*, 87(2): 363–403.

Deem, R. (Ed.) (1984): *Coeducation Reconsidered*, Milton Keynes: Open University Press.

Delphy, C. and Leonard, D. (1992): *Familiar Exploitation*, Cambridge: Polity Press.

Department of Education (1966): *Investment in Education*, Dublin: Stationery Office.

Department of Education (1969): *Ár nDaltaí Uile: All Our Children*, Dublin: Stationery Office.

Department of Education (1979): *Tuarascáil Staitistiúil 1978/79*, Dublin: The Stationery Office.

Department of Education (1988): *Tuarascáil Staitistiúil 1987/88*, Dublin: The Stationery Office.

Department of Education (1990): *Tuarascáil Staitistiúil 1989/90*, Dublin: The Stationery Office.

Department of Education (1994): *Tuarascáil Staitistiúil 1992/93*, Dublin: The Stationery Office.

Department of Education (1995): *Tuarascáil Staitistiúil 1993/94*, Dublin: The Stationery Office.

Department of Education (1995): *Charting Our Education Future: White Paper on Education*, Dublin: Stationery Office.

Department of Education (various years): *Rules and Programmes for Secondary Schools*, Dublin: Stationery Office.

Ditchburn, G. and Martin, J. (1986): *Education for Girls in Catholic and Independent Schools in the Western Suburbs of Melbourne and Gippsland*, Victoria: Non-Government Schools Participation and Equity Project.

Dreeben, R. (1968): *On What is Learned in School*, Reading, MA: Addison-Wesley.

Drudy, S. and Lynch, K. (1993): *Schools and Society in Ireland*, Dublin: Gill and Macmillan.

Duncan, O.D., Featherman, D.L. and Duncan, B. (1972): *Socioeconomic Background and Achievement*, New York: Seminar Press.

Dusek, J.B. and Flaherty, J.F. (1981): "The Development of Self-Concept During Adolescent Years", *Monograph of Social Research on Child Development*, 46(4): 191.

Eccles, J.S., Adler, T., Futterman, R., Goff, S.B., Kaczala, C.M., Meece, J.I. and Midgley, C. (1983): "Expectations, Values and Academic Behaviours" in Spence, J. (Ed.), op. cit.

Eccles, J.S., Adler, T. and Meece, J. (1984): "Sex Differences in Achievement: A Test of Alternate Theories", *Journal of Personality and*

Social Psychology, 46: 26–43.

Eccles, J.S., Wigfield, A., Harold, R.D. and Blumenfeld, P. (1993): "Age and Gender Differences in Children's Self and Task Perceptions During Elementary School", *Child Development*, 64: 830–47.

Epstein, C.F. (1988): *Deceptive Distinctions: Sex, Gender and the Social Order*, New Haven, CT: Yale University Press.

Erickson, E.H. (1968): *Identity, Youth and Crisis*, New York: Norton.

Feather, N.T. (1974): "Coeducation, Values and Satisfaction with School", *Journal of Educational Psychology*, 66(1): 9–15.

Fennema, E. and Peterson, C. (1986): "Teacher–Student Interaction and Sex-Related Differences in Learning Mathematics", *Teaching and Teacher Education*, 2(1): 19–42.

Fennema, E. and Sherman, J. (1977a): "The Study of Mathematics by High School Girls and Boys: Related Variables", *American Educational Research Journal*, 14: 159–168.

Fennema, E. and Sherman, J. (1977b):. "Sex-Related Differences in Mathematics and Achievement, Spatial Visualisation, and Affective Factors", *American Educational Research Journal*, 14: 51–71.

Finn, J. (1980): "Sex Differences in Educational Outcomes: A Cross-National Study", *Sex Roles*, 6: 1.

Finn, J.D. and Achilles, C.M. (1990): "Answers and Questions about Class Size", *American Educational Research Journal*, 27: 557–77.

Fiske, E.B. (1990): "Lessons", *New York Times*, 11 April: B6.

Fitzgerald, L.F. and Crites, J. (1980): "Towards a Career Psychology of Women: What Do We Know? What Do We Need to Know?", *Journal of Counselling Psychology*, 17(1): 44–62.

Foon, A.E. (1988): "The Relationship Between School Type and Adolescent Self Esteem, Attribution Styles and Affiliation Needs: Implications for Educational Outcome", *British Journal of Educational Psychology*, 58: 44–54.

Gamoran, R. (1991): "Schooling and Achievement: Additive versus Interactive Models", in Raudenbush, S.W. and Willms, J.D. (Eds.), *Schools, Classrooms and Pupils*, San Diego, CA: Academic Press.

Gamoran, R. and Dreeben, A. (1986): "Race Instruction and Learning", *American Sociological Review*, 51(5): 660–70.

Gardner, H. (1987): *Frames of Mind: The Theory of Multiple Intelligence*, London: Fontana.

Garrett, S. (1987): *Gender*, London: Tavistock.

Gill, J. (1992): "Re-phrasing the Question about Single-Sex Schooling", in Reid, A. and Johnson, B. (Eds.), *Critical Issues in Australian Education in the 1990s*, Adelaide: Painters Prints.

Giorgi, L. and Marsh, C. (1990): "The Protestant Work Ethic as a Cultural Phenomenon", *European Journal of Social Psychology*, 20: 499–517.

Glass, G.V., Cahan, L.S. Smith, M.L. and Filby, N.N. (1982): *School Class Size: Research and Policy*, Thousand Oaks, CA: Sage.

Goldberg, D. (1972): *The Detection of Psychiatric Illness by Questionnaire*, London: Oxford University Press.

Goldberg, D. (1978): *Manual for the General Health Questionnaire*, Windsor: National Foundation for Educational Research.

Goldstein, H. (1987): *Multilevel Models in Educational and Social Research*, London: Charles Griffin and Co.

Goldstein, H. (1995): *Multilevel Statistical Models*, London: Edward Arnold.

Goldstein, H., Rasbash, J., Yang, M., Woodhouse, G., Pan, H., Nuttall, D. and Thomas, S. (1993): "A Multilevel Analysis of School Examination Results", *Oxford Review of Education*, 19(4): 425–33.

Government of Ireland (1992): *Green Paper: Education for a Changing World*, Dublin: The Stationery Office.

Guilford, J.P. (1954): *Psychometric Methods*, New York: McGraw-Hill.

Hallinan, M. (1992): "The Organization of Students for Instruction in the Middle School", *Sociology of Education*, 65: 114–27.

Hallinan, M. (1994): "School Differences in Tracking Effects on Achievement", *Social Forces*, 72(3): 799–820.

Hallinan, M. and Sorensen, A. (1985): "Class Size, Ability Group Size and Student Achievement", *American Journal of Education*, 94(1): 71–89.

Halpern, D.F. (1986): *Sex Differences in Cognitive Abilities*, London: Lawrence Erlbaum Associates.

Halsey, A. (1972): *Trends in British Society Since 1900*, London: Macmillan.

Halsey, A. (1975): "Education and Social Mobility in Britain Since World War Two", *OECD Seminar: Inequality and Life Chances*, 97(2): 501–509.

Halsey, A., Heath, A. and Ridge, J. (1980): *Origins and Destinations: Family, Class and Education in Modern Britain*, Oxford: Clarendon Press.

Hanafin, J. (1992): "Coeducation and Attainment: A Study of the Gender Effects of Mixed and Single-Sex Schooling on Examination Performance", Ph.D. Thesis, University of Limerick.

Hanafin, J. and Ní Chárthaigh, D. (1993): *Coeducation and Attainment*, Limerick: Plassey.

Hannan, D.F. (1979): *Displacement and Development: Class, Kinship and Social Change in Irish Rural Communities*, Dublin: ESRI General Research Series, Paper No. 96.

Hannan, D.F., with Boyle, M. (1987): *Schooling Decisions: The Origins and Consequences of Selection and Streaming in Irish Schools*, Dublin: ESRI General Research Series, Paper No. 153.

Hannan, D.F., Breen, R., Murphy, B., Watson, D., Hardiman, N. and O'Higgins, K. (1983): *Schooling and Sex Roles: Sex Differences in Subject Provision and Student Choice in Irish Post-Primary Schools*, Dublin: ESRI General Research Series, Paper No. 113.

Hannan, D.F. and Hardiman, N. (1978): *Peasant Proprietorship and Changes in Marriage Rates in the Late Nineteenth Century*, Dublin: ESRI, Unpublished Paper.

Hannan, D.F. and Ó Riain, S. (1993): *Pathways to Adulthood in Ireland*, Dublin: ESRI General Research Series, Paper No. 161.

Hannan, D.F. and Shortall, S. (1991): *The Quality of Their Education: School Leavers' Views of Educational Objectives and Outcomes*, Dublin: ESRI General Research Series, No.153.

Hardin, J. and Dede, C. (1973): "Discriminations Against Women in Science Education", *Science Teacher*, 40: 18–21.

Hargreaves, D. (1967): *Social Relations in a Secondary School*, London: Routledge and Kegan Paul.

Haveman, R., Wolfe, B. and Spaulding, J. (1991): "Childhood Events and Circumstances Influencing High School Completion", *Demography*, 28: 133–57.

Head, J. (1987): "A Model to Link Personality Characteristics to a Preference for Science", in Kelly, A. (Ed.), *Science for Girls?*, Milton Keynes: Open University Press.

Heath, A. and Clifford, P. (1990). "Class Inequalities in Education in the Twentieth Century", *Education and Training Policies for Economic and Social Development*, NESC.

Heynes, B. and Catsambis, S. (1986): "Mothers' Employment and Children's Achievement: A Critique", *Sociology of Education*, 59: 140–51.

Higher Education Authority (1995): *Interim Report of the Steering Committee's Technical Working Group*, Dublin: Higher Education Authority.

Hoffer, T., Greeley, A.M. and Coleman, J.S. (1985): "Achievement Growth in Public and Catholic Schools", *Sociology of Education*, 58(2): 74–97.

Hoffman, L.W. (1989): "Effects of Maternal Employment in the Two-Parent Family", *American Psychologist*, 44: 283–92.

Hollinger, D. and Adamson, R. (Eds.) (1993): *Single-Sex Schooling: Perspectives from Practice and Research* (special report from the Office of Education Research and Improvement, US Department of Education, Vol. 1), Washington, DC: US Department of Education.

Hudson, B. (1984): "Femininity and Adolescence", in McRobbie, A. and Nava, M. (Ed.), *Gender and Generation*, London: Macmillan: 31–53.

Hunt, S. and Hilton, J. (1981): *Individual Development and Social Experience*, London: George Allen and Unwin.

Inner London Education Authority (1990): *Differences in Examination Performance*. RS 1277/90.

Jencks, C., Smith, M., Bane, M., Cohen, D., Gintis, H., Heynes, B. and Michelson, S. (1972): *Inequality: A Reassessment of the Effects of Family and Schooling in America*, New York: Basic Books.

Jones, C. (1985): "Sexual Tyranny in Mixed-Sex Schools: An In-Depth Study of Male Violence", in Weiner, G. (Ed.), *Just A Bunch of Girls*, Milton Keynes: Open University Press.

Jones, J., Kyle, N. and Black, J. (1987): "The Tidy Classroom: An Assessment of the Change from Single-Sex to Coeducation in NS Wales", *Australian Journal of Education*, 31(3): 284–302.

Jones, K. (1991): *Multi-Level Models for Geographical Research*, Norwich: University of East Anglia.

Jones, K. (1992): "Using Multi-Level Models for Survey Analysis", in Westlake, A., Banks, R., Payne, C. and Orchard, T. (Eds.), *Survey and Statistical Computing*, Amsterdam: North-Holland.

Kahle, J.B. and Lakes, M. (1983): "The Myth of Equality in Science Classrooms", *Journal of Research in Science Teaching*, 20: 131–40.

Kalmijn, M. (1994): "Mother's Occupational Status and Children's Schooling", *American Sociological Review*, 59: 257–75.

Kandel, D. and Lesser, G. (1972): *Youth in Two Worlds*, San Francisco, CA: Jossey-Bass.

Karabel, J. and Halsey, A.H. (Eds.) (1977): *Power and Ideology in Education*, Oxford: Oxford University Press.

Keith, P.M. (Ed.) (1988): "The Relationship of Self-Esteem, Maternal Employment and Work/Family Plans to Sex-Role Orientations of Late Adolescents", *Adolescence*, 23: 959–66.

Kellaghan, T. and Dwan, B. (1995a): *An Analysis of the 1994 Leaving Certificate Examination Results*, Dublin: National Council for Curriculum and Assessment.

Kellaghan, T. and Dwan, B.(1995b): *An Analysis of the 1994 Junior Certificate Examination Results*, Dublin: National Council for Curriculum and Assessment.

Kellaghan, T. and Fontes, P.J. (1988): "Gender Differences in the Scholastic Self-Concept of Irish Pupils", *Irish Journal of Education*, 22: 42–52.

Kellaghan, T., Weir, S., Ó hUallacháin, S. and Morgan, M. (1995): *Educational Disadvantage in Ireland*, Dublin: Department of Education, Combat Poverty Agency, Educational Research Centre.

Kelly, A. (1978): *Girls and Science*, Stockholm: Almquist and Wiksell.

Kelly, A. (1981): *The Missing Half: Girls and Science Education*, Manchester: Manchester University Press.

Kelly, A. (Ed.) (1987): *Science for Girls?*, Milton Keynes, Open University Press.

Keys, W. and Ormerod, M. (1976): "A Comparison of the Pattern of Science Subject Choice for Boys and Girls in the Light of

Pupils' Own Expressed Subject Preference", *Social Science Review*, 58(203): 348–50.

Kimball, M. (1989): "A New Perspective on Women's Maths Achievement", *Psychological Bulletin*, 105: 198–214.

Kohn, M.L. and Schooler, C. (1982): "Job Conditions and Personality: A Longitudinal Assessment of the Reciprocal Effects", *American Journal of Sociology*, 87(6): 1257–86.

Krupnick, C. (1985): "Women and Men in the Classroom: Inequality and Its Remedies", *On Teaching and Learning*: Journal of the Harvard Danforth Center, Cambridge, MA: 18(25).

Landsbaum, J. and Willis, R. (1971): "Conformity in Early and Late Adolescence", *Developmental Psychology*, 4: 334–7.

Leahy, R. (Ed.) (1985): *Development of the Self*, San Diego, CA: Academic Press.

Lee, V.E. and Bryk, A.S. (1986): "Effects of Single Sex Secondary Schools on Student Achievement and Attitudes", *Journal of Educational Psychology*, 78(5): 381–95.

Lee, V.E. and Bryk, A.S. (1989): "Effects of Single-Sex Schools: A Response to Marsh", *Journal of Educational Psychology*, 81: 647–50.

Lee, V.E. and Lockheed, M. (1990): "The Effects of Single-Sex Schooling on Student Achievements and Attitudes in Nigeria", *Comparative Educational Review*, 43(2): 209–31.

Lee, V.E., Marks, H. and Byrd, T. (1994): "Sexism in Single-Sex and Coeducational Independent Secondary School Classrooms", *Sociology of Education*, 67: 92–120.

Lees, S. (1993): *Sugar and Spice: Sexuality and Adolescent Girls*, Harmondsworth: Penguin.

Lewin, M. and Tragos, L.M. (1987): "Has the Feminist Movement Influenced Adolescent Sex Role Attitudes? A Reassessment After a Quarter of a Century", *Sex Roles*, 16: 125–36.

Lewis, M. and Kellaghan, T. (1993): *Exploring the Gender Gap in Primary Schools*, Dublin: Educational Research Centre.

Linn, M.C. and Petersen, A.C. (1985): "Emergence and Characterisation of Sex Differences in Spatial Ability: A Meta-Analysis", *Child Development*, 56: 1479–98.

Lynch, K. (1989a): "The Ethos of Girls' Schools: An Analysis of Differences Between Male and Female Schools", *Social Studies*, 10: 11–81.

Lynch, K. (1989b) *The Hidden Curriculum: Reproduction in Education*, London: Falmer.

Lynch, K., Close, S. and Oldham, E. (1994): "The Republic of Ireland", in Burton, L. (Ed.) op. cit..

Mac an Ghaill, M. (1994): *The Making of Men: Masculinities, Sexualities and Schooling*, Buckingham: Open University Press.

McRobbie, A. (1991): *Feminism and Youth Culture*, London: Macmillan.

MacSween, M. (1993): *Anorexic Bodies*, London: Routledge and Kegan Paul.

Maccoby, E.E. (1988): "Gender as a Social Category", *Developmental Psychology*, 26: 755–65.

Maccoby, E.E. (1990): "Gender Relationships: A Developmental Account", *American Psychologist*, 45: 513–20.

Maccoby, E.E. and Jacklin, C. (1974): *The Psychology of Sex Differences*, Stanford, CA: Stanford University Press.

Madaus, G., Airasian, P. and Kellaghan, T. (1980): *School Effectiveness*, New York: McGraw-Hill.

Madaus, G.F., Kellaghan, T., Rakow, E.A. and King, D. (1979): "The Sensitivity of Measures of School Effectiveness", *Harvard Educational Review*, 49: 207–30.

Mahony, P. (1985): *Schools for the Boys? Coeducation Reassessed*, London: Hutchinson.

Mare, R.D. (1981): "Change and Stability in Educational Stratification", *American Sociological Review*, 46: 72–87.

Marsh, H. (1989a): "The Effects of Attending Single-Sex and Catholic Coeducational High Schools on Achievement, Attitudes and Behaviours and on Sex Differences", *Journal of Educational Psychology*, 81: 70–85.

Marsh, H. (1989b): "The Effects of Single-Sex and Co-Educational Schools: A Response to Lee and Bryk", *Journal of Educational Psychology*, 81: 651–653.

Marsh, H. (1989c): "Sex Differences in the Development of Verbal and Mathematics Constricts: The High School and Beyond Study", *American Educational Research Journal*, 26: 191–225.

Marsh, H. (1991): "Public, Catholic Single-Sex and Catholic Coeducational High Schools: Their Effects on Achievement, Affect and Behaviours", *American Journal of Education*, 99: 320–56.

Marsh, H., Smith, D., Marsh, M. and Owens, L. (1988): "The Transition from Single-Sex to Coeducational High Schools: Effects on Multiple Dimensions of Self-Concept and on Academic Achievement", *American Educational Research Journal*, 25: 237–69.

Martin, M.O., Hickey, B.L. and Murchan, D.P. (1992): "The Second International Assessment of Educational Progress: Mathematics and Science Findings in Ireland", *The Irish Journal of Education*, 26, Special Issue.

Martin, M.O. and Morgan, M. (1994): "Reading Literacy in Irish Schools: A Comparative Analysis", *The Irish Journal of Education*, 28, Special Issue.

Medrich, E.A, Roizen, J., Rubin, V. and Buckley, S. (1982): *The Serious Business of Growing Up: A Study of Children's Lives Outside School*, Berkeley, CA: University of California Press.

Mexcca, A.M., Smelsera, N.J. and Vasconouos, J. (Eds.) (1989): *The Social Importance of Self-Esteem*, Berkeley, CA: University of California.

Moore, M., Piper, V and Schaefer, E. (1993): "Single-Sex Schooling and Educational Effectiveness: A Research Overview", in Hollinger, D. and Adamson, R. (Eds.) op. cit.: 7–68

Mortimore, D., Sammons, P., Stoll, L., Lewis, D. and Ecob, R. (1988): *School Matters: The Junior Years*, Wells: Open Books.

Murnane, R.J., Maynard, R.A. and Ohls, J.C. (1981): "Home Resources and Children's Achievement", *Review of Economics and Statistics*, 63: 369–77.

National Education Convention (1994): *Report on the National Education Convention*, Dublin: The Convention Secretariat.

NCCA (1994): *Assessment and Certification in the Senior Cycle*, Dublin: NCCA.

Nuttall, D., Goldstein, H., Prosser, R. and Rasbash, J. (1990): "Differential School Effectiveness", *International Journal of Educational Research*, 13(7): 769–76.

Nuttall, D.L., Thomas, S. and Goldstein, H. (1992): *Report on Analysis of 1990 Examination Results*, AMA EO Circular 92/13.

Nye, F.I. and Hoffman, L.W. (1963): "The Unemployed Mother in America", in Oakley, A. (Ed.), op. cit.

Oakes, J. (1985): *Keeping Track: How Schools Structure Inequality*,

New Haven, CT: Yale University Press.

Oakes, J. (1990): "Opportunities, Achievement and Choice: Women and Minority Students in Science and Mathematics", *Review of Research in Education*, American Educational Research Association, Washington, DC, 16: 153–222.

Oakley, A. (Ed.) (1985): *Sex, Gender and Society*, Aldershot: Gower.

O'Connor, S. (1968): "Post-Primary Education: Now and in the Future", *Studies*, 27: 233–51.

OECD (1992): *Education at a Glance: OECD Indicators*, Paris: OECD.

OECD (1995): *Education At a Glance*, Paris: OECD.

Orbach, S. (1986): *Hunger Strike*, London: Faber and Faber.

Orlofosky, J.L. (1977): "Sex Role Orientation, Identity Formation and Self-Esteem in College Men and Women", *Sex Roles*, 3: 561–75.

Ormerod, M.B. (1975): "Subject Preference and Choice in Co-educational and Single-Sex Secondary Schools", *British Journal of Educational Psychology*, 45: 257–67.

Ormerod, M.B. and Duckworth, D. (1975): *Pupils' Attitude to Science: A Review of Research*, Slough: NFER.

Owens, T.J. (1994): "Two Dimensions of Self-Esteem: Reciprocal Effects of Positive Self-Worth and Self-Deprecation on Adolescent Problems", *American Sociological Review*, 59(3): 391–408.

Pallas, A., Entwisle, D., Alexander, K. and Stluka, F. (1994): "Ability-Group Effects: Instructional, Social or Institutional?", *Sociology of Education*, 67: 27–46.

Pearlin, L. (1989): "The Sociological Study of Stress", *Journal of Health and Social Behaviour*, 30: 241–56.

Pearlin, L., Menaghan, E., Leiberman, M. and Mullan, J. (1981): "The Stress Process", *Journal of Health and Social Behaviour*, 22: 337–51.

Pearson, J.L. and Ferguson, L.R. (1989): "Gender Differences in Patterns of Spatial Ability, Environmental Cognition and Maths and Engineering Achievement in Late Adolescence", *Adolescence*, 24: 421–30.

Phares, E.J. (1976): *Locus-of-Control and Personality*, Morristown, NJ: Silver Burdett.

Pilling, D. And Pringle, M.K. (1978): *Controversial Issues in Child Development*, London: National Children's Bureau, Paul Elek.

Postlethwaite, N. and Ross, K. (1992): *Effective Schools in Reading*, The Hague: International Association for the Evaluation of Educational Achievement.

Pratt, J. (1985): "The Attitude of Teachers", in Whyte, J. et al. (Eds.) op. cit.

Rhodes, R. (1986): "Women in the Family in Post-Famine Ireland: Status and Opportunity in a Patriarchal Society", Ph.D. Thesis, University of Illinois.

Riddell, S. (1992): *Gender and the Politics of the Curriculum*, London: Routledge and Kegan Paul.

Rosenberg, M. and Pearlin, A. (1978): "Social Class and Self-Esteem Among Children and Adults", *American Journal of Sociology*, 84(1): 53–77.

Rosenberg, M. (1985): "Self Concept and Psychological Well-Being in Adolescence", in Leahy, R. (Ed) op. cit.

Rosenberg, M., Schoenbach, C., Schooler, C. and Rosenberg, F. (1995): "Global Self-Esteem and Specific Self-Esteem: Different Concepts, Different Outcomes", *American Sociological Review*, 60: 141–56.

Rosenberg, M., Schooler, C. and Schoenbach, C. (1989): "Self-Esteem and Adolescent Problems: Modelling Reciprocal Effects", *American Sociological Review*, 54: 1004–18.

Ross, C.E. and Mirowsky, J. (1989): "Explaining Social Patterns of Depression: Control and Problem Solving — or Support and Talking?", *Journal of Health and Social Behaviour*, 30: 206–19.

Rowe, K. (1988): "Single Sex and Mixed Sex Classes: The Effect of Class Type on Student Achievement, Confidence and Participation in Maths", *Australian Journal of Education*, 32(2): 180–202.

Rowe, K.J. and Hill, P.W. (1994): "Multilevel Modelling in School Effectiveness Research: How Many Levels?", Seventh International Congress for School Effectiveness and Improvement, Melbourne.

Rutter, M. and Madge, N. (1976): *Cycles of Disadvantage: A Review of Research*, London: Heinemann.

Rutter, M., Maughan, B., Mortimore, P., Outson, J. and Smith, A.

(1979): *Fifteen Thousand Hours, Secondary Schools and Their Effects on Children*, Cambridge, MA: Harvard University Press.

Sammons, P., Hillman, J. and Mortimore, P. (1995): *Key Characteristics of Effective Schools*, London: Institute of Education.

Sampson, S.N. (1989): "Australian Research on Gender in Education", *Evaluation and Research in Education*, 3 (3): 133–41.

Schneider, F. and Coutts, L. (1982): "The High-School Environment: A Comparison of Coeducational and Single-Sex Schools", *Journal of Educational Psychology*, 74(6): 898–906.

Schneider, F., Coutts, L.M. and Starr, M.W. (1988): "In Favour of Coeducation: the Educational Attitudes from Coeducational and Single-Sex High Schools", *Canadian Journal of Education*, 13(4): 479–96.

Sears, P.S. and Feldman, D.H. (1974): "Teacher Reactions With Boys and With Girls", in Stacey, J. (Ed.), *And Jill Came Tumbling After: Sexism in American Education*, New York: 1974.

Sewell, W.H., Haller, A. and Portes, A. (1969): "The Educational and Early Occupational Attainment Process", *American Sociological Review*, 34: 82–92.

Sewell, W.H., Haller, A. and Ohlendorf, G. (1970): "The Educational and Early Occupational Status Attainment Process: Replication and Revision", *American Sociological Review*, 35: 1014–27.

Sewell, W.H. and Hauser, R.M. (1975): *Education, Occupation and Earnings: Achievement in the Early Career*, New York: Academic Press.

Shavit, Y. (1984): "Tracking and Ethnicity in Israel: Secondary Education", *Sociology of Education*, 49: 210–20.

Shavit, Y. (1990): "Segregation, Tracking and the Educational Attainment of Minorities", *American Sociological Review*, 55(1): 115–26.

Shavit, Y., Muller, W., Krans, V., Katz-Gerro, T. (1994): "Vocational Education and the Transition of Men from School to Work in Israel, Italy and Germany", ESF Working Paper.

Shaw, J. (1976): "Finishing School: Some Implication of Sex Segregated Education", in Barker, D. and Allen, S. (Eds.), *Sexual Divisions in Society: Process and Change*, London: Tavistock.

Skaalvik, E.M. (1990): "Gender Differences in General Academic Self-Esteem and in Success Expectations on Defined Academic Problems", *Journal of Educational Psychology*, 82(3): 593–8.

Smelser, N.J. (Ed.) (1986): *Handbook of Sociology*, Newbury Park, CA: Sage.

Smelser, N.J. (1989): "Self-Esteem and Social Problems: An Introduction", in Mexcca, A.M, Smelser, N.J. and Vasconcouos, J. (Eds.): 1–23.

Smith, D. and Tomlinson, S. (1989): *The School Effect*, London: Policy Studies Institute.

Smith, S. (1980): "Should They Be Kept Apart?", *Times Educational Supplement*, London.

Sorensen, A. and Hallinan, M. (1984): "A Reconceptualization of School Effects", *Sociology of Education*, 50: 273–89.

Spearman, C. (1904): "'General Intelligence', Objectively Determined and Measured", *American Journal of Psychology*, 15: 201–93.

Spearman, C. (1927): *Abilities of Man*, New York: Macmillan.

Spence, J. (Ed.) (1983): *Achievement and Achievement Motives*, San Francisco, CA: Freeman.

Spender, D. (1982): *Invisible Women: The Schooling Scandal*, London: Writers and Readers Publishing Co-operative Society Ltd.

Spender, D. and Sarah, E. (Eds.) (1980): *Learning to Lose: Sexism and Education*, London: The Women's Press.

Stables, A. (1990): "Differences Between Pupils from Mixed and Single Sex Schools in Their Enjoyment of School Subjects and in Their Attitudes to Sciences and to School", *Education Review*, 42(93): 221–230.

Stanworth, M. (1983): *Gender and Schooling*, London: Hutchinson.

Steedman, J. (1983a): *Examination Results in Mixed and Single-Sex Schools*, Manchester: Equal Opportunities Commission.

Steedman, J. (1983b): *Examination Results in Selective and Non-Selective Schools*, London: National Children's Bureau.

Steinberg, L., Blinde, P. and Chan, K. (1984): "Dropping Out Among Language Minority Youth", *Review of Educational Research*, 54: 113–32.

Stipek, D. (1984): "Sex Differences in Children's Attributions for Success and Failure on Maths and Spelling Tests", *Sex Roles*, 11: 969–81.

Thomas, S., Nuttall, D.L. and Goldstein, H. (1993): *Report on Analysis of 1991 Examination Results*, AMA EO Circular 93/24.

Thomas, S., Pan, H. and Goldstein, H. (1994): *Report on Analysis of 1992 Examination Results*, AMA and Institute of Education, University of London.

Thurstone, L.L. (1935): *Vectors of Mind*, Chicago: University of Chicago Press.

Thurstone, L.L. (1947): *Multiple Factor Analysis*, Chicago: University of Chicago Press.

Tracey, D. (1987): "Toys, Spatial Ability and Science and Maths Achievement: Are they Related?", *Sex Roles*, 17: 115–38.

Trickett, E. et al. (1983): "The Independent School Experience: Aspects of the Normative Environments of Single-Sex and Co-education Secondary Schools", *Journal of Educational Psychology*, 74(3): 374–81.

Turritin, A., Anisef, P. and MacKinnon, N. (1983): "Gender Differences in Educational Achievement: A Study of Social Inequality", *Canadian Journal of Sociology*, 8(4): 395–419.

Vockell, E.L. and Lobonc, S. (1981): "Sex-role Stereotyping by High School Females in Science", *Journal of Research in Science Teaching*, 18: 209–19.

Walshok, M. (1978): "Occupational Values and Family Roles", reprinted in Berk, L.E. (Ed) (1989), op cit.

Weinreich, H. (1978): "Sex Differences in 'Fear of Success' Among British Students", *British Journal of Social and Clinical Psychology*, 17(1): 37–42.

Wernersson, I. (1991): "Sweden", in Wilson, M. (Ed.), *Girls and Young Women in Education: A European Perspective*, Oxford: Pergamon Press.

Wetter, R. (1977): "Levels of Self-Efficacy Associated with Four Sex Role Categories", Reprinted in Keith, P.M. (Ed.) (1988), op. cit.

Whelan, C., Hannan, D.F. and Creighton, S. (1991): *Unemployment, Poverty and Psychological Distress*, Dublin: ESRI General Research Series, Paper No. 150.

Whyte, J. (1986): *Girls Into Science and Technology: The Story of a Project*, London: Routledge and Kegan Paul.

Whyte, J., Deem, R. Kant, L. and Cruickshank, M. (Eds.) (1985): *Girl Friendly Schooling*, London: Methuen.

Willis, P. (1977): *Learning to Labour*, Aldershot: Saxon House.

Willis, S. and Kenway, J. (1986): "On Overcoming Sexism in

Schooling: To Marginalise or Mainstream?", *Australian Journal of Education*, 30: 132–49.

Willms, J.D. (1985): "The Balance Thesis: Contextual Effects of Ability on Pupils' O-Grade Examination Results", *Oxford Review of Education*, 11(1): 33–41.

Wilson, M. (Ed.) (1991): *Girls and Young Women in Education: A European Perspective*, Oxford: Pergamon Press.

Winefield, A. (1993): *Growing Up With Unemployment: A Longitudinal Study of its Psychological Impact*, London: Routledge.

Winefield, A.H. and Tiggeman, M. (1989): "Job Loss versus Failure to Find Work as Psychological Stressors in the Young Unemployed", *Journal of Occupational Psychology*, 62(1): 79–85.

Witkin, H., Lewis, H., Hertzman, M., Machover, K., Meissner, P. and Wapner, S. (1954): *Personality Through Perception*, New York: Harper and Row.

Wittig, M.A. and Peterson, A. (1979): *Sex-Related Differences in Cognitive Functioning*, New York: Academic Press.

Wolleat, P.L., Pedro, J.D., Becker, A.D. and Pennema, E. (1980): "Sex Differences in High School Students' Causal Attributions on Performance in Mathematics", *Journal of Research in Mathematics Education*, 11: 356–66.

Wolpe, A. (1988): *Within School Walls: The Role of Discipline, Sexuality and the Curriculum*, London: Routledge and Kegan Paul.

Wrigley, J. (1992): *Education and Gender Equality*, Philadelphia, PA: Falmer Press.

Yates, J. and Firkin, J. (1986): *Student Participation in Mathematics*, Victoria: Curriculum Assessment Board.

Young, D. (1994): "Single-Sex Schools and Physics Achievement: Are Girls Really Advantaged?", *International Journal of Science Education*, 16(3): 315–25.

Young, D.J. and Fraser, B.J. (1990): "Science Achievement of Girls in Single-Sex and Co-educational Schools", *Research in Science and Technology Education*, 8(1): 5–20.

Youniss, J. and Smollar, J. (1985): *Adolescent Relations with Mothers, Fathers and Friends*, Chicago, IL: University of Chicago Press.